REPUTATION

REPUTATION
—Portraits in Power—

MARJORIE WILLIAMS

Edited by Timothy Noah

PublicAffairs
New York

Published in the United States by PublicAffairs™,
a Member of the Perseus Books Group.

PublicAffairs books are available at special discounts for bulk
purchases in the U.S. by corporations, institutions, and other
organizations. For more information, please contact the Special Markets
Department at the Perseus Books Group, 2300 Chestnut Street, Suite 200,
Philadelphia, PA 19103, call (800) 810-4145, ext. 5000,
or e-mail special.markets@perseusbooks.com.

Designed by Trish Wilkinson
Text set in 11-point Goudy

A CIP catalog record for this book
is available from the Library of Congress.
ISBN-13: 978-1-58648-679-2
First Edition

10 9 8 7 6 5 4 3 2 1

Once again, for Will and Alice.

CONTENTS

Should they whisper false of you,
Never trouble to deny;
Should the words they say be true,
Weep and storm and swear they lie.

—DOROTHY PARKER

INTRODUCTION

Timothy Noah

In November 2005 I published a collection of writings by my wife, Marjorie Williams. Marjorie, a Washington-based journalist for *Vanity Fair* and the *Washington Post,* had died ten months earlier, at age forty-seven, after a three-year battle with liver cancer. Immediately following her death I was flooded with requests from friends and admirers to make available an anthology of Marjorie's profiles and essays. I started editing the book one month after the funeral; it provided, among other benefits, a vessel for my grief. Assuming this would be my only chance to collect Marjorie's work, I initially prepared a plump "best-of" omnibus. Wiser heads pointed out that little demand existed for a seven-hundred-page anthology celebrating a writer who, though much loved inside the capital and among fellow journalists, was little known to the book-buying public. Reluctantly, I trimmed the manuscript down to more manageable length and hoped circumstances might afford the chance to publish a successor volume. *The Woman at the Washington Zoo* (the title came from a favorite poem of Marjorie's by Randall Jarrell) proved a success, both critically and commercially, beyond—well, perhaps not beyond my wildest imaginings—but certainly beyond my earthbound expectations, creating the opportunity I'd wished for to collect and publish the rest of Marjorie's best.

Before *The Woman at the Washington Zoo* appeared, Marjorie was known chiefly as a writer of incisive political profiles. When Peter Osnos of PublicAffairs first approached me about putting out an anthology, the book he had in mind probably didn't much resemble what I turned in three months later. *Zoo* purported to be a wry anthropological skewering of official Washington, but closer inspection revealed it to be a memoir in disguise. The first half contained some of the sharpest profiles Marjorie had written, but these were overshadowed in the second half by a handful of exquisite personal essays, two of them previously unpublished. Readers were affected most deeply by "Hit by Lightning," Marjorie's bracingly candid narrative essay about discovering, and coming to terms with, her terminal disease. (A slightly shorter version published in *Vanity Fair* immediately prior to *Zoo*'s publication won Marjorie a posthumous National Magazine Award and later was reprinted in Houghton Mifflin's *The Best American Essays 2006*.) Other essays explored Marjorie's richly complex feelings about getting and staying married, giving herself over to motherhood, and her own mother's death. The frank intimacy of these writings lent *Zoo* an intensely personal tone that tended to obscure the cooler intelligence on display in the profiles.

Reputation is a very different sort of book. It consists entirely of profiles (apart from the prologue). The mood is more playful, and Marjorie's wicked humor is more abundantly in evidence. In the title story, Marjorie observes that in the time it takes Clark Clifford to pronounce the word *re-pu-taaaaaay-shun*, "you could run downstairs to buy a paper and back." In "The Story of a Good Girl," Marjorie quotes an old-school *New York Times* editor griping about the corporate sensitivity seminars introduced by publisher Arthur Sulzberger Jr.: "I've been hugged by people I don't even want to shake hands with." In "Here Comes the Groom," Marjorie finds Larry King, in person, "unexpectedly pink."

This new collection provides ample opportunity to marvel at Marjorie's eye for novelistic detail. In "The Game," Jim Baker's smile is "what the dental hygienist asks you to emulate when she wants to get at your back molars." In "The Story of a Bad Boy," Lee

Atwater, who squirms madly while he's talking, "sits much stiller when he listens, his brow puckered into a pit that could grip a small marble." Another wonder is Marjorie's ear for dialogue. In "Before the Fall," Charles J. Kelly is the "number-one white booster" for a Colin Powell presidency. (The time was 1995, during the if-you-blinked-you-missed-it Powell boomlet.) Kelly is no doubt sincere in his admiration for Powell, but he gives himself away when he tells Marjorie that a black man in the White House would convey the message, "Kwitcherbitchin. If I can do it, you can do it. Don't run around talking about how the world owes you a living."

In Washington, the worst thing they can call you is a human being. Marjorie delighted in getting past her subject's white-marble edifice, pushing aside the freeze-dried human-interest morsels tossed out by some press aide to throw her off the scent, and identifying real flesh and bone. In some cases, what she found was even chillier than the bland mask of eminence. In "Mother's Milk," Terry McAuliffe flees the hospital room where his wife is about to give birth so he can attend a party the *Washington Post* is throwing for its gossip columnist. In "The Story of a Bad Boy," George H. W. Bush tells a key operative in his 1980 presidential campaign, "I do want you to understand that, if I win, we don't want any people like you in the government." These portraits possess not only the rhetorical flair but also the moral complexity more typically associated with classic short fiction.

What ties them together is a sense of a particular American moment. Readers glimpsed this aspect of Marjorie's writing in *Zoo*. Although I chose the profiles in that book to represent timeless Washington archetypes rather than the spirit of the specific dozen years when they were written, Marjorie's gift is not so easily pigeonholed. Those pieces also conveyed a sense of how Washingtonians, in a style characteristic of the late twentieth century, muddied the distinction between doing good and doing well. In Marjorie's obituary, *Washington Post* writer David Von Drehle (now with *Time*) compared her body of work to Plutarch's *Lives*. This volume attempts, as unpretentiously as I can manage, to follow that train of thought. Less grandly, one might compare *Reputation* to *Seven Men*, Max Beerbohm's humorous collection of

late-nineteenth-century character sketches, with the significant difference that Beerbohm's representative Britons were fictional, whereas
Marjorie's representative Americans are real.

If, as the novelist L. P. Hartley wrote, the past is a foreign country,
then the near past is more like Canada than Bhutan. The challenge
is to look beyond overwhelming similarities to the world we inhabit
and tease out subtle differences. Marjorie's active years as a newspaper and magazine writer began in 1987 and ended in 2001. This
was an era that historians are only beginning to distinguish from our
own. Sean Wilentz of Princeton recently christened it the "Age of
Reagan,"* designating the starting point at 1974 and the end point
at 2008 (which may be wishful thinking). In Wilentz's view, President Ronald Reagan (or at least the idea of Reagan) dominated this
stretch of American history in the same way that president Franklin
Roosevelt and his New Deal legacy dominated the four decades that
preceded it. The time period covered in *Reputation* is the decade following Reagan's presidency, but Reagan's presence is pervasive. Various people profiled in this book came to Washington because of
Reagan's 1980 election—George H. W. Bush, of course, and Jim
Baker, but also (for divergent reasons) Lawrence Walsh, Mary
Matalin, and Laura Ingraham. Two others—Lee Atwater and Colin
Powell—were ushered onto the national stage when they joined the
Reagan White House. Clark Clifford and Patricia Duff had little regard for Reagan—Clifford tagged him an "amiable dunce," and Duff
worked for Democratic candidates throughout his presidency—but
their lives, too, were shaped by Reagan's policies. Clifford benefited
financially from the lax regulation of banks; Duff, less directly,
achieved wealth through the lax regulation of corporate mergers
(because it made her future husband, Ron Perelman, a billionaire).
Both Cinderella stories end unhappily, providing, perhaps, a stern
lesson about the Reagan era's fevered money culture.

A rival definition of the era described in this book, set forth by
Washington think-tanker Derek Chollet and George Washington

The Age of Reagan: A History, 1974–2008 (HarperCollins, 2008).

University political scientist James Goldgeier, is that the 1990s were an interwar period not unlike the 1920s, bracketed in this instance by the end of the Cold War and the start of America's wars in Afghanistan and Iraq.* Such epochs are defined less by what occurred *during* them than by lingering memories of what happened *before* and a failure to anticipate what would happen *after*. Nostalgia for or disgust with the Reagan presidency (see, respectively, Ingraham and Walsh) might be two examples of the temptation to look backward. Frivolity (the softball-pitching King) is one crime of which interwar eras typically stand accused; a fixation on money (Clifford, Duff, McAuliffe) is another. The Janus-like structure of *Reputation*, I'm pleased to observe, fits neatly with Chollet and Goldgeier's interwar template. The book begins with Clark Clifford, aging symbol of a bygone probity that was always an illusion, and ends with Colin Powell, whose halo will be dented by the second Iraq war—but whose brief potential to become the first black president foreshadows the candidacy of Barack Obama. The profiles in between follow no chronological order, which somehow fits, too. (And, no, Anna Quindlen does not dwell within Washington's orbit; she's included here to illustrate where feminism stood during this period—a function also performed, somewhat differently, by the profile of Laura Ingraham. It's also a great piece.)

Our understanding of fin de siècle Washington is not, at this moment, fixed. Marjorie herself was no historian in the retrospective sense; she was a writer of present history. It was her habit, whenever possible, to show rather than tell. And so I leave it, finally, to Marjorie to set the scene in the prologue that follows.

America Between the Wars: From 11/9–9/11, the Misunderstood Years Between the Fall of the Berlin Wall and the Start of the War on Terror (PublicAffairs, 2008).

PROLOGUE

Welcome to Washington

"Washington City is the poorest place in the United States from which to judge the temper of the nation," wrote a columnist named Frank Carpenter in 1882. "Its citizens have a different outlook on life than those of the individual states, and the atmosphere is artificial and enervating."

Two centuries after the city's founding, Carpenter's observation makes a good starting point for a tour of the capital's soul. For Washington is a much-maligned city, butt of a thousand campaign slurs and target of resentment by the legions of Americans who feel estranged from their government. And no one dumps on the city more than the people who live here. This is not, we tell ourselves guiltily, the real America. The population is too transient, we say, too obsessively focused on government. The city is provincial, we add: the theater is still second-rate at best, the food—despite the ethnic enclave and a small if growing number of inspired restaurants—a pale shade of the diversity that New York or Chicago can offer. As for women's fashion . . . well, isn't Washington one of the best markets in the country for Talbots, home of the grosgrain hair band, the plaid skirt, and the boiled-wool jacket?

The wise defender of Washington knows that you will get nowhere by trying to refute the common criticisms; you must begin by embracing them. To love Washington is to champion its amateur status as a city.

Washington is unfashionable, and God bless it. Despite the grandly conceived boulevards and circles, laid out by Pierre L'Enfant in 1791, the city feels more suburban than urban—in design, in atmosphere, in ethos. It is still a one-industry town, although it is true that one of the major changes of the 1980s was that Washington developed a sizable business culture for the first time, powered by a real estate boom and the area's growing popularity as a headquarters for such corporate giants as Mobil and General Dynamics. But the exception proves the rule: these companies moved here to be close to the policy makers. In Washington, the government and its satellites—the media, the lobbyists, the policy jocks—blot out all else. It is a very small world. This, above all, is what natives feel duty bound to decry about the city. Secretly, it is what they love most.

Gore Vidal wrote, correctly, of the "calculated dowdiness" of old-line Washington society—a description that still applies to the city's most prominent citizens. From Katharine Graham, with her boarding-school-headmistress coif and the dull-brown Mercedes that pilots her to and from the *Washington Post*; to House Speaker Tom Foley, who can be seen at the "social" Safeway (the supermarket branch that serves Georgetown) pushing his shopping cart past the paper-towel bargains; to Miss Manners (a.k.a. Judith Martin), who presides over lunch at the stodgy Cosmos Club in her timeless Gibson Girl bun, this is a town of the comfortably, proudly un-chic.*

When Washington does feint in the direction of trendiness, it comes across like a man in midlife crisis sporting bell-bottoms and a bolo tie. Consider the latest success on the restaurant scene, Red Sage, an import from Santa Fe. The food is wonderful, but the decor—rumored to have cost close to $3 million—is ruthlessly Southwestern, with barbed wire appearing as a motif in everything from the chandeliers to the swizzle sticks.

---

*This essay was written in 1993. Katharine Graham had retired as chair of the Washington Post Co. two years earlier but remained a visible presence at the paper and on Washington's social circuit.

Though Washingtonians have flocked to try out Red Sage—President Clinton took Hillary here for Valentine's Day—it remains blatantly unassimilated. If it disappeared tomorrow, the waters would close over it instantly. No true Washingtonian would mourn it as a trusted part of city life—not the way they mourn Mel Krupin's, which closed its doors in 1988. A pricey upscale deli with forgettable food, Mel's was a place where you would run into bureau chiefs and publishers, former ambassadors and current White House aides.*

Washington's priorities are simply different from those of other cities. Although there are a great many six-figure salaries here, the super-rich are almost absent, and along with them the need for plumage. Washington is less about money than—exactly as the flabby clichés insist—about power. Its credit system is proximity; its currency, information.

There are two distinct Washingtons—the local city and the national capital. The former is the actual community made up of the District of Columbia and its booming suburbs. It is one of America's youngest great cities, and one of its most paradoxical stories of urban success and failure. Supported by the steady engine of federal spending, greater Washington has become the richest metropolitan area in America, measured by education level and household income. Washington is also the murder capital of the country, measured on a per capita basis.**

Race relations follow the same pattern. The area is home to a huge proportion of middle- and upper-income blacks, but the city itself retains a depressing level of informal segregation. Washington proper is a mecca for African Americans, with a thriving black culture, but white Washingtonians know little about this side of the city. Unlike the federal government, the city is largely black-run, from Mayor Sharon Pratt Kelly and congressional delegate Eleanor

---

*Red Sage did indeed attract little notice when it shut down in 2006.

**Washington's per capita murder rate peaked in the early 1990s. Since then it has dropped to number seven, behind Detroit, Baltimore, New Orleans, Newark, St. Louis, and Oakland.

Holmes Norton down through the top ranks of city government and the majority of the city council.

To the hordes who are drawn to the city by ambition, however, it is Washington's other life—its role as the national capital—that has the most vivid reality. This split personality is the continuing legacy of Washington's birth, for it was a capital before it was a city, selected by George Washington in 1791 on behalf of a bickering Congress. Only after the location was chosen, for its ambidextrous appeal to both the North and the South, was Pierre L'Enfant commissioned to make it real.

How far apart the two Washingtons lie was rather poignantly suggested in 1990, when federal authorities set up an undercover drug purchase in Lafayette Park, just across the street from the White House, in order to provide a prop—a seized bag of crack cocaine—for a televised speech by president George H. W. Bush. (The president intended to hold up the bag of crack and intone sadly that drugs were sold everywhere—even across the street from 1600 Pennsylvania Avenue.) Alas, when the order went forth to find the evidence, it turned out that crack arrests were unknown in the heavily policed blocks surrounding the president's home. In the end, someone had to be induced to sell crack across the street from the White House. When the Drug Enforcement Administration instructed its mark, a local dealer, that the buy would take place in Lafayette Park, he said, "Uh, where?"

Across the street from the White House, the agents explained.

"Where the fuck is the White House?" asked the dealer, who had grown up in southeast D.C.

To the city's striving political class, of course, the White House is and always will be the center of the universe. This state of mind is summed up, for me, by the view from the Presidential Suite of the Hay-Adams Hotel, where Bill Clinton spent his first night in Washington as president-elect. If you gaze out the south-facing window in the sitting room, across petite Lafayette Park, the White House is a thing of marzipan, improbably near and intimate in scale. To the initiated, Washington is a place where power seems just this seductively close at hand.

I spent my wedding night in the same suite at the Hay-Adams and keep a rich memory of it. I like to imagine that late at night, after meeting with the outgoing president, fending off the press, and dining with a few dozen ambitious strangers, Bill and Hillary turned out all the lights and stole over to the window in their bathrobes to assimilate at last the awesome turn in their lives.

The fables of power in Washington are, of course, 95 percent hooey; the truth is far more prosaic. Policy is made by a thousand tiny engines. A cabinet secretary has social firepower, but it's the analysts who report to the deputy assistant secretaries who are really writing the rules, along with certain staff members on certain Senate and House subcommittees—the men and women who live for the day the *Post* will describe them as "key staffers." And they aren't out at Hollywood's idea of a Glittering Washington Party; they're back at their scrungy government-issue desks, scarfing down a Domino's pizza over another late-night assignment.

These foot soldiers have far more social cachet under the policy-smitten Clinton regime than they ever had under Republican rule. But some things never change. Under either party, late-night revelry is unknown to "official" Washington. (It's been suggested that one reason sex scandals have such an explosive impact on Washington is that there is so little sex going on here in the first place.) Yet features editors have recently been running article after article about young Clintonites who party at dives such as Chief Ike's Mambo Room. The trend is curious: Where else but Washington would the sudden appearance of young people hanging out in bars make the newspaper, not to mention the paper of record, the *New York Times?*

Washingtonians love to build up a mythology of how their private lives mingle with the common, public life. Remember when the Kennedys were just that nice young couple who lived around the corner on N Street in Georgetown? As often as not, these memories are decisively improved by the passage of time. But there is the rare communal moment, like the time visiting Soviet leader Mikhail Gorbachev ordered his limousine to a halt so that he could shake hands at one of downtown's busiest intersections. Lobbyists in $300 loafers could be seen glowing and gawping just like the secretaries on their lunch breaks and the bicycle messengers on their rounds.*

A different kind of myth obscures Washington's charm for the casual visitor, who may find that the city's most renowned features are some of its most overrated. The cherry blossoms may be beautiful, yes; but the area around the Tidal Basin is always mobbed while they are in flower, and the glory lasts for only a few days before the scene disintegrates into what looks like bare trees banked in patches of wadded Kleenex. (Far better to spend an afternoon in the gardens of Georgetown's glorious Dumbarton Oaks.) The Museum of American History at the Smithsonian surprises you with the feel of a crowded attic. (Try, instead, a Sunday afternoon at the Phillips Collection.) The Washington Monument is the biggest bust of all. Walks to the top are prohibited because of all the graffiti left by climbers past, so you must first endure a long, long wait for the massive elevator, which finally disgorges its passengers beneath a ring of tiny windows made of blurry Plexiglas.**

Of the city's monuments and public spaces, the best are those that have been transformed by the visible use others have made of them. The Mall, which forms the great spine of L'Enfant's original plan for the city, is in fact a rather dull, naked rectangle—until you reach the Reflecting Pool and your mind's eye summons the sea of humanity that crowded around it to hear Martin Luther King Jr. describe his dream. This is why the Vietnam Veterans Memorial is the single mandatory stop on any visitor's trip. The sense of action there, of being embraced by a live event, is unexpectedly powerful—especially for the visitor who pays attention to the tributes left daily by mothers and buddies and sons and strangers at the foot of the black granite wall.

By far the largest part of Washington's charm, however, lies in the ease of life in the city. Though few Washingtonians would be caught dead admitting it, this place has a grace that we love and need.

---

*This was December 1987, at the height of the Soviet general secretary's historic economic reforms (*perestroika*).

**These problems were eventually addressed during extensive renovations in the late 1990s.

Washington is probably the cleanest big city in America, formed as it was without heavy industry; with its strict zoning, it is also one of the most open, physically. (Those who hate it here tend to be those who love the muscular, modern architecture of New York and Chicago.) Large parts of the city proper are more suburban than urban, wreathed in the green that advertises one of the country's best gardening climates.

The mix of city and suburb is at its most pleasant in Cleveland Park—now defined as an in-town neighborhood but high enough up a hill, some three miles northwest of the White House, that it was a summer retreat in Grover Cleveland's era. A two-block stretch of Newark Street, lined with clapboard houses so large they have the gravity of small hotels, summarizes all that is generous about life in Washington.

Washington's most well-known address, Georgetown, retains its slightly self-conscious beauty—but a gathering tension between its insular residents and its rowdy visitors is, for the first time in this neighborhood's long history, marking it with controversy. Homeowners here have always considered their neighborhood to be a "Brigadoon," with its quaint old shops: Scheele's Market since 1891; Martin's Tavern since 1933; the Francis Scott Key Book Shop since 1939.* Once each spring residents even throw open their impeccable doors to the public for the famous Georgetown House Tour. Yet their ire has been raised by the twentysomethings who crowd M and Wisconsin Streets on weekends.

Perhaps the most stunning place in the city is Rock Creek Park—a dramatic defile, a forest, really, that stretches from the Potomac straight up through the city to Maryland. A leafy parkway takes a driver all the way from the Lincoln Memorial, past Cleveland Park and Shepherd Park, and finally across the Maryland state line, with only two stoplights along the way.

A change of administration—especially a change like the recent one, when a new party as well as a new president moves into the

---

*The Francis Scott Key Book Shop closed its doors in 1995.

White House—sets off a mad scramble for status. With this administration, though, the status grab was shoved aside by President Clinton's rocky start,* and by the president himself, whose populist
rhetoric and conspicuous common-man preferences made him hard
to read. In fact, six months into the Clinton era, the administration's
style—particularly its idea of status—is still evolving. While the First
Couple, for instance, chose to send Chelsea to Sidwell Friends
School, the city's school for children of political gentry, they have es-
chewed most of the other trappings of "elitist" life. Too busy with the
national health care plan, Hillary has yet to change the White House
china (although she did change her name back to Rodham Clinton
after the election). And while her husband makes occasional appearances at the city's popular restaurants, such as Galileo, he has also ordered the White House mess to stay up as late as he does.

This is an administration that is frenzied (Clinton is late to
nearly every appointment) and folksy (one advisor, at the urging of
vice president Al Gore, actually flashed his Texas Longhorn boxer
shorts in front of the president, seated at his Oval Office desk). On-
lookers, both locally and nationally, still find the passions of the
president paradoxical, yet charming. He may be building a jogging
track in the White House backyard, but his penchant for McDon-
ald's (just around the corner) has not faded. His bedside table is
stacked with both mysteries (*The Search for Temperance Moon* by
Douglas C. Jones) and intellectual nonfiction (*Preparing for the
Twenty-first Century* by Paul Kennedy).

Yes, transplanted Arkansans have replaced many of the high-
spending Republicans as figures in the city, and the "Mack" McLar-
tys make quite a different statement from the Robert Mosbachers.**

---

*Clinton fumbled an attempt to integrate gays into the military and couldn't
persuade Congress to pass his economic-stimulus package.

**McLarty was Clinton's first White House chief of staff. Mosbacher was com-
merce secretary to the first President Bush. Both were energy company executives, but Mosbacher cut a more dashing social figure, mainly because of his
glamorous wife, Georgette, a habitué of New York's charity-ball circuit who
owned a successful cosmetics firm.

But perhaps the most interesting dance to watch is the courtship between the new, imported powers and the leaders of Washington society.

The membrane between society and Washington's power crowd is porous. Some new presidents, like George H. W. Bush, are already creatures of Washington when they move into the White House. Others, such as Ronald Reagan, must court the locals like the ambitious son of a banker wooing the daughter of old aristocracy. He badly wants her cachet, to take the edge off his raw money; her secret is that she wants his money just as badly.

Every rung of the social ladder has its counterpart on the power ladder: the president first, of course. Below him the White House chief of staff (who only has delegated power, to be sure, but remember, proximity is all) and the top three cabinet members—the secretaries of state, defense, and treasury. A senior senator who chairs a powerful committee ranks near the top (though a more junior senator can transcend an unsexy committee assignment with charm), as does a justice of the Supreme Court. Even justices, though, must parcel out their social capital wisely. Antonin Scalia is considered a highly desirable dinner guest, whereas Sandra Day O'Connor attended social functions—receptions, openings, teas, screenings—so indiscriminately upon arrival in Washington that she earned one of the in-crowd's most withering insults: "She would go to the opening of a door."

Each president, of course, puts his own stamp on the hierarchy. Clinton's most notable move was giving his wife unprecedented policy clout. His own managerial style relies less on the traditional power structure and more on what some of his staffers call "liberation management." Clinton administration job titles are often ambiguous, to circumvent the bureaucracy, and roles are given to staffers on a case-by-case basis. Health care policy is being shaped not by the Health and Human Services department but by Hillary Rodham Clinton and her advisor, Ira Magaziner.* Russian relations aren't dominated by the

---

*Their health care reform plan failed to acquire sufficient congressional support and was shelved in September 2004.

secretary of state; Strobe Talbott—a former journalist, the president's friend, and a new ambassador at large—also has a great deal of say. When tensions arise—as they do in any work situation where boundaries are vague—Vice President Gore says problem solving involves "talking things through."*

Perhaps most formidable in the power structure, though, is someone like Democratic grande dame Pamela Harriman, who, not coincidentally, gave one of the first two dinners Bill Clinton attended in Washington as president-elect. Harriman has not only money and a good Washington pedigree (both legacies of the late W. Averell Harriman) but the ancillary charm of a British background. (Washingtonians are hopeless Anglophiles.) She used these assets to make herself a force in the political world, raising millions for the dispirited Democratic Party all through the 1980s. Her Georgetown house seemed destined to be the center of the Clintonian social universe, but her nomination to be ambassador to France has left the social pinnacle up for grabs by the likes of Esther Coopersmith and Elizabeth Bagley, wife of tobacco heir Smith Bagley. Katharine Graham, it will be noted, does not need to compete. The *Washington Post* constitutes a power base that Metternich himself would have killed for.

Though a common complaint is the city's transience—no one who figures in official Washington is *from* here, after all—the truth is that many newcomers stay forever, secretly at home in the city everyone loves to hate. As each administration departs, it leaves behind a layer of flotsam on the shore—lobbyists, lawyers, public relations people—all now too smitten or too connected ever to move away.

The city happily absorbs its quadrennial infusions of new blood. But Washington always does more to change its newcomers than the newcomers do to change it.

—*June 1993*

---

*Talbott was appointed deputy secretary of state the following year.

REPUTATION

(CLARK CLIFFORD)

If you could see out the windows of his twelfth-floor office, you would be able to see the Jefferson Memorial and Washington Monument. You could see the Capitol, where he rode with Harry Truman when Truman went to deliver the speech Clark Clifford had drafted, the speech that would become known as the Doctrine. You could see Lafayette Square and, beyond it, the White House, to which Clifford used to amble whenever Jack Kennedy's secretary called. You could see the Potomac, and look toward the Pentagon, where Clifford moved when Lyndon Johnson needed a new secretary of defense in the last desperate year of his presidency.

But Clifford is too sensitive to bright light, a legacy of hepatitis, which he contracted during a trip to Vietnam in 1967. And so his office is perpetually dimmed by heavy tan curtains that close out the radiance of the day; visitors must content themselves with his own, more subtle luster. He closes his eyes and covers them with his vast right hand, as if with a cool compress.

"All I can say to you," he confides in his laborious baritone, "is it has been the most dif-fi-cult pe-ri-od in my life." Now the hands, so long the fingers seem to have four or five knuckles apiece, join in the steeple that is his trademark gesture. It says thoughtfulness, judiciousness, probity. "I've prac-ticed law for sixty-two years," he continues. "This is the first time that an-y cloud has ever been associated with my name or my reputation." *Re-pu-taaaaaay-shun*, he says. In

1

the time it takes Clark Clifford to state his grief, you could run downstairs to buy a paper and back.

Clifford is famously deliberate, famously theatrical, in his every word and gesture. But perhaps only Clifford's voice could give that word—*reputation*—the weight it deserves just now, near the end of his life, in the midst of his troubles. For it is Clifford's golden reputation that is suddenly threatened after forty-six years in Washington. And it was Clifford's reputation, and his willingness to lend it to an unsavory client, that brought him into the bank scandal that now sullies his image as the prototype of the respectable Washington lawyer. Time was, this was the kind of trouble for which you called Clark Clifford. Johnson aide Walter Jenkins, House Speaker Jim Wright, former CIA director Richard Helms, Carter administration budget director Bert Lance: men who had legal problems with political dimensions, or political problems with legal dimensions, all called Clark Clifford, who was a master at tweezing one from the other—and then defusing both. But today it is Clifford who, at eighty-four, is entangled in investigations—by the Federal Reserve Board, the Justice Department, and the Manhattan district attorney. These authorities are following up a shadowy foreign bank's admission that it illegally acquired a controlling share in First American Bankshares, a Washington-area bank holding company chaired by Clifford. They are also examining whether Clifford either knowingly or unknowingly misled state and federal regulators ten years ago when he laid his prestige on the line to assure them that the foreign bank would not be involved in First American's acquisition by a group of Middle Eastern investors. The two banks, and their relationships with Clifford and his law firm, have been under ever-sharper scrutiny since 1989, when executives of the foreign bank pleaded guilty to laundering drug money—some of it through accounts at Clifford's First American Bank.

Clifford has said that at worst he was misled by the foreign bank with which his name is now linked. But revelations keep coming. On Sunday the *Washington Post* reported that he profited personally from stock transactions, to the tune of more than $6 million, that were financed by the foreign bank he claims to have been duped by. Clifford's embarrassment comes just as he is preparing to cement his legend with a memoir, *Counsel to the President*, for which Random House paid him $1 million. What was to be his triumphant act of self-definition threatens instead to be an ironic comment on the evanescence of image. "It is," says an old friend, "one of the grand falls."

Establishment Washington is stunned by the turn of events. Not just surprised or—in the cases of the many people who bear Clifford a genuine fondness or respect—saddened, but truly shocked. Because Clifford has been a kind of local totem, basic to the status hierarchy of postwar Washington. In the words of Democratic lawyer Berl Bernhard, "He has held this position at the pinnacle of—it's not really just power—it's the pinnacle of *respectability*." And he has guarded that summit carefully. Although he has made himself a multimillionaire, his true capital is in the name Clark Clifford and what it stands for. This is what his investors knew, in hiring him to represent their deal. It is what the bank regulators accepted, in weighing Clifford's assurances against their own doubts. The worst possible scenario under investigation is that Clifford knowingly misrepresented the deal to those regulators. The best is that he was duped, lied to by his investors and lured into lending them his prestige. For a man who has made a career of knowing the score, it is hard to say which would be the more painful choice.

"I can't put Clifford together in my mind with either stupidity or unethical behavior," says Harry McPherson, a former Johnson aide and fellow attorney. But, he concedes, if news reports to date accurately reflect investigators' findings, "this required either a failure of intellect or a failure of ethical reasoning, I guess." On a human level, Clifford's is a relatively simple story of a driven man who came to Washington and made good—made history—but who nursed one ambition too many. The particular engines of this story are as old as Clifford is, and their insistent noise can be heard all through the decades of his career. They may help solve the mystery of how a man as smart and as wealthy as Clark Clifford came to ally himself with clients who could bring about his downfall.

But there is another mystery in Clifford's history: the intriguing question of how Washington came to repose so much confidence in a corporate lawyer-lobbyist, making him the personification, the very definition, of integrity. The answer to that mystery lies in the story of how he made himself the monumental figure he is—and of how eager Washington always is to think of its fixers as statesmen. This is the history of a Washington reputation.

⁓

Lloyd Cutler, another prominent Democratic lawyer, measures Clifford's reputation in an anecdote. In 1979, at the nadir of Jimmy Carter's presidency, Cutler was asked to become counsel to the president. "When the president asked me to become counsel, I asked what did he expect from me. And he said, 'I want you to perform a Clark Clifford role. To do what Clark Clifford did for Harry Truman.'" These words, from a president who ran against the Washington establishment Clifford had long symbolized, described a relationship that was then almost thirty years in the past. Cutler continues: "I got it in writing. And after that, whenever a meeting went on that I wasn't invited to . . . I would go to President Carter or to [chief of staff] Hamilton Jordan and say, 'I think Harry Truman would have wanted Clark Clifford to be at this meeting.' It was like saying 'Open Sesame.' Really, it opened every door."

Clifford describes his meteoric start in Washington, in 1945, as almost accidental. A native of Missouri, he was a successful St. Louis trial lawyer, a pillar of the city who planned to stay there, when America joined World War II. Although old enough to be exempt from service, Clifford volunteered for the navy and was commissioned as a lieutenant in 1944. An old associate from Missouri who was serving as the new president's naval aide had Clifford assigned to Washington temporarily as his assistant in the summer of 1945. Clifford recognized immediately that there was a power vacuum around Truman. After Franklin D. Roosevelt's death, Roosevelt's old associates, tired from long service and in many cases contemptuous of the new president, had deserted the White House in droves.

Clifford moved quickly. While his own boss was at the Potsdam Conference with the president, he attached himself to Samuel I. Rosenman, the special counsel to the president who was one of the few FDR holdovers. He did whatever chores he was allowed to do, and eventually he was promoted to replace the naval aide. Clifford was given responsibility for arranging Truman's regular poker weekends on the presidential yacht *Williamsburg*, games that became an important part of his bond with Truman and an important rite of access to the president, which Clifford controlled. The first thing he did was study a poker manual until his game improved, a small price to pay for the bonds he forged with the likes of W. Averell Harriman, future chief justice Fred Vinson, and then-Rep. Lyndon Baines Johnson. By the time Rosenman left to return to his New York law practice, Clifford had begun to establish himself as a speechwriter and all-purpose advisor. In June 1946 he became Truman's special counsel. He was thirty-nine, and he had been in Washington less than a year.

After a time there was no area of policy he did not touch. He was soon the subject of fawning magazine profiles as the power behind the president, a new breed of White House aide. The aura was born. Even today, Clifford is a notably handsome man. At thirty-nine, he was devastating: blue-eyed and imposingly tall, with blond hair he was sometimes accused of styling into its wheaty waves and the flashing smile of a man who knows he has perfect teeth. With his wife, Marny, he became socially sought after. "Just to look at them," gushed a society columnist in the *Washington Post,* "makes you feel you've just gone through an ocean spray."

Clifford's willingness to work was his seed capital. He worked seventy- and eighty-hour weeks, and according to his wife, he sometimes fell asleep at parties. Clifford's autobiography plays up the more statesmanly functions of his job—an emphasis he would make all through his career. He was deeply involved in the first building blocks of what would become the Cold War policy of containment:

the Truman Doctrine, the Four Points, the Marshall Plan.* And Clifford's book suggests that he was crucial to Truman's decision, in 1948, to grant immediate recognition to the new state of Israel. In domestic policy, the president's counsel was perceived as liberals' chief conduit to the president. But Clifford, who had had no interest in government at the time Roosevelt launched the New Deal, guarded his own views very closely. In *Counsel to the President,* Clifford writes in the clinical argot of the pragmatist. He refers scathingly to "'professional liberals' whose ardor and search for ideological purity outweighed their discretion and their judgment."

Clifford's pragmatism determined his attitude toward the early manifestations of communist witch-hunting in 1946 and 1947: he supported Truman's Loyalty Program. The infamous Executive Order 9835, issued in March 1947, established "loyalty boards" empowered to examine federal employees, who could be fired on the basis of anonymous accusations to J. Edgar Hoover's FBI, and without any specific finding that they had done anything disloyal. Thousands of federal employees were hauled before loyalty hearings, many forced from the government under circumstances that made it almost impossible for them to find other jobs. His failure to head this off, Clifford writes, is one of the greatest regrets of his career. Truman "felt that without the loyalty program, the political pressures would have been much greater, and more difficult to resist. At the time, I agreed with him; later I would come to a different conclusion." But his precise role in the affair is left vague. The executive order, Clifford writes, was drafted by the FBI and the Justice Department and "passed through my office before it was approved by the president."

It is a selective reporting of his role. As every good bureaucrat knows, ducking involvement in a controversial issue can require as

---

*The Truman Doctrine established that the United States would oppose any further projection of Soviet power. The Four Points pledged U.S. support for the United Nations, postwar economic recovery abroad, political freedom abroad, and Third World development. The Marshall Plan financed Europe's rebuilding after World War II.

much finesse as joining the fray. At least one liberal friend, assistant secretary of the Interior C. Girard Davidson, entreated Clifford to use his influence against the gathering forces of red-baiting. In late 1947 he wrote Clifford a long, confidential letter arguing that the Loyalty Program must be redesigned to guarantee employees the standard rights of due process: to confront their accusers, to hear the charges against them, to present witnesses on their own behalf, and to appeal. Clifford forwarded the letter to the presidential assistant in charge of the program with a bland covering memo saying, "I shall appreciate having your comments on his letter, and your advice as to how I should reply." The letter somehow leaked, causing a raft of editorials calling for Davidson's firing. Davidson never heard from Clifford.

The climax of Clifford's service to Truman came with the hairsbreadth victory of 1948. Clifford was widely perceived as the author of Truman's impossible, come-from-behind win, including the grueling "whistle-stop" train tour. After it, he decided to leave the White House and strike out on his own. All power in Washington ultimately flows from politics. Thus Clifford's role in the 1948 election, observes another Democratic lawyer, "launched him into the absolute most upper echelons of the Washington power scene. And he knew how to handle that. He knew how to get there, and he knew what it took to stay there. . . . He knew what he could be, and he became it."

Clifford's aura flows, first, from his role in the history of his times. But it is hard to separate his contributions from the legend he has built up around them and from his great skill at capitalizing on his natural gifts—his voice, his bearing, even the alliterative good luck of his name. He wears double-breasted, pin-striped suits with sharp, upswept lapels; he has worn them steadily for decades, lending them his own dignity when the whims of fashion condemned them as inappropriate on other men. Folded into his great leather desk chair, with his polished wingtips planted flat on the floor, he has physical fabric to spare. His knees sit higher than his thighs, and his arms are so long that, with his elbows planted on the chair's arms, his hands can meet up at chin level. The presence is polished off by the deep, rich voice, deployed so slowly it almost parodies itself. "There's that soft, confidential, complimentary tone," says George Reedy, former press secretary to Lyndon Johnson. "All your defenses go down." Reedy summarizes the total effect: "He radiates prudence, more than anyone else I have ever met in Washington. He *has* at least as much prudence as others, but he definitely *radiates* it more." A close associate describes Clifford's aura as "a totally conscious construction. Totally."

For forty-one of his forty-six years here Clifford has been a lawyer-lobbyist, like the handful of men who preceded him in the field or were his peers (Tommy "the Cork" Corcoran, Abe Fortas, James Rowe), and like the thousands of men and women who have since flourished on K Street. But he is "like" these others only by category. His genius has consisted largely of making himself seem as unlike them as possible, in the eyes of his clients, of the government officials who are his targets, and of the press. Through his intermittent work as advisor and problem solver to presidents, he has made himself appear a lifelong public servant who only incidentally practices hardball Washington law.

If you were to codify Clifford's achievement, it could be reduced to five simple rules:

One. Resist characterization as a lobbyist or influence peddler, however much truth those labels might hold. Others *lobby*. Clifford *counsels*.

Two. Develop something more lasting than influence, which perishes with each change of administration. Because Clifford has prestige, influence follows.

Three. Shun the accountability and dependence (not to mention the pay scale) of a government job. For Clifford, who served only one year in government in the past four decades, the half-dozen presidential job offers he turned down would have been demotions.

Four. Hone your wisdom in foreign, not domestic, policy. It's easier to influence behind the scenes, it's worth more status points, and it's far less likely to conflict with a corporate law practice.

Five. Above all, avoid appearing to seek power. There's no one the power-hungry creatures of Washington admire more than someone for whom power looks effortless; the idea is that power begs an audience with Clifford because he's just so damn smart. "Clifford's view of himself is that power sought him—that he never sought power," says a close associate. "At a certain point in a person's life, when he has said something like this long enough, he believes it when he says it. Even if on a daily basis he does things that suggest otherwise."

On leaving the Truman administration, Clifford went into partnership with a friend who had worked in the antitrust division of the Justice Department. He immediately developed a little speech that he delivered to every prospective client. "I do not consider that this firm will have any influence of any kind here in Washington. . . . If you want influence, you should consider going elsewhere. What we can offer you is an extensive knowledge of how to deal with the government on your problems."

Within a year of leaving office, he was representing RCA, Standard Oil, the Pennsylvania Railroad, the Republic of Indonesia, El Paso Natural Gas, TWA, and Phillips Petroleum, whose chairman he had met through a good friend, Oklahoma Sen. Robert S. Kerr. Not until 1969 did any member of his firm register as a lobbyist. Not until 1975, when the Justice Department made a minor fuss over the firm's four-year-old representation of Algerian oil interests, did Clifford register as the agent of any foreign government. His was, he said then and says now, an *advisory* firm. Of course, Clifford well knew that his clients regarded him as a big wheel at the White House. He remained close to President Truman, sometimes joining him on vacations in Key West, and continuing to be responsible for arranging Truman's cherished poker weekends. And when Republican Dwight D. Eisenhower took office, there was still the Democratic Congress to deal with. Clifford was already best friends with Missouri Sen. Stuart Symington, whom he had known in St. Louis. He made tight associations, too, with junior Sen. John F. Kennedy, with future Senate Majority Leader Johnson, and with Kerr—who was arguably as powerful a figure as Johnson. In Symington, Kennedy, and Johnson, Clifford had as friends three of the party's future presidential contenders.

He became known as the Washington lawyer who had a special skill, who could succeed where others failed—and by the 1960s he was rumored to be the first lawyer in America to make more than a million dollars a year. (He disputes the statement that he was first, without quarreling with the million-dollar figure.) Perhaps his most famous success was in saving millions of dollars for DuPont family interests on the court-ordered divestiture of a huge block of General Motors stock. He was able to push through Congress a bill enabling DuPont's shareholders to pay capital gains taxes, rather than the much higher ordinary income tax, on the shares that were distributed to them. And he did it without lobbying Congress personally, instead directing an imaginative lobbying campaign by DuPont's president.

At the same time, he was seen as a man who could give counsel on delicate, quasi-political problems. In 1957, Sen. Kennedy asked him to counter an accusation by columnist Drew Pearson that Kennedy aide Theodore Sorensen was the real author of Kennedy's Pulitzer Prize–winning book, *Profiles in Courage*. Pearson had made the charge on an ABC broadcast. It was clear, from notes and manuscripts, that Sorensen had at least given Kennedy extensive help in research and writing. But Clifford not only obtained a network apology, he got an ABC vice president to read on the air the groveling statement that Clifford had drafted—with Sorensen. Clifford became JFK's personal lawyer, performing services for him even while supporting rival presidential candidate Symington in the 1960 campaign. Already, Clifford had a special status. Where another man would have been exiled for his service to an opponent, Clifford was respected for a usefulness that transcended political combat. After the election, Kennedy asked Clifford to manage his transition.

To this day Clifford carries secrets about the services he performed as JFK's personal lawyer. But he writes in his book about the political advice he tendered. For example, it was Clifford whom JFK called in, in the fall of 1961, while the family pondered whether twenty-nine-year-old Ted Kennedy should run the following year for the president's old Senate seat. A family friend was keeping it warm for the next Kennedy, and the decision seemed certain but for one thing: Teddy had cheated on two Spanish exams at Harvard ten years earlier. "The president and Bobby wanted my judgment as to its effect on their brother's possible candidacy," Clifford explains in his book, "and recommendations as to how to deal with it publicly if the family concluded that he should make the race." Clifford researched the matter in his lawyerly way, questioning Ted and the classmate who took the exams for him, and concluded the race could be won anyway. Teddy, he counseled, should arrange to explain the incident, as if spontaneously, in answer to a question from a journalist. "The president decided that Teddy should follow the suggestion I had made to surface the matter through an interview with a friendly journalist," Clifford writes. "The man chosen, Robert Healy of the *Boston Globe,* wrote the story on March 30, 1962." Perhaps his strangest assignment, early in the new administration, was JFK's request that he travel to New York to talk to Joseph P. Kennedy Sr., to try to dissuade him from his insistence that Robert F. Kennedy become attorney general. Clifford would not succeed, as surely JFK knew in advance; it seems likely he wanted to preview for his father, in the person of Clifford, the likely reaction of "establishment" Washington to the controversial appointment.

Just once, President Kennedy leaned heavily on Clifford's contacts with industry. In 1962, the big steel companies raised prices on the heels of major union wage concessions, in violation of what Kennedy believed was a solid understanding that the companies, too, would show restraint. The president sent Clifford to stare them down, threatening them with antitrust investigations, tax audits, and defense contract boycotts.

The new administration cemented Clifford's credentials as a "wise man." In an administration striking for its youth, Clifford was able, in his midfifties, to seem an elder statesman, and he played it for all it was worth. His canniest decision was not to join the administration. As transition director he said flatly that he would accept no job in the new administration. Only in that way, he said, could he adjudicate among power-hungry job candidates. He turned aside JFK's tentative suggestions that he become CIA director or chief arms control negotiator. Kennedy understood perfectly the nature of Clifford's use to him, and his to Clifford. "Clark is a wonderful fellow," Kennedy was fond of saying. "In a day when many are seeking a reward for what they contributed to the return of the Democrats to the White House, you don't hear Clark clamoring. All he asked in return was that we advertise his law firm on the backs of one-dollar bills."

Clifford's relationship with Lyndon Johnson had cooled during the Kennedy years. But when LBJ became president, Clifford once again became one of Johnson's chief outside advisors. As always, some of his advice concerned rough-and-tumble political difficulties. Shortly before the 1964 campaign, for example, Clifford and Abe Fortas were called in when LBJ's close aide Walter Jenkins was arrested in a homosexual incident at the District YMCA. Clifford and Fortas visited the city's major newspapers to argue (though unsuccessfully) that the matter should be kept out of the news. The same year, LBJ was worried that the party would demand the vice presidential nomination for Bobby Kennedy—a prospect the president loathed. It was Clifford who drafted a "talking paper" on how to let Bobby down gently, and Johnson, in his anxiety to handle Kennedy carefully, simply read the paper aloud to RFK.

LBJ was far more apt than President Kennedy to call Clifford in on matters of policy. He was a part of White House deliberations all through the Six-Day War, for example. Clifford's book is larded with references to such scenes as joining Johnson in the Situation Room while Johnson talked to Soviet premier Aleksei Kosygin on the hot line. But unlike Fortas, who was intensely involved in Johnson's Great Society, Clifford had little part in the roiling domestic policy of those years.

Clifford handled Johnson astutely. Over and above his own reluctance to return to government, Clifford understood that Johnson was a manipulator and a bully, and he was careful never to put himself directly under LBJ's power. "I had the feeling that from my standpoint, at that period," he says judiciously, "I would serve him better as an independent advisor than actually going into a job which placed me under his control." He turned down—again—the job of CIA director ("I knew that's not what I wanted to do"). He turned down UN ambassador ("I slipped out of that one very quickly") and attorney general—twice. (*Especially* attorney general. A good part of Clifford's practice was antitrust law, a major area of concern for the Justice Department. "I gave as my reason," he says demurely, "that that was not where my principal interest in government lay.") He turned down national security advisor and undersecretary of state.

And then came the day, in 1968, when LBJ issued his direct, very presidential request that Clifford kindly join the administration as Robert McNamara's successor at the Pentagon. "He did not ask me," recalls Clifford. "He proceeded on the assumption that we already had an agreement." Johnson had snared him for what was possibly the hardest job in Washington: the management of the Vietnam War. Three years before, in the summer of 1965, Clifford had warned LBJ against escalating the war. He wrote the president that Vietnam could be a "quagmire," and that 50,000 American soldiers could die—a remarkably prescient prediction. But once LBJ rejected the advice, Clifford decided to pay the price he had to in order to stay at the table. He decided, he says, that "it does me no good to get off in the corner and sulk because he disagreed with me." Johnson had made his choice, Clifford says, so "it became our country's policy and I went ahead and I supported it." He supported it with such vigor that by the time he became secretary of defense, in the days after the Tet Offensive, he was known as one of the most fervent hawks in the president's inner circle. But once assigned personal responsibility for the prosecution of the war, his opinion shifted rapidly, back to his original stance.

General William Westmoreland had just requested an additional 206,000 troops. In the course of reviewing that request, the new secretary conducted a reappraisal of the entire war effort. He concluded that the United States simply had no feasible plan to win the war. Clark Clifford made up his mind to try to get president and country out of Vietnam. Finally, the frustrated doves in the Pentagon and the White House had an ally of sufficient clout to get through to the president. "It was like being in a John Ford movie," recalls Harry McPherson, then Johnson's assistant and chief speechwriter. "It was like the cavalry rode in."

But one did not change Lyndon Johnson's mind through frontal assault. Clifford instead bent his every wile to a campaign for change. Richard Fryklund, a former deputy assistant secretary of public affairs at the Pentagon, remembers the detail with which Clifford plotted his course. Before a meeting in which he hoped to score points, "he'd be leaning back in his chair looking up at the ceiling, as if the script were there, and walking himself through it, as we critiqued it," recalls Fryklund. He rehearsed "down to the little pleasantries. He'd say, 'At this point, I'll turn to Dean [Rusk, secretary of state], and I'll wink.' And then he'd make a remark—some in joke between the two guys—'And then I'll turn back to the president and say—.' And he would have gestures in there." Knowing that Johnson had been encouraged to prosecute the war in meetings with various "Wise Men"—men like Dean Acheson, Douglas Dillon, Cyrus Vance, and Omar Bradley—Clifford arranged for Johnson to host a dinner to hear these men's opinions afresh. It was a ploy, as he knew that Acheson, Dillon, and others had changed their views on Vietnam, and it had the shocking effect on Johnson that Clifford had hoped. Johnson had planned a speech on Vietnam for late March. Clifford, with the help of McPherson and others, used it as an opportunity to redirect the policy. By the time March

31 rolled around, Johnson was ready to announce that the United States would halt almost all bombing and propose peace talks.

"Without question, Clifford played a preeminent—and I believe the decisive—role" in changing Johnson's policy, wrote former undersecretary of the Air Force Townsend Hoopes in his book *The Limits of Intervention*.

> He was the single most powerful and effective catalyst of change. . . . He rallied and gave authoritative voice to the informed and restless opposition within the government, pressing the case for change with intellectual daring, high moral courage, inspired ingenuity, and sheer stubborn persistence. It was one of the great individual performances in recent American history, and achieved in the remarkably taut time span of thirty days.

Johnson also announced on March 31 that he would not seek reelection. Clifford was caught completely by surprise but continued to the end of the administration to tug a string here, push his luck there, and do everything possible to commit the United States to winding down the war. By the time of President Nixon's inauguration, peace talks were under way. And although Nixon continued to press the war, expanding it into Laos and Cambodia, Clifford's work had at least limited the American effort.

Clifford's acts made him a hero to an entire generation of Democrats in Washington who had watched in horror as their party's presidents tied the nation's fate to the Vietnam War. His relationship with Lyndon Johnson, on the other hand, never recovered. Though persuaded by Clifford's campaign, Johnson felt it was a betrayal. As secretary of defense, accountable to history for his acts, Clifford traded away his most cherished resource—the confidence of the president—for what he perceived as the correct course. It was the kind of conflict Clifford's Five Commandments were devised to avoid. It was the finest hour of his career.

With Nixon elected, Clifford went back to full-time private practice. And though the Republicans now controlled the White House, Clifford's prestige was at an all-time high. He was sixty-two.

He was known as a man of both principle and pragmatism. The stage seemed set for the kind of twilight career Washington offers its favorite sons: a selective practice, golf at Burning Tree, a trade mission here, and a special diplomatic assignment there. A gradual, dignified retirement. Two decades later Clifford would be working twelve-hour days, around the clock and around the year, at a new career. He would not go gentle into that good night. He would be driven, instead, toward the darkness of personal scandal.

Margery Pepperell Kimball Clifford, known to her friends as Marny, has a reputation for plain speaking. She is explaining what a difficult time her husband has had lately. How painful it is for him to hear his good name, after all these years, linked to wrongdoing. How much he has aged since investigators began asking how this revered elder statesman came to be fronting for a group of Middle Eastern investors who apparently circumvented U.S. banking laws. How tired he is of saying, over and over, that things are not what they seem. "The trouble is," she explains, "you'd say exactly the same things if you were guilty. Think about it—you would." She has summarized Clark Clifford's problem more neatly than reams of investigators' reports ever could.

"I just find it totally hard to believe he's gotten into any kind of problems," says Democratic lawyer Berl Bernhard, voicing the commonsensical puzzlement that is almost universally shared in Washington: "One, he doesn't need to. And two, you know, the thought that someone in some way misled or deceived him—it's possible, but it makes me say, Good Lord, these people must be very clever. Because he is not what you'd call ingenuous." *These people* are the high-rolling bankers who Clifford says may—*may*, he emphasizes— have taken advantage of his good name.

The story is complicated in its details, but simple in its essence. In the late 1970s a group orchestrated by a Luxembourg-based bank, Bank of Credit and Commerce International (BCCI), tried to buy a

Washington-based bank holding company, Financial General Bank-shares. BCCI was a sprawling and secretive international bank, with tendrils everywhere but little accountability to any nation that might regulate its operations. The American bank resisted, and the deal disintegrated under a mass of lawsuits. Subsequently, a group of Middle Eastern investors—all of them banking clients of BCCI—offered to buy the bank. Federal and state regulators were concerned. Were these investors fronting for BCCI? No, the feds were told. Was BCCI lending them money to buy the bank? No—and furthermore the investors intended to be passive investors, with no interest in the running of the bank. Would BCCI be in any way involved in the running of Financial General? No. Its only possible role was to be an occasional advisor to the investors, who after all were long-term BCCI clients.

The man who made all these representations on the investors' behalf was Clark Clifford. Other lawyers were involved, of course, and some of the wealthy investors themselves traveled from Saudi Arabia and Kuwait to explain their intentions to a special meeting of Federal Reserve Board officials and state banking regulators in April 1981. But it was Clark Clifford, silver-haired and silken-voiced elder statesman, who introduced the investors, vouched for them, and gave the regulators his personal assurance that the deal was in order. "There is no function of any kind on the part of BCCI," Clifford told the hearing. "I know of no present relationship. I know of no planned future relationship that exists." He himself had agreed, he added, to act as chairman of the bank, ensuring an important layer of insulation between the day-to-day operations of the bank and the passive investors in the Middle East. He had already recruited, for the prospective board of directors, such distinguished Americans as his friend Stuart Symington, former senator from Missouri. "I am comforted," he told the hearing about the deal, "that I know that it's good for our country."

The deal went through; the company was renamed First American Bankshares; and Clifford, at seventy-five, became chairman of the largest bank holding company in the Washington area. Robert A.

Altman, thirty-three, his closest colleague in the law firm Clifford &
Warnke, became president. Neither of them had ever run any business larger than a twenty-lawyer law firm. Today, First American
Bankshares is an $11 billion enterprise with subsidiaries in six states
and the District of Columbia, and more than 180 bank branches in
the Washington area alone.* But rumors have surrounded the real
ownership of the company ever since its sale. In 1988, a BCCI officer
arrested in a federal money-laundering sting operation told a wired
undercover agent that BCCI owned First American. Clark Clifford,
he said, was BCCI's attorney in Washington, and a formidable figure.
"I mean," the man said, "Clark Clifford is sort of the godfather of the
Democratic Party." The rumors were borne out early this year when
BCCI, under new management and under pressure from investigators, acknowledged illegally owning a controlling interest in First
American. At several points, an audit showed, First American's
nominal investors bought new shares in First American's holding
company, financing the purchases with loans from BCCI. The investors never paid off the loans, and so BCCI gained control of the
shares by default. The Federal Reserve Board ordered BCCI to divest
itself of whatever shares it holds in First American.

The complexity of the relationship between the two banks is increased by the fact that Clifford's law firm represented both BCCI
and First American for most of the 1980s. Clifford and Altman
played a leading role in shaping BCCI's defense against the money-
laundering charges. These charges added a lurid taint to the story
when investigators learned that some of the laundered money, funds
of Panamanian strongman Manuel Noriega, was moved through an
account in First American. Yet Clifford and his partner have dis-
claimed any knowledge of BCCI involvement in First American's
affairs. They still speak of the problem in the subjunctive voice,
about the shares BCCI *allegedly*, or *possibly*, controls. Clifford has

---

*A much-diminished First American Bankshares was bought out in 1993 by
First Union Corp. First Union, in turn, was acquired in 2001 by Wachovia Corp.

been in full operating control of the bank, he says. *If* any illegality took place, Clifford says, it was done behind his back. "It wasn't anything that *we* did. We haven't done a thing. We've run the bank and run it honestly."

There has been, in friends' and allies' comments about Clifford, a faith that his problems will work out, that somehow Clark will explain everything. His friend and longtime client Pamela Harriman said, "It seems incredible to me, with all of Clark's long knowledge of people, that this was possible. But I'm absolutely convinced that there was no wrongdoing done with his knowledge." That was before the *Washington Post* reported that Clifford and Altman were able to buy stock in First American's holding company in 1986 and 1987 with money loaned to them almost risk-free by BCCI. Between them they have made $ 9.8 million—two-thirds to Clifford and one-third to Altman—in pretax profit by reselling 60 percent of the stock to a man who also financed the purchase with a loan from BCCI.

Here, too, Clifford and Altman say everything is aboveboard. They bought stock in lieu of compensation, they say. Clifford has been paid only $50,000 in salary each year, and Altman has not drawn a salary. They paid interest and fees on the loans. They had the permission of the directors of First American's holding company and filed the required notices of the stock purchases with American banking authorities. But the directors of the holding company, who approved the deal, numbered only four. Two of them were longtime friends of Clifford's—Symington and retired Lt. Gen. Elwood P. Quesada, onetime director of the Federal Aviation Administration. The other two were Clark Clifford and Robert Altman.

The most striking things about the deal are that Clifford and Altman never had to put up any money of their own, and that they were able to sell the stock for three times what they paid for it. It is the development that takes the story beyond the realm of international wire transfers and the complexities of offshore banking and into the readily grasped realm of political nightmare. "I think it makes everything that much worse," says one heavyweight lawyer. "Because it reflects on his statements, and Altman's statements, that they were operating the bank independent of BCCI. Why would BCCI, in effect, give them that money? It makes it all much stickier."

———

How could a man who valued his reputation so highly have been either seduced or gulled into lending that reputation to clients who used it so crassly? Why did a man in his seventies and eighties, after a career like Clifford's, borrow this trouble? For every unanswered question, some admirers of Clifford's like to steer a reporter toward a single answer: that his problems are the fault of his younger partner. *Go get Altman,* they whisper, off the record, at interview's end. *It's got to be Altman.*

For the past decade and more, Altman has been Clifford's closest associate, working with him on his most important cases and handling the day-to-day business of running the bank. And whereas Clifford had been a millionaire for decades at the time the bank deal was struck, Clifford's friends say, Altman was a nakedly ambitious young man still on the verge of the big time. Perhaps he pushed Clifford into the deal, they say, or misled him along the way about the true nature of First American's relationship with BCCI.

Clifford and Altman appear a study in contrasts. Altman, forty-four, is married to actress Lynda Carter, who played Wonder Woman on TV and passes, in Washington, for glitz. He lives in an enormous new mansion in Potomac, where he throws parties for an enormous collection of new friends. When Altman and Clifford work cases together, it is said in the legal community, they are a formidable tag team. Clifford is the genial good cop who calls up and confers the compliment of humbly introducing himself to a new adversary. Altman is the one who calls later and threatens scorched earth if you don't back down. It could be seen as the familiar case of the powerful man who assigns his more disagreeable deeds to a surrogate, as President George H. W. Bush did with Lee Atwater.* But the bond

---

*See "The Story of a Bad Boy," p. 205.

between Clifford and Altman is also a personal one. At this point Altman may be his mentor's chief intimate. Clifford was best man at Altman's wedding and became the godfather of Altman's son, James Clifford Altman. "It's almost like a father–son relationship, in a way," confirms Marny Clifford. Clifford is the father of three daughters and very much a man of his generation where gender roles are concerned. His firm has no women partners, and he is given to referring to female support staff as "girls." Altman says, "I suppose he wanted to pass on to someone that which he had learned over fifty or sixty years."

Clifford firmly closes off any implication that Altman could have acted at any point without his knowledge. "I have been in charge of the matter," he says firmly. "I have set the policy and he has complied with the policy I have set." Altman echoes that statement—and minimizes his own role in the pair's decision to become involved in the operations of the bank, saying, "I think the whole idea kind of challenged [Clifford]. He took it on and I went along for the ride." He amends himself quickly: "Well, that's a little casual."

Since the stock deal was revealed, only a few of Clifford's friends cling to some hope that Altman will be shown to have abused Clifford's trust. But all along, those tempted to attribute the scandal to the hunger of the younger man have underestimated the role of Clifford's own drive, a force so insistent that it has kept him working long past the point where other men, willingly or not, have come to rest. To understand what kept Clifford striving, you would have to go far back, to the era before radio. To a time when lamplighters walked the neighborhoods of St. Louis in the evening, a day when little boys read Horatio Alger books for ideas of how to be men.

In his great gift for self-presentation, Clifford carries most visibly the legacy of his mother, Georgia McAdams Clifford. She was the sister of the dashing liberal editor of the *St. Louis Post-Dispatch*, Clark McAdams, and her family were all vibrant, colorful souls.

Georgia Clifford was a professional storyteller. She was president of the National Story Tellers' League, and in the 1930s she had her own show on the CBS radio network. Quite deliberately, she taught Clifford and his sister to revere language and to present themselves with flair. He believes she is one of the reasons he was drawn to the high dramatics of trial law as his first career and the source of the subtler thespian gifts he brought to his role in Washington.

But the most important legacy was his father's. Clifford's bond with his father was a powerful one. It was not until his father died, he writes, that he felt free to join the navy, setting in motion his entire new career. Neither in person nor in his book does Clifford use the word "failure" to describe his father, but this is the sense that hangs heavy in his descriptions. "It's going to sound queer," Clifford says, "but I think he felt that the greatest accomplishment of his life was getting my mother." Frank Clifford's career was with the Missouri Pacific Railroad, and as Clifford grew up his father was making the slow rise through the executive ranks—partly by virtue of having as a mentor the railroad's executive vice president. "The railroad was my father's whole life," Clifford recalls. "He never worked for anybody else." But the boss died suddenly, of a heart attack. New management was brought in, and Frank Clifford's career was swiftly, permanently sidetracked. His spirit, his son says, was crushed.

"The spring went out of his step and the sparkle went out of his eye," Clifford recalls, "and I was old enough then that he could talk with me about it. . . . And the lesson from that my father passed on to me—and he *meant* to pass it on to me—was, try to plan your life so that it is not dependent upon others. . . . The more you can construct and structure your own life based upon your own efforts and the less subject your life is to the direction and control of others, the happier you're going to be." The lesson, absorbed when the son was in college, can be traced through Clifford's entire career. Going into law and then setting up his own firm, where no single client could make or break him. Resisting government appointments by Kennedy and especially by the domineering Johnson.

But even before Frank Clifford's career collapsed, he had striven to give his son a stern message about work. "From the time I was four or five," Clifford writes, "he began to impress me with the fact that to live was to work." Look at Clifford's life through the lens of that proposition, and a pattern announces itself. He graduated from high school at fifteen. He had ulcers by the time he was in his thirties. The word he uses most often to characterize his life is *discipline*.

"He's a true workaholic," says Marny Clifford, "one of the worst I've ever seen. He's on a treadmill—he can't get off it." Pamela Harriman agrees. "Except for golf, I can't think of anything he really enjoys outside of the office." Paul Warnke calculates that his eighty-four-year-old law partner "is here certainly always five days a week, usually six and sometimes seven." Marny explains: "He doesn't like vacations. Hates them." For years, Clifford took only a week's vacation every year—an all-male golf trip to a Fort Lauderdale, Florida, house made available to him by Phillips Petroleum, on whose board he used to sit. For the past nine years, since he began running the bank, he says proudly, he hasn't taken *any* vacation.

Clark Clifford can't possibly need the money. This is the bedrock, puzzled response to Clifford's troubles, in living rooms and law firms all around Washington. And it's true. Not only does he have more money than he needs; he doesn't especially seem to enjoy the money he has. The house where the Cliffords have lived since 1950 appears to bear this out. It is a historic landmark, a nineteenth-century clapboard farmhouse where J. E. B. Stuart's men were bivouacked during the Civil War. The land it occupies, just off Rockville Pike, is quite valuable. And yes, the Cliffords have servants, including the man who answers the door and later brings iced tea on a little round platter to Marny and her visitor. And yes, there are sleek, dark cars in the garage, a dowdy Fleetwood and a more dashing black Jaguar. But there are few other signs of wealth in this house, which displays the confident negligence of the upper class. Paint is cracking on the wall of the main stairway. In the living room the slipcovers are worn dull, having served their masters since 1931. In the dining room there are small tendrils of dust on the walls, near the ceiling. Pointing out her collection of Chinese porcelain, displayed on the walls of the room, Marny Clifford says, with reflexive Yankee frugality, that of course these are pieces she's had for ages. They've gotten so expensive she can't afford to buy any more.

Clark Clifford just doesn't care much about possessions, or social life, or any of the things that most Americans think of as sources of pleasure. "Clark is a very simple soul, he really is," Marny explains. "I can't remember him ever, in all the years I've been married to him, wanting something. I can think of a thousand things I want; most people can. But he is very strange that way."

There is, however, something he needs.

She finishes her tour of the house in the den, where the memorabilia of his career are displayed. She points at the photos on the wall nearest the front of the house, of the friends and acquaintances who enlivened five decades of life in Washington. They are all pictures of dead men. "Stu," says Marny Clifford sadly, at the photo of the late Stuart Symington, for decades Clifford's best friend. "Omar Bradley, he's dead." She points, and points again. "Tom Clark's dead. Bill Douglas is dead." She shakes her head. "Bob Lovett, Averell. Jimmy Forrestal, he's dead."

Clifford had outlived, by 1981, almost all of his old colleagues. He had outlived his presidents and, in a way, his party, which had lost a landslide to Ronald Reagan. Although he had been consulted from time to time by President Carter, assigned the odd trouble-shooting trip abroad, it had been years since he was a White House regular. He had even outlived many of his clients. "I think that as you get to be mid-seventies, you look around and all of a sudden your clients have retired," says partner Warnke. "The [corporate] general counsels are years younger than you are, so as a result your younger partners are much more apt to get new business than you are. And Clark, I think, did not want to have nothing to do." It seems possible, then, that the Arab buyers of Financial General Bankshares had something incalculably valuable to offer the seventy-five-year-old Clark Clifford.

To live is to work.

"I think, at the time, without considering, I was looking at other contemporaries who were seventy-five, looking to see what they did," Clifford says. "Some of them would go with their wives each morning to the market and help with the marketing, help pushing those carts and all. Well, I didn't find that very appealing. Another was to go down to the post office every morning and get the mail. That wasn't anything that excited me much. A lot of them go to Florida and disappear. Some of them just sit on the front porch and rock and wait to *die*." He infuses the syllable with drama, then adds the dryly comic punctuation: "That didn't appeal to me either."

Both the darkness and the humor of this meditation have a calculated quality. If a true feeling animates it, it sounds like contempt for all those cart pushers and mail fetchers. Clifford recalls that "back when I used to take vacations, about the second or third or fourth day I would have had enough." He gestures around at his dusky office, cocooned by its heavy drapes. "This is my life here. This is what I do."

~~~

"I had been *me-tic-u-lous-ly* careful through the years that I not get involved in a posture that would be embarrassing for me," says Clark Clifford, tapping a long finger on his desk. "It is very easy to do in Washington. And it didn't happen to me. I've been here all these years, you see, then I ran into this recent problem."

This recent problem. In a series of interviews, Clifford replies to questions about the bank with a quality that looks very much like bafflement. Again and again, he makes arguments that run counter to everything Clark Clifford has stood for in more than four decades of Washington life. "When people say, 'Oh, Clifford must have known,' the fact is, I would have been the *last* one to know," says Clifford. "I would have been the last one [BCCI] would have told. . . . Because maybe they did use my good name at the beginning. Maybe they did depend to some extent upon my reputation. All right, if that's an asset then it's an asset. But they wouldn't tell me what was going on, because the day they would have told me was the day that I would have left them." *I was blind,* says the man who made a career of seeing around corners.

"At the time, under the conditions that existed, it all seemed perfectly appropriate," he says of his stock deal. "Let me add that there's nothing illegal in any way with the deal regarding the purchase of the stocks." *I am within the letter of the law,* says the man who always understood—who taught some of the most powerful men of his time—that in Washington, once you are reduced to arguing the law you have already lost the case.

Only one, or at most two, people know what really happened in Clifford's stewardship of the bank, down to his most personal motives. Whether he led or followed; whether he was involved from the start in a foreign bank's scheme to gain control of an American outlet, or passively allowed it to develop behind his unassailable image; whether Clifford was lied to or deluded himself. But the truth is that Clifford is proud of his bank. His picture has graced its annual reports. He once even appeared in a First American commercial. When his friend and fellow lawyer Edward Bennett Williams was dying of cancer, Clifford was anxious to show him around the bank before he was too ill to go out. Lawyer Bob Strauss describes how he, Clifford, and Williams had lunch at the bank's offices, in the shadow of the great, grave oil portrait of Clark Clifford, Bank Chairman. "It was almost like a father showing off accomplishments to his son," says Strauss.

Clark Clifford's ultimate mistake may have been that, after a lifetime of making Washington believe in his legend, he fully believed in it himself. Clifford came along in an era when great corporate wealth was learning how to counter a whole new generation of government regulation. He became the fig leaf assuring postwar Washingtonians that all the profitable transactions here between public and private power, business as usual, are simply the workings of a mighty democracy. If Clark Clifford could be what he was—"advisor to the presidents"—at the same time he was making millions of dollars, year in and year out, working for the biggest corporations in America; if he could nip across Lafayette Square from his office to help Lyndon Johnson sort out the Six-Day War in between helping General Electric and McDonnell-Douglas and Knight-Ridder and scores more to palliate the wearisome meddling of the federal government; if Clark Clifford could do all this, then surely the . . . *friendly* relationship of political power and corporate wealth in Washington is just the natural order of things.

As Mr. Integrity, the man who wrote the warranty of Washington's basic virtue, Clifford has been selling his reputation for a long, long time. It was as heady a role as exists in Washington, perhaps in all of corporate America. He seems baffled, so late in life, that the safe haven of his reputation cannot protect the man who needs it now.

Clifford says he regrets nothing. He looks back a decade, to his initial involvement in the bank, and says, "Given the facts as I knew them then, I would make the same decision." But sitting in his curtained office, closed away from the White House, the Capitol, the power centers of the city he once owned, he does say he is full of misgiving. "I'm mystified," says Clark Clifford. "And I want to tell you that in the process I've lost something that I worked for for sixty-two years. To a certain extent I've lost my good name, and I'm deeply sorry about that."

—*May 8 and 9, 1991*

POSTSCRIPT (FOUR MONTHS LATER): THE HEARING

He shambled in clutching an old gray fedora, of the kind (perhaps the very hat) he wears in photos from the 1940s, where he smiles from his deferential spot a few steps astern of Harry Truman's shoulder. He never put the hat on his head yesterday, but that wasn't the point. Clark Clifford, master of gesture, had come to defend himself before the House Banking Committee, theater of the absurd. As usual, he left nothing to chance.

It can't have been an accident that Marny Clifford and Lynda Carter—starlet-wife of Clifford's protégé and law partner Robert Altman—came in first, dressed in black. Or that Clifford made notations on his documents with a humble pencil. Or that the pair's long-awaited first public testimony about the widening bank scandal they find themselves in opened with a long, chatty narrative from Clifford himself that threw a moist blanket of pathos over the fiery oratory of the committee members.

He was the elderly trial lawyer, bringing all his skills to the summation of his last, most important case. He was a ventriloquist, playing straight man to a partner assigned the riskier lines. He was Grampy, telling the kids about how he built the homestead in aught-four—a statesman reminding a roomful of aspirants that he was present at the creation of their universe. He was everything he had to be if he hoped to persuade the committee—and the vastly more important television audience beyond—that he was, in a word he stressed, *mystified* to find himself at the helm of an institution secretly owned by an outlaw foreign bank.

"Now, I recognize as I listen to you gentlemen we have a formidable task in persuading many of you of our innocence in this," Clifford told the committee in buckling down to his opening statement, an hour-and-a-half-long tale that walked his audience from his service in Truman's White House up through his twilight career as chairman of First American Bankshares. "But I approach it willingly. I approach it with a desire to have this hearing.

"Each of you at some time in your career has been attacked and you've recognized the difficulty with how you respond to the attack. You don't own a newspaper through which you can speak and neither do we. You don't have persons who will rise to your defense and neither do we." Never mind that he was anxiously flanked by some of the most serious Washington and New York legal talent money can buy. Clark Clifford brings an epic sincerity to all he says. In the high ivory expanse of the Rayburn House Office Building's Wright Patman Room, his musical voice rang clear, an instrument more complicated than normal human voices. "The whole atmosphere of the public, all the proceedings that have taken place, all would be against us. And yet, we appear here so that you can hear our side. And I suggest to you that it is my deep conviction that when you have heard us, you will at least in some way have a different attitude."

He told them that "our consciences are clear." He told them, "You have my *word* for it." He told them he took on the management of a major bank holding company a decade ago, at the age of seventy-five, because he needed the challenge. "Maybe it's kept me alive for nine more years," he said, with a smile that shyly conceded his great age.

In the end, he let himself be at a loss for words. He paused. He lifted his skeletal, elongated, always-busy fingers in a gesture of confusion. "My judgment is questionable," he said sadly. "I guess I should have learned [of BCCI's ownership] some way. . . . I'd give a lot if somebody had told me, back in 1984, that this operation was the kind that it was. I would have given anything if I could have avoided what I've gone through this past year." When he was done, he fell into the profound stillness from which he marshals his energy after eighty-four years. Sitting back, eyes closed, the articulate hands for once at rest, he seemed impossibly old, the famous hair a pure white, the skin a rosy map of crinkled tissue. His brows and lashes seemed dusted by snow.

"Mr. Clifford is most impressive," said ranking minority member Chalmers P. Wylie (R–Ohio) out in the hallway, after a full morning of this. "Mr. Clifford could sell hams in a synagogue."

It wasn't so much the things he said. Although it was Clifford's first public testimony about the relationship between BCCI and First American Bankshares, which Clifford chaired until his resignation in August 1991, there were no major developments in yesterday's hearing. There were no shocking revelations about the scandal, which flows from intensive investigations by the Federal Reserve, the Manhattan district attorney, and a Senate committee. No important new twists in the explanations offered by Clifford or Altman, First American's former president.

It was the clash of imperatives that made it a classic piece of Washington drama. On one side, Clifford and Altman, pressing their public defense. On the other, a committee of fifty-two men and women who, for the past couple of years, have labored in the gloomy shade of the savings and loan scandal.* The House Banking Committee—formerly a prestigious assignment—has come in for a major share of blame for regulatory laxity. Clark Clifford, then, represented a wonderful opportunity for the thirty-odd members who put in appearances. Indignation! Righteousness! Few constituents understand what the BCCI scandal is all about, but surely they know it's bad. What could be better than a chance to admonish the scandal's two leading American players?

"It pains me to say this," said Rep. Toby Roth (R–Wis.), painlessly. "Others may believe your story, but I must say I don't believe a word of it. I've looked at this case and my conclusion is that you knew and that you made millions."

"Mr. Chairman," said Rep. Charles Schumer (D–N.Y.), "Mr. Altman and Mr. Clifford are asking us to believe that when their house was on fire, they didn't smell the smoke, feel the heat, or hear the alarms."

Schumer knows how to get maximum mileage from a hearing. After the committee broke for lunch, he told me: "When you listen to Clifford and all his achievements, my heart wants to believe him, but my head says it's very hard to." Then he rushed away to the TV microphones set up in the lobby of the Rayburn Building's east entrance. "When I listen to Clifford and think about his achievement," Schumer said, "my heart wants to believe him, but my head says no." When the hearing resumed after lunch, Schumer told Clifford, "After listening to your presentation, I guess I would say to you that my heart wants to believe you, but my head says no."

---

*During the 1980s a combination of reckless lending practices and ill-considered federal deregulation set up the savings and loan industry for massive failures. The government ended up spending $124 billion to clean up the mess, in what is often described as the biggest financial scandal in U.S. history.

When Clifford first reached the witness table he handed the hat to Marny, who stowed it beneath her chair with the aplomb of a woman who's been serving as assistant prop master for sixty years.

Lynda Carter's role was more prominent. At the hearing's start, as Clifford and Altman entered through the northernmost door, the former Wonder Woman sprang to the threshold to give her man a photogenic kiss. Awkwardly, there were no cameras there, so she also gave him a kiss when the proceedings broke for lunch. On their way out of the room, Altman and Carter paused for photographs, and she murmured some supportive words about the relief of hearing her husband granted a chance to air the truth. As they swept down the marble hallway, the cameras helplessly trailed this unaccustomed glamour. When the Cliffords came out, no cameras remained to record the fact that they were holding hands.

Altman himself dominated the afternoon, answering most of the members' prolix and somewhat redundant questions. It fell to him to perform the high-wire act of answering most of the more specific inquiries, citing the nitty-gritty specifics of dates and times and laws and letters. It was a fascinating chance to watch the symbiotic bond of Clifford and Altman, who together make up a third character in the drama. If one looks improbably old, the other seems improbably young. Altman, like Clifford, wore a double-breasted, pin-striped suit with upswept lapels, a white shirt, and French cuffs. Altman shadows Clifford's hand gestures, sometimes mimicking at the very same time Clifford's steepled gesture, in which the fingers all meet in thoughtful comity.

The room reverberated with the kind of irony in which Washington specializes. Fourteen years ago this week, Clifford starred in a different hearing, across the Hill, concerning a different banking scandal. Only then he was Bert Lance's lawyer—writing his client's aggressive, give-no-quarter opening statement, and then teaching him how to modulate his later responses to include grateful praise of the senators who had given him the opportunity to clear the air.*

---

*Lance, White House budget chief under president Jimmy Carter, was forced to resign over allegations of earlier corruption when he was chairman of a Georgia bank. In a subsequent criminal trial, Lance was cleared of all charges.

Lance was so impressed by Clifford's skills that he recommended him to Agha Hasan Abedi, the Pakistani banker who eventually embroiled Clifford in BCCI.

And how must it feel to Clifford to receive lèse majesté from the likes of Rep. Joseph P. Kennedy II (D–Mass.)? Kennedy opened with a statement praising everyone involved in the case, including Clark Clifford, whom he called "one of the greatest public servants in modern American history. . . . His record of courageous service to our country is legendary and needs no introduction." One imagined Clifford thinking, *You young pup*; thinking of how he had kept the most private secrets of the congressman's uncle, President Kennedy, had vainly tried to explain to the grandfather—the first Joe Kennedy—that the father, Bobby Kennedy, would never do for attorney general.

This was, after all, just the House of Representatives. Not the place Clifford ever had his closest contacts. Not worth that investment of his time. But this was the place chosen for his star turn. And so it was worth enduring, stoically, a certain amount of denunciation.

Rep. Maxine Waters (D–Calif.), a freshman member, went beyond fulmination into something like passion. "Let me just say that as a new member of this committee, I am thoroughly disgusted with the high and mighty, with the privileged," she said. "I come from a district where people are poor, where people are struggling, where people go to jail when they steal a loaf of bread. They're shot by cops if they dare to make a wrong move. . . . The high and the mighty and the rich are getting away with unusual criminal activity, and I'm anxious to be involved in these hearings. I do not intend to be nice to anybody."

In the midst of her statement, Clifford elaborately cleared his throat, a troubling, phlegmy sound he made no effort to direct away from the microphone. And for the whole morning, he addressed the "gentlemen of the committee," or "you men," excluding not only Waters but also Reps. Mary Rose Oakar (D–Ohio) and Marge Roukema (R–N.J.). Each time, Waters smiled a wintry smile. Could this just be the reflexive sexism of an eighty-four-year-old man?

It seemed likely until the lunch break, when Clifford was coaxed to the TV microphones in the lobby. Some committee members had said very harsh things, a reporter observed: Did it bother him?

"I think everyone's entitled to—" and Clifford paused slightly, the tired gent suddenly falling away to be replaced by a younger, more dangerous man, "—*his* opinion," he concluded with an acid smile.

Before the day was out, the testimony would raise other populist eyebrows. Rep. Clifford B. Stearns (R–Fla.) asked Altman about reports that BCCI's Abedi had given Lynda Carter a Jaguar as a wedding gift. "It is true that he gave my wife a very generous gift," he said. "That is the kind of thing that is done in the circles in which he operated in the Middle East, but as far as a personal relationship, our dealings were almost entirely business." Toward hearing's end, Clifford was addressed by the lone socialist member of Congress, Bernie Sanders (Vt.), about the BCCI loans that enabled him to purchase First American stock that he later sold at great profit. "Tell the American people and the working people making eight or ten bucks an hour whose standard of living is declining," Sanders said, "what it's about when prominent Americans work for Middle Eastern billionaire dictators who provide $10 million lines of credit, and as a result of that they are able to make many, many millions of dollars in a couple of years. . . . What should they believe in that type of system?"

Clifford pointed out that there was nothing illegal about his representing the foreign investors he believed to be First American's shareholders. With patient hauteur, he explained that "these people abroad decide that they want to acquire this bank holding company. So they get together and they come up with around $200 million. Now, this may be difficult for citizens in Vermont who make $8, $10 an hour to understand, but it happens all the time."

The lunch break lasted two hours, at the advance request of Clifford's attorneys, so that Clifford could take a nap. As the questions dragged on in the afternoon session, it was apparent the hearing couldn't end by 5:00 p.m., so there was another break in the late afternoon.

It was after 7:00 p.m. when chairman Henry B. Gonzales (D–Tex.) finally gaveled the hearing to a close. "I know it's been long," he told Clifford and Altman. "This committee is large. You can look at it this way: it's a fifty-two-member committee. It's as if you had appeared before half of the Senate, plus two."

Just as lawyer Clifford would have advised, witness Clifford thanked the committee for its courtesy before shambling out, for the last time, to the Cadillac that would bear him home.*

—September 12, 1991

---

*Altman eventually went on trial for bank fraud in New York and was acquitted. Clifford was also indicted, but managed to avoid standing trial because of ill health. The two men paid $5 million to settle a legal action brought by the Federal Reserve Board. Clifford died in 1998 at the age of ninety-one.

HERE COMES THE GROOM

(LARRY KING)

This one, you see, is different.

"I have never been with a person like Shawn," says Larry King, about the actress and infomercial entrepreneur with whom he will make his seventh trip to the altar in September, "who I like as much as I love. I've loved people without liking 'em. Liked people without loving 'em. . . . She's not only beautiful outwardly," he continues, "but beautiful inwardly. So I, like, adore her. I wouldn't hurt her for the world. And I've changed with her!"

In person, Larry King is unexpectedly pink. From his open shirt collar up to the crest of fine hair that is artfully poufed each morning at a Georgetown hair salon, his skin has the too-scrubbed rosy softness peculiar to TV stars who go in and out of thick makeup nearly every day. The heavy, square glasses seem less enormous than they do on television, and so do the brown eyes they frame. Peering out from this famous face, placidly friendly, they seem the small eyes of an ordinary man who is hiding inside the wild colors and iconic features of a Larry King costume. On his feet, this noon, are blue suede shoes, two shades darker than a Miami sky.

And here is the amazing thing: King is discussing his impending marriage, to thirty-seven-year-old Shawn Southwick, as if it were a genuine surprise. "If you had told me eight months ago, 'You're going to meet someone twenty-six years younger than you, and might

like to have a baby again'—ha ha! I had just told David Frost
. . . 'I'll never marry again.'"

He says this as if he were not the only person in America who believed, eight months earlier, that Larry King would never again propose marriage, impulsively, passionately, as he had at least eight
times before (counting the two engagements that were made and
broken since the end of his last marriage). As if he were not a man
whose best friend has observed that he marries so often he has rice
scars.

"I mean, what do I need it for?" asks King rhetorically. For excitement, say his friends and former loves. "He's like one of those Vietnam guys who re-ups and re-ups, because they're hooked on the
adrenaline of it," says Rama Fox, who was engaged but never married
to King. For affirmation. For company. "There's something about
Larry that's almost a little poignant," says a Washington woman who
has seen him casually over the years. "He's a lonely man."

He is also, according to friends and colleagues, a man of chaotic
and boundless needs. "He is a very sweet man, and he is desperate to
connect with people," says Tom Farmer, former executive producer
of *Larry King Live*. In the view of those who like the sixty-three-
year-old King, he is genial, well intentioned, generous to a fault.
The worst you can say about their version of Larry King is that there
is pathos to him.

Some, however, see a darker Larry King. This is the man who was
once arrested for larceny, who scammed loans from banks, who has
compulsively deceived the women he loves, who has been the target
and the instigator of litigation in four different states, who declared
bankruptcy not once but twice.

They are, of course, the same Larry King: the same eager, starving
presence that comes live, six nights a week at 9:00 p.m., eastern
standard time, into America's living rooms. After forty years in
broadcasting—most of them on radio—and twelve years on CNN,
King is a bona fide TV star, host of the highest-rated show on his
network. Many critics have tried unsuccessfully to put a finger (or
lay a glove) on King's appeal; they point to his gruffly ingratiating
voice and his ability to project intense interest in his guests and the

way he immerses the famous in a warm bath of reassurance and re-spect. *New York Times* columnist Maureen Dowd may have come closest when she called him "the resort area of American journal-ism, the media's Palm Springs, where politicians and other figures of controversy or celebrity can go to unwind." But his success is, fi-nally, one of those self-validating miracles of television culture. He has made himself, through sheer desire, the mayor of Celebrityville.

It is not an accident that women move through King's life almost as rapidly as guests move in and out of the chair that faces his across the little desk in CNN's Studio 11C. "All the qualities that make Larry a great interviewer make him really bad husband material," says a close friend. "All the curiosity, the 'Who's the most interest-ing person in the room, and who's the latest, the newest?'" The man's personality perfectly reflects the demands of the media and the network that made him rich and famous.

It is King's job to elide the gap between hard news and entertain-ment, to allow CNN—the no-frills network born of Ted Turner's conviction that America could be fed all news, all the time, unem-bellished by stars and pretty faces—to traffic in our baser appetites. And it isn't easy to dignify the proposition that Sylvester Stallone equals the president of the United States equals Kathie Lee equals Yasser Arafat equals Kato Kaelin equals Ross Perot. It is not easy to insist, day in and day out, that our interest in the North American Free Trade Agreement is no more or less ennobling than our interest in the murder of JonBenet Ramsey. To pull off this trick, it helps to be someone who has only a nodding acquaintance with reality, whose own inner life is as obscure to him as the lunar tides of a dis-tant planet.

Having a conversation with King is like sitting with someone on sodium pentothal. It all comes burbling out, the shallow stream of his consciousness, the most profound feelings of his life followed by the glancing encounters with celebrities, quickly pursued by the well-worn stories of his fabled youth in Brooklyn. "She has no guile," he says of Southwick. "I never met anyone like that. Like, incapable of lying. Don Shula was that way. That's why I respected him so much."

On the air, at lunch in Washington, over breakfast in Beverly Hills, King disgorges famous names with the efficiency of a gum-ball machine: "Anthony Quinn was on my television show . . . I like Sam Donaldson . . . I remember [Billy] Graham telling me once . . . I know Ben Bradlee . . . Walter Matthau, great guy . . . George Bush told me . . . I flew out to Houston with Elizabeth Dole. . . ."

King's show—always a modest hit for CNN—reached a new level of success in the 1992 presidential campaign. After Ross Perot chose King as his confidant, declaring on the show in February of that year his willingness to run for president, *Larry King Live* was suddenly the hottest thing in politics. Once scorned as the lightweight celebrity-monger down the hall from CNN's Washington newsroom, King was learning to play a canny game, in which his political interviews validated the show for more glamorous guests and viewers, and his celebrity side glamorized the show for wing-tipped Washington folks. This year alone, he will make cameo appearances in seven films, affording Hollywood an easy shorthand for a movie character's rise to a certain level of stardom.

But if the show's success relies on its mixture of subjects, King is clearly most excited by the celebrity side. In some essential way, the proximity of fame validates the man who was once Lawrence Harvey Zeiger, of Brooklyn's Bensonhurst. In his 1989 book about his heart attack and quintuple-bypass surgery, he records the vast number of celebrities who sent him flowers: not only "these incredible orchids from Raymond Burr," but a card and a floral display—*a $200 floral display*—from Frank Sinatra.

King likes his luxuries, but his drive is not really about money. Despite an income of around $4 million a year, he has lived in the same Virginia high-rise, overlooking Washington, D.C., for more than a decade—an apartment friends describe as resembling a hotel suite decorated ten years ago or "a duplex pad that Sammy Davis Jr. or Peter Lawford could have crashed in."* No, his drive is about attention—of any kind. "The most genuine he is is when he's on the

---

*That was then. Today King lives in a $12 million gated estate in Beverly Hills.

air," says Tom Farmer, who worked with King from 1991 to 1994. "The rest of the time he could be kind of deflated, like a Macy's balloon that is sort of put away between parades. Then, when he gets on the air, that's his oxygen."

"It truly is his only life, the only thing that matters to him," says Chuck Conconi, a Washington journalist who used to be a close friend. "Once, I said to Sharon [Mrs. King from 1976 to 1983] that I didn't know what to get Larry for his birthday. And Sharon said, 'Get him an "On The Air" sign for his bedroom.'" Acquaintances describe his behavior at an election-night party at the home of Washington humorist Mark Russell. When the local TV stations sent crews to film a little color there, King was first in line with a sound bite. "Larry kept running up to be interviewed by anyone who would do it," says another Russell guest. "This guy's on TV every day, and it's *never* enough."

For his first ten years at CNN, King maintained the national radio show he had started in 1978, which was his first large step toward becoming a household name. Though he cut his radio show from five and a half hours to three in 1987, CNN executives felt strongly that he was spread too thin. "We put in this new contract an amount of money that would enable him to give up radio," says network president Tom Johnson of the five-year contract that runs through 2000. "We picked up that whole piece of his income and gave him eight weeks of vacation. Unfortunately, he manages to use most of that up going around and speaking," doing dozens of appearances a year for profit and charity. "When you make someone laugh—I don't know if 'orgasmic' is the word, but it's close," says King. "If you get a big laugh with that first joke, you immediately know that the next forty minutes are going to be the best forty minutes of your life."

In Washington, King doesn't have many true friends; he is far more showbiz than most in a company town whose industry is government. To the powerful folks who go on his show, says one woman who is an occasional guest, "it's like going to your gynecologist. You hope you won't see him socially." But King has always had an active romantic life in the capital. There are women in Washington who can bring each other to weeping laughter by reciting their favorite Larry King pickup lines. "I think there's real chemistry here," he is apt to say on a first date. "Do you feel the chemistry?" Or, "Do you believe in love at first sight?" King is so widely known as a would-be Lothario that comedian Jon Stewart worked him into his remarks at last April's dinner of the White House Correspondents' Association. Noting the presence of Ellen DeGeneres, Stewart praised her for coming out of the closet. "Although I still believe," he added, "it's an elaborate ruse to keep Larry King from hitting on her."

Sandra McElwaine, a Washington journalist, recalls a visit to King's apartment to interview him for a magazine. "And he's sitting at one end of this big glass coffee table, and I'm sitting at the other end, and we're doing this interview," she recounts. "At the end, I said, 'Is there something you want to do with your life that you haven't done?' At which point, he says, 'Yes!' and the next thing I know this creature in a jumpsuit has flung himself across a glass coffee table filled with sort of spiky objects. And I hear in my ear, 'I want to kiss you,' as this person lands on top of me. I was stunned! . . . It was funny afterwards," she says. "I have dined out on it for years. But it wasn't funny when it was happening." ("To the best of my recollection, I've never leapt across a table to kiss anyone except Angie Dickinson," King responds, "and that was like magic.")

There is definitely a Larry King type. "If you had all our pictures lined up, you would think we were all from one very large, large family," says a statuesque blonde he has pursued. As King himself wrote in 1989, he likes women who are "blonde, blue-eyed, [with] straight features, pretty. . . . The girl you couldn't get as a kid. The girl who wouldn't give you a second look." King has been remarkably successful, as an adult, at getting that girl. He has dated or been romantically linked with Dickinson, New York newscaster Marlene Sanders, and Cyndy Garvey, the ex-wife of ballplayer Steve Garvey; during the first O. J. Simpson trial, when King's show spent weeks at a time in Los Angeles, he simultaneously dated Suzanne Childs, spokeswoman for the district attorney's office, and Jo-Ellan Dimitrius, the jury consultant for the defense. "Hey," says a friend of King's, "there aren't a lot of charming, rich, heterosexual fifty- to sixty-five-year-olds who can take you to dinner with Yasser Arafat and Frank Sinatra."

"He makes you feel like you are the only woman on this earth," says a former flame. He is lavishly generous, buying his girlfriends Chanel bags, Hermès scarves, jewelry from Tiffany's and Cartier. Someone familiar with King's methods describes him as conferring "this all-enveloping attention. Flowers every day, limos, this, that—just incredible. And then, overnight, stopping."

"You want to have a man pay attention to you, have a Larry King experience," says Alicia Mundy, Washington bureau chief for *Mediaweek*, who describes her only date with King a few years ago. He was attentive, interesting, even sweet, she says, but the evening was not a success. King took her to Duke Zeibert's—a downtown power restaurant that has since gone out of business—and enlivened the dinner hour by taking Mundy's hand, gazing into her eyes, and singing. "Star Dust," as she recalls, and then "St. Louis Blues." "He's going, 'Do you recognize that? Hoagy Carmichael?' . . . I'm like, *Oh God, let me die now*. He's holding my right hand, which has my fork, with a piece of sauced crab cake. I finally had to, like, wrestle the fork free. At one point I actually took a bite with our two hands holding the fork." Mercifully, King had to get to CNN to do his show. As he and Mundy were preparing to leave, one of the proprietors—a man she knew—reproved her: "You know, Alicia, most women stop eating when Larry starts singing."

The first Mrs. King, née Frada Miller, was a Brooklyn girl he married at nineteen, when he was at loose ends—not yet launched on his career, but without the grades to go to college. He describes this marriage vaguely as lasting "a year, half a year," and says, "I wouldn't recognize her if I saw her. . . . I don't even remember living with Frada."

King's second and fourth marriages were to Alene Akins, a Playboy Bunny he met in his salad days as a Miami radio star. They were first married in 1962, divorced a year later, remarried in 1967, and divorced again in 1971. King adopted her son, Andy, and the couple together had a daughter, Chaia, now twenty-nine.

The third Mrs. King was Mickey Sutphin. She and King were married from 1963 to 1966. They had a daughter, Kelly, who at the age of nine was adopted by Sutphin's subsequent husband and has never since been a part of King's life.

King's fifth marriage was to Sharon Lepore, a former math teacher. Their union ran from 1976 to 1983 and seems to have been his closest brush with stability. Sharon, whom he has repeatedly courted since their parting, is said by many of those close to King to be the love of his life. "They've had more reconciliations than I can count," says Chuck Conconi. "That relationship is a fascinating, deadly strange relationship. . . . He won't see her for a long time, and he'll desperately want her."

King said "I do" for the sixth time with Julia Alexander, a Philadelphia legal headhunter to whom he proposed after a three-week courtship that took place almost entirely by telephone. They married in 1989, amid volcanic publicity, at Duke Zeibert's. ("What Julie and I both know—and this is what experience gives you—is there can never be anything after this, or anything as strong," he wrote shortly before the wedding.) At the reception, which was photographed exclusively by *People* magazine, guests placed bets— literally placed bets, with cash on the bar—about the likely date of the marriage's end. The couple separated in 1990, reunited twice, and then split for good in 1991.

King has occasionally floated a more flattering version of his marital history, in which he has been married only four, or even three, times (the first he apparently discounts because it was annulled at the insistence of the couple's parents, the third because of the child's adoption, and the fourth because it was Alene's second tour). But then, he has, in general, a casual way with the facts of his life. In 1991, *Washington Post* reporter David Finkel decided to fact-check one of King's Brooklyn tales, a shaggy-dog story about driving to New Haven in the dead of winter to check the price of Carvel ice cream with two old pals, including his close chum Sandy Koufax, who went on to fame as the Dodgers' pitcher. "I've never been to New Haven," Koufax told Finkel. Nor, he said, did he meet King until both were long past their Brooklyn years.

King seems to relate to the actual facts and episodes of his life, as retailed in eight books and endless interviews and monologues, as if they were barnacles on a mighty ship. Does the ship keep track? One of his many book collaborators recalls that it was like pulling teeth to get King to read the final product. "He'd moved on. In his mind, he had done what you need to do, and he'd moved on. He'd told the story. 'So then you have to go back and correct the story? What's that?' It just wasn't in his makeup."

On the one hand, he is supremely self-involved. "If we were walking down Connecticut Avenue and I stepped off a curb and got smashed by a bus," says someone who knows him well, "his reaction would be, 'How could you do this to me? You know I have a bad heart!'" On the other hand, he is entirely without the introspective impulse. "So here's this guy who's on TV every night asking people to reflect on themselves, and he doesn't do it himself," says a long-time associate. "He's incapable of doing it."

In fact, his life has been so chaotic that it is difficult to see it whole. It contains entire lawsuits, scandals, even children, whose existence isn't widely known. Careful readers of King's column in USA Today recently noted the sudden appearance of a son named Larry King Jr. He was, it turns out, the fruit of a brief fling in King's early Miami days. Some of King's closest associates and friends had never heard of the thirty-five-year-old Larry junior, who re-entered King's life about four years ago. And even this dramatic development King explains in a somewhat slippery way. "She married," King narrates, of the young man's mother, "he had a stepfather all those years, she was dying of lung cancer, she called and said, 'Y'know, you had a son.' I never checked it—never took a DNA test, whatever they do. 'Well, he's grown up now, he's getting married, and before I die, I'd like you to know him.' So immediately you're suspicious. Well, my lawyer went down to Florida, met her, met the kid. And he's the greatest. He's obviously my son: he laughs like me, he looks like me. And the kid wants nothing. . . . It was a gift from heaven."

When King and I meet again ten days later, I press him for further details about the young man's mother. This time, as he tells the story, it has one significant difference: he first learned of his son's existence, he acknowledges, when the mother was pregnant. "She called me up one day and said, 'Y'know, I'm having a baby, and it's yours,'" he explains. "And then she called me back later and said, 'I've named him Larry King Jr., and he looks just like you. . . . I said, 'OK, but I'm not—' and she said, 'I'm not going to bug you.' . . . I knew he was out there somewhere, but I never—he never bothered me, never asked for anything."

What the two accounts have in common is their emphasis on King's fear of being imposed upon.

—————

The true story of King's life begins with two deaths. The first preceded his birth, and the second prematurely ended his childhood. In 1932, Eddie and Jennie Zeiger—immigrants from Russia who had met in America—lost their first son, Irwin, to appendicitis. They had been slow in getting the six-year-old to the hospital; by the time doctors saw him, his appendix had already burst. Larry was born the following year, in November, to parents still drowning in grief and remorse. King phrases this in a striking way: "My father consumed me," he says. "He wanted a son so bad." As for King's mother, according to friends, she hovered, doted, and protected, vigilant now against anything that might claim her second child, or the brother born three years later.

For nearly ten years of his life, King was his hungry father's boon companion. He hung out at the bar his father operated in Brownsville ("He was like a Brooklyn Toots Shor," King says, "without any money"), went to ball games, lived "in a man's world." But three days after D-Day, his father—who had sold the bar to work in a defense plant—died suddenly of a heart attack at age forty-four.

"Everything about me changed," recalls King. "I went from being a good student to a bad student. . . . I went from feeling very secure to very insecure." Smarting from what felt to him like paternal abandonment, Larry became the family's bad boy.

Without the father's income, the Zeigers tumbled from their toehold in the middle class. They moved to Bensonhurst, a slightly better neighborhood, but had to live in an attic apartment. Mrs. Zeiger went on welfare, secretly taking in sewing to help make ends meet. Larry and his brother both remember, with perfect clarity, the visits from the "relief worker" whose job it was to double-check that their mother wasn't buying high-quality meat.

King's mother stepped up her vigilance toward what remained of her family, and spoiled them—"What you could spoil on $34 a week," recalls Larry. "I think at that point she was just hanging on," says someone who knows King well. "Anytime he got in trouble, it was always forgiven. So he never had to learn to deal with consequences." King is the first to admit that he was never confronted by any limits on his behavior. "If I were to blow up a bank and kill twenty-six people," he wrote in his 1982 autobiography, *Larry King,* "my mother would have said, 'Well, Larry made a mistake, but I'm sure those people at the bank did something to provoke him.'" When Larry graduated from high school, it was his mother, not he, who proudly began wearing his high-school ring. Twenty-five years later, she was buried with it still on her finger.

King has mined his childhood endlessly for entertainment, even writing a heavily nostalgic book about the old neighborhood and the gang of boys he ran with. But beneath these bright reminiscences, clearly, was a difficult youth, in which his chief solace was the magic of radio, the disembodied voices of Arthur Godfrey and Red Barber. King wasn't athletic, and he wasn't great to look at—he once described himself as "acne-faced" and overweight—but his mimicry of the radio stars, he recalls, commanded attention. "One thing I always had," he says, "was glibness."

To this day, King's best friends are guys he knew in high school. Whenever he is in Los Angeles, where most of these old pals now live, they meet every morning at Nate 'n Al's, the famed deli in

Beverly Hills, to talk baseball and shoot the breeze. On a recent Friday, King was joined there by Sid Young, who runs a construction firm, and Asher Dann, a real estate broker. I asked them to tell me about King as a boy.

"As a kid?" asked Sid. "A real nerd."

"What do you mean, as a kid?" joked Asher.

Larry chimed in. "But I wasn't smart. Nerds are supposed to be smart."

"Yeah, he wasn't smart," agreed Asher.

"But he was socially inept," Sid pointed out.

Larry: "Yeah, we discovered girls at seventeen."

To which Sid and Asher cried, in unison, "*You* discovered girls at seventeen!"

There was something touching about the scene, his friends' obvious affection for King; they seemed to embrace him with their jests as he sat in the booth, slumped as always, his arms protectively crossed over his belly. "His focus of continuity is that circle of aging eighth-graders," observes a female friend of King's. "If you're not his girlfriend, you get the best part of Larry."

King moved to Miami at age twenty-three on the advice of an acquaintance, hoping to break into radio, and got hired by a tiny AM station as morning DJ, for $55 a week. It was there, at the station manager's insistence, that he changed his surname to King. By 1961 he was working for the hottest station in the market, doing a nighttime interview show, and by the midsixties he owned Miami. Though best known on radio, he also hosted a TV interview show and wrote a Winchell-esque column for the *Miami Herald*.

Miami was a booming town then, a prime touring stop for star entertainers. Truly, this was the place and time where Larry King came of age, and his tastes were molded by the talents he interviewed there. Frank Sinatra. Jackie Gleason. Don Rickles. Vic Damone. Mel Torme. Some of King's books and stories evoke that period in his life with such vividness one can almost see the young Larry King knifing through the soft night air in the new car he bought every year, on top of the world. But hungry as King was to be noticed, he seems to have had an even greater drive toward self-destruction—overspending wildly, betting on horses, skipping his taxes. "When I made $100 a week, I spent $150," he says. "When I should have had a Mercury, I had a Cadillac." He filed for bankruptcy in 1960, then promptly plunged even deeper into debt.

"It's a real test of your professionalism to go on the air while sheriffs are at your home repossessing your property," he noted dryly in *Larry King*. That book, written before his huge TV celebrity, doesn't pretty up many of the darker passages of his career. It describes, for example, how he would coax loans from new banks. First he would ask the president out for lunch, to solicit his advice for an imaginary feature story on the banking industry. Then, a few weeks later, he would call the man again to thank him. And "oh, by the way . . . my mother is quite ill and I need five thousand dollars for an operation—can you tell me the best place to get a loan for that quickly?" Naturally, the bank president would take care of it personally, circumventing the usual credit checks.

Into this quagmire came Lou Wolfson, a Florida financier who was under investigation for securities violations. (His name became famous in 1969, when Justice Abe Fortas was forced to resign from the Supreme Court following the revelation that a Wolfson foundation had been paying him a stipend.) King and Wolfson launched an improbable scheme to bankroll New Orleans district attorney Jim Garrison's investigation of President Kennedy's assassination. King, who had met Garrison through his radio show, was to be one of the conduits for Wolfson to send Garrison $5,000 a month. But King inevitably pocketed some of this money, to help sustain his frantic financial juggling act, and three years later, Wolfson would charge him with grand larceny—because of his fury over King's role in an even wilder scheme.

In 1967 and 1968 Wolfson was convicted of securities violations. At the end of 1968 he asked King to intercede with President-elect Nixon, whom King knew through a mutual friend, Bebe Rebozo. Nixon referred King's request to Attorney General Designate John Mitchell, who turned King down. But rather than tell Wolfson this,

King pretended that Mitchell was willing to help, and that Mitchell's law firm would need money to look into the case. The money Wolfson ponied up went, instead, into King's pocket. When King finally confessed to Wolfson that the new administration was not going to let him off the hook, Wolfson was irate. In 1971, after finishing his prison sentence, he got back at King by charging him with theft in the Garrison affair.

Wolfson's charge of grand larceny against King was ultimately dismissed on statute-of-limitations grounds, but King's rise was stopped cold. The only broadcasting work he could find was at a Shreveport, Louisiana, racetrack; it was not until 1975 that he returned to Miami and cajoled his way back onto the air. Even that exile did not change his ways. From 1961 through 1978, according to records filed in his second bankruptcy, King was involved in more than forty legal actions, mostly lawsuits from unsatisfied creditors. It was only after his 1976 marriage to Sharon Lepore—to whom he had lied about both his income and his debts—that he finally put his financial affairs in order. When she discovered the extent of the mess, she insisted that he declare bankruptcy again and start anew. When he did, his debts totaled $352,246, including unpaid taxes. Among the creditors left holding the bag were six banks, various hotels, restaurants, stores, and the Riverside Memorial.

King seems to be a genius at getting the people around him to take care of him and pick up the pieces. "It's up to all of us who try to, I guess, surround Larry to keep him in some kind of balance," frets a solicitous Tom Johnson. A loyal cadre ensures that King never has to do what he hates most: say no. He will be happy to speak at your charity's dinner if you ask him . . . and then his assistant will call to tell you no, regrettably, he is already busy that night. He would love to have you as a guest on his show, he'll tell you . . . and his producers will later tactfully explain that, well, they're a trifle overbooked.

"Once you work with him, you become very protective of him," says former producer Farmer. "Suddenly you are worried about Larry's cars, and Larry's diet, and how much outside work he is accepting, and whether Larry is sleeping well. All his producers end up taking care of him in ways that you wouldn't take care of, say, Pat Buchanan down the hall. Because you want to help this guy. Because he needs you!"

One of the most oft-told of the Larry Stories that circulate at CNN concerns his take-out order when he eats dinner at his desk, before the show. His favorite dish, from a local Chinese restaurant, is chicken with cashews—without the fat-laden cashews. When the food arrives, a young intern or production assistant is charged with combing through it to remove any errant nuts; then he or she has to swaddle the chicken in paper towels and squeeze out any excess oil. This is part of the iron discipline King now maintains over his diet. Where his survival is at stake, he is capable of total control. He gave up smoking after his 1987 heart attack, for example. And when he began making real money again, after his second bankruptcy, he gave over control of his financial affairs to a trusted advisor. The self-destructive urges that derailed him decades ago seem to be channeled into the only area of his life that can't be turned over to a surrogate: his love life.

As soon as King has successfully wooed a woman, according to people who know him well, he almost immediately turns to another one—keeping the first on a string. For instance, when he met Julia Alexander and began courting her, a friend says, he was on the verge of reuniting with ex-wife Sharon Lepore; they had even been house hunting together. And then, within weeks of his marriage to Alexander, he was again courting Lepore. "Larry has to have relationships upon relationships, so he always has a place where that stimulation is going on," says ex-fiancée Rama Fox. "Larry is astonishing in the things he finds to lie about and deny. To me, he's a Sports Liar."

King has been engaged to two women since his split with Alexander—in 1992 and 1993 to Fox, a minister in the Movement of Spiritual Inner Awareness (the cult made famous by Arianna Huffington, among others), and in 1995 to Deanna Lund, a fifty-something television actress (star of the 1960s show *Land of the*

Giants), who was introduced to King in a restaurant by the actress Connie Stevens and to whom he reportedly proposed on the second date. Neither of these relationships got as far as the altar, and the one with Fox, which lasted on and off for three years, resulted in bitter litigation in Los Angeles.

The immediate cause of action, on both sides, was money. He wanted Fox to repay him $50,000 in escrow money for a house they had almost bought together, and she wanted him to make good on a repeated promise that he would give her $400,000 to compensate for all the time and anguish she had put into their relationship. But Fox's real grievance against King was what she termed "persistent philandering" with two of his ex-wives, Alexander and Lepore. At one point, according to Fox, King had her and Alexander—with whom he was briefly reconciled—house hunting on opposite coasts for homes to buy with him. (King's divorce from Alexander was ultimately completed in 1992, with a large financial settlement; he later sued her for slander—a suit that was settled in 1994 with a court-ordered silence on both sides and the sealing of the records in the case.)

King appears to acknowledge his duplicity in documents filed in the Fox case. In August 1992 she apparently persuaded him to commit to paper some thoughts on how he treated women. These notes, titled "My Pattern with Women," are rendered in brief phrases in a spiral-bound notebook. "Need to step into danger," he wrote. "Something to bring me adrenaline—a rush. I lie—pretend—mislead—equivocate— I will have two or more women going at the same time. . . . I have secret compartmentalized little worlds I keep away from each other. I put up a front to people important in my life—if questioned I feel desperate—attacked—threatened. Like I'm going to lose something. I'll say and do almost anything to keep it from coming. Most of the time I split. . . . Don't look at consequences—operate under false pretenses."

Fox today describes King's life as "a spiderweb that is about ten dimensions deep, and you think you know, and then you see behind it, and you go, Oh, this is what's behind it—but then there's something behind that." Interestingly, one other woman from King's past also described her involvement with him as a "web." "He's very artful at gaslighting," says this person. "You feel like you're the one that's going crazy—like you're the one who's done something wrong."

King v. Fox is one of those legal proceedings that reveal a good deal about the adversaries—showing, in King's case, the angry man who lives inside the genial, easygoing legend. In his deposition, taken last year, he rails at both Fox and his ex-wife Julia Alexander. Calling Fox "a greedy, money-grabbing hooker," he rages that "she's bullshit. She's bullshit when she smiles to you." Again and again he comments bitterly that he is the only person in any of these relationships who has to work for a living. (It's worth noting that the acrimony of King's breakups has increased in lockstep with his salary.)

King's attorneys claimed in court documents that Fox wrung promises from King under duress, "exploiting King's exhaustion during heavy work schedules, his susceptibility and vulnerability as a result of the powerful medications he was on, his emotional hardship stemming from his then pending divorce litigation." Specifically, King was dependent on the sleeping pill Halcion through much of his relationship with Fox. It had been prescribed by his doctors after his heart surgery in 1987, and he stopped taking it in 1993. King and Fox both say that most of the issues in the lawsuit have been settled on terms more favorable to King than to Fox. But in exposing so much of King's private life to scrutiny, Fox—who still contemplates writing a book about him—may have gained the ultimate satisfaction. When confronted, in his deposition, with his own scribbled thoughts on his relationships with women, King called them "the inner deep-most feelings of a person trying to get a grip on his life, a very generous, nice, caring person." As the notes near their end, they become briefer and more disjointed: "When I feel close I start thinking negatively to prevent it," he wrote. And later:

Live in a pretend world.
Aloneness??
Self-punishment.
Pleasure in self-hate. . . .
Jewish—homely—glasses—rejected—not wanted.

The last page contains only two observations. The first is "Giving over control is not good." And then, on a separate line, "Don't feel anything." It is hard to know whether to read that final sentence as a description of, or an instruction to, himself.

Enter Shawn Southwick, wearing on her ring finger a Harry Winston diamond bigger than a pistachio nut. She is breathtaking: five feet eleven, with intense blue eyes and a spill of amber hair and a smile your dentist sees in his dreams. She is also nice, in a coltish, all-American way, asking the waiter in the grand dining room at the Beverly Wilshire hotel for a dish of maraschino cherries to eat and suddenly plucking out a swatch of what looks like her hair to show me the Luxurious Hair clip-on extension that she invented and sold on infomercials in the late '80s. Laughing over the complicated planning involved in throwing a wedding for three hundred, she explains the difficulty of limiting the guest list. "Especially if you're marrying someone like Larry, who every time someone comes on the show, he says"—and here she grips my shoulder and drops her voice to a comically deep emulation of his Brooklyn rasp—"*You'll come to the wedding.*'"

They met outside Tiffany's, in January, literally bumped into each other. And he made a pass, and he took her to dinner that night with Al Pacino and Beverly D'Angelo, and he called her, and he sent her gifts every day, and by April she was saying yes. Though they first planned the wedding for December, they have moved it up to September 6.

"It is fast, faster than I would have thought," she concedes. Does she have any concerns about his track record? "Nope," she answers. "I'm aware of it. He's a sixty-three-year-old man, and I wouldn't expect him to not have been married before. I've been married, too—twice. . . . What I focus on is our future. I don't want to be puffy and goopy. But I feel like the luckiest woman ever." A pause, then she continues levelly. "I know there have been lucky women before me. But, dammit, I'm going to be the last one."

Just now, King makes his entrance, resplendent in a bright-orange linen shirt. They kiss. "She's the best," says Larry, gazing. "The best angel that walked the earth." She signals him, across the table, that he has her lipstick on his face.

"Do you like the shoes I got you this morning?" he prompts. He's had a busy morning in Beverly Hills: Armani shoes for Southwick. Elsa Peretti earrings from Tiffany's for one of his producers, who turns thirty today, to match a necklace he had bought for her on another occasion. He begins to talk about how much he loves to buy presents, how good he is at picking things out for people. His publicist, Juli Mortz, pushes back her hair to display the earrings he once bought for her, also at Tiffany's.

"So, Larry," teases Shawn. "If you ever lose your job, you can be a personal shopper."

"I was always generous to a fault," Larry says a few minutes later. "I still am. The only difference is, I can't outspend myself now. Can't outspend what I make."

Watching the lovebirds together, I think back to my earlier conversation with King. Whatever he may consciously decide to withhold from you, he is, at times, the most unconsciously honest man in America. "This I know," he said in our first interview. "She's the only person I've ever known who, if you came to me right now and said, 'Here's the situation: she has to be with you every moment of the rest of your life. That is, she'll go to work with you, she'll—except when you go to the bathroom—she'll be with you every second,' that's OK. That would be OK."

He offered an example of how he's changed, with Southwick. "I'm much more patient. I'm an impatient person that's patient with her," he said. "I'm always clock-aware; I always know what time it is. Shawn's late. Other people in my life, at different stages in my life, I would say, 'Hey, one more time, forget it.' [With Shawn] it don't bother me at all." He stopped himself. "It bothers me, but it's of such less import to the overall picture. Don't bother me. I mean, it's such a *minute* bother."

Anyway, this time is different. He just knows it. The couple plans to live most of the year in L.A., and King hopes to include, in his next contract, the right to broadcast as many as 70 percent of his shows out of CNN's Sunset Boulevard studio. But network president Johnson makes it clear that he is not happy about this prospect; he feels the show has to stay in Washington at least 50 percent of the time. It would be an irony if, having been made a star by politics, King remained shackled to that identity, forever hobbled in his pursuit of the celebrities who are his true passion. For now, King and his future bride have taken a six-month rental in Los Angeles. They have a condominium in Utah, where Southwick's fifteen-year-old son from her first marriage lives with his father. And King talks vaguely of getting a bigger apartment in Washington. If it all seems a little impermanent—well, his sincerity is nonetheless complete.

"I don't think he feels guilty about anything," says someone who knows King very, very well. "That would imply he was capable of understanding what he'd done. . . . If he were capable of knowing what he'd done, people would hate him a lot more." Instead, King has a way of making all his transgressions seem as harmless as his blue suede shoes. And perhaps you have to have a special vulnerability to be taken in by Larry King, whether in business or in love. But it's interesting to note how neatly the common picture of King—as an easygoing, somewhat hapless man who poses no threat except the professional one of running a toothless interview show for newsmakers—inverts reality.

Even now, King seems merely puzzled by the wreckage in his wake. "I never feel like I have to perform" with Shawn, he enthused at our first interview. "I, like, always found in other people some things I liked, but she is . . . ." He broke off, arrested in mid-thought. "But, you know, I guess if you'd have stopped me when I first met Sharon, I might have said the same thing." For a portion of a second he lingered there, on the threshold of insight, and then rushed on, toward another doorway. "Although Sharon and I had fights when we were dating," he concluded. Shawn, she's another story. "We never fight," King tells me, in her presence. "I love her too much to fight with her."*

—*September 1997*

---

*Eleven years after this profile was first published, Southwick and King are still married. They have two sons: Chance, born in 1999, and Cannon, born in 2000.

THE GAME
(JAMES BAKER)

His smile is what the dental hygienist asks you to emulate when she
wants to get at your back molars. Teeth bared, cheeks pulled straight
back toward the ears, it seems a function strictly of the facial mus-
cles; the fellow-feeling sketched in that smile rarely spreads as far as
the eyes.

"I graduated with honors, and I graduated right at the 10 percent
mark," James A. Baker III is saying, in response to a general question
about his performance as a law student at the University of Texas.
He is just warming up. "I'll tell you what I think is a true story. They
have something called Order of the Coif, which is the top 10 percent. And of course having had a good but not spectacular first year,
my second and third years had to be really good if I was going to
make Order of the Coif.

"I had good second and third years," he goes on, but these other
guys, two or three of them, flunked the final semester. Which reduced the size of the class just enough to reduce by one the number
of students who could be counted in the top 10 percent. As a result,
says Baker, "I missed it by one." This is where the chilly smile comes
up, as he raises a hand, his thumb and index finger an inch apart.
"I missed it by *that* much. And that was sort of a disappointment at
the time."

It is the smile of a man who has never lived down a defeat. Never
mind that he made law review, and won the law prize his last semester,

and assumed his destined place at the top of the Houston legal establishment. That he went on to a meteoric second career in government,
became chief of staff to the most popular president in decades,*
stepped up to the cabinet as secretary of the treasury. Never mind that,
at fifty-eight, on the threshold of four or eight years** as secretary of
state, and as an old friend and longtime advisor to the president of the
United States, he is perhaps the most powerful unelected man in
America.

When just the first of these small consolations is mentioned to
him—*you made law review, right?*—he nods. "I made law review, and
I was an officer of the law review," he says. But after the scantest
pause, he circles back, helpless to avoid the far tougher interrogator
who lives in his head. "And I was basically in the top 10 and a *half*
percent of the class."

It is rare for Baker to allow such an extended glimpse into the
ceaseless workings of the machinery that has powered him, or driven
him, to the top. Here, for a long moment, he shows not only his
competitiveness—the single Baker characteristic on which everyone
agrees—but also his obsession with control. It's bad enough to lose;
it's horrible to lose because some other guys flunked out. Invited to
talk about her husband's achievements, Susan Baker, too, reaches
back to the image of the student grind. "He will be an overachiever
until he dies," she says placidly. "That's in his bones. He's built that
way." He is a high-performance engine uninterested in pretending to
be anything else.

This part of Baker's nature is an important reason for his success
in Washington. But this part would make him successful anywhere.
The extraordinary acclaim he draws in Washington has as much to
do with Washington's nature as with Baker's, and is properly understood as an expression of both.

Jim Baker, man of the sterling reputation, has come to represent a
Washington ideal. A competitor, in a city whose weightiest transac-

---

*Ronald Reagan.

**It ended up being not quite four.

tions are commonly described as a game; a gentleman, in an establishment whose highest value is that antagonists be able to drink together after 6:00 p.m.; a corporate lawyer, in a culture that reserves its harshest punishments for the incautious, he has much to tell us about Washington's values. And Baker—a lifelong workaholic, a man in whom drive is more important than destination, a loner with few close friends—also has much to tell us about Washington's demands on the humanity of its actors and about a culture's choice of illusions.

Washington is not the only city that lauds and rewards a gifted manager. But only Washington, gazing on that package of skill, energy, calculation, and discipline that constitutes the successful "player," insists on calling it virtue.

———

During the transition, Jim Baker declined the security detail that is routinely assigned to a secretary of state-designate. Well into his second career, he is leagues too secure to bother with the trappings that many people here confuse with the goals of the game. He shows none of the frailties that have devastated some of the people closest to him, seems prey to none of the garden-variety ambitions that have seduced or destroyed so many of his peers. An era that shattered a Robert "Bud" McFarlane, gulled a Michael Deaver, and tripped up numerous Ed Meeses and Richard Allens and Anne Burfords, has seen Baker churn smoothly toward the top.*

---

*Bud McFarlane was President Reagan's national security advisor. Disgraced by his role in the Iran-Contra scandal (see "The End of the Affair," page 179), he tried, unsuccessfully, to commit suicide. Michael Deaver, a former top Reagan aide, was convicted of perjury in 1987 in connection with an investigation into lobbying activities he'd taken up after leaving the White House. Attorney General Ed Meese resigned in 1988 amid various controversies about his personal ethics. Richard Allen, who preceded McFarlane as national security advisor, quit the White House in 1982 after it was revealed that he had accepted $1,000 in gifts from a Japanese magazine. Anne Burford was Environmental Protection Agency administrator. She resigned after refusing to hand over to Congress a large number of documents concerning toxic waste cleanups.

This assurance can be chalked up, in part, to a hidden Baker asset: his patrician background. In spite of—or perhaps because of— its heterogeneous leadership class, Washington retains a furtive love of the aristocracy. Baker's punctilious affability undercuts any suggestion that he is an unapproachable blue blood. For every touch that bespeaks his background (he wears crisp button-down shirts that say "JAB III" on the breast pocket), he sends a countervailing signal that he is a regular guy (he drinks beer from the can at black-tie dinners). Yet his class, in turn, overrides any suggestion that he is a mere politician.

His family is the Baker of Baker & Botts, said to be the second-oldest law firm west of the Mississippi. Bakers founded some of Houston's banks, trusts, and utilities; wrote the real estate deals and loaned the money that created the city center; and helped plot the city's growth from cow town to metropolis. Today Baker keeps up his listing in the Houston *Social Register* and belongs to the Bayou Club (adjacent to the Houston Polo Club, it is the most exclusive in town) and the Houston Country Club (bigger, but still more exclusive than River Oaks, where mere money hangs out).

James A. Baker III is actually the fourth James Addison Baker. The first, his great-grandfather, was a Civil War veteran and district judge who moved to Houston after the war to become a partner in the young firm. After Judge Baker came Captain Baker, who earned his title in the largely ceremonial Houston Light Guard. After him came the current Jim Baker's father. In Houston today they liken "Jimmy" Baker not to his father, but to his grandfather. "Captain Jim" was the Baker who built the law firm into a national power, the first in Texas to have strong ties to Wall Street, and who started the tradition of sending sons east for Ivy League polish. He was a founder and chairman of the board of the Texas Commerce Bank (originally the South Texas Commercial National, on whose board a Baker was represented every year but two from 1890 to 1980) and of the Guardian Trust Company (a forerunner of MBank). But most dramatically, he uncovered the murder of his client William Marsh Rice, the industrialist whose bequest would found Rice University. On hearing of Rice's death in New York, legend has it, Captain Baker sped east in his private railroad car and helped the police prosecute the butler and lawyer who had colluded in the murder and prepared a false will. Having saved the Rice fortune, he spun it into an endowment that could support an ambitious university—just the cultural adornment Houston lacked—and chaired the board until his death in 1941.

The Baker men were raised on a creed of purest propriety. The bulk of Baker & Botts's business, at the end of the nineteenth century and the early part of the twentieth, lay in the epochal westward expansion of the railroads. Only lawyers of impeccable reputation could persuasively defend the rapacious frontier capitalism of clients like Jay Gould and E. H. Harriman. Captain Baker told a group of young lawyers in 1937: "Work hard, study and apply yourself closely, stay on the job and keep out of politics." Preston Moore, Baker's first cousin, says, "I think we were brought up to feel . . . that whatever kind of mind you had, you ought to try to develop it; that you had a good body, and you ought to take care of it. But more than that, you had a good name, and you always ought to remember that."

"If there's one great skill Jim Baker has," says former White House political director Ed Rollins, it's that he's "one of the most disciplined men I have met in political life." Even by Washington standards, Baker is phenomenally hardworking. He puts in long, long days, touching more people—by telephone or in person—than others manage to do. He stays at work until 9:00 or 9:30 at night to return calls from members of Congress. (So much the better if they've gone home to dinner. The point isn't to speak to them, it's "to make sure that Senator so-and-so knows that Baker tried to reach him," in the words of an aide.) Finding himself on Capitol Hill with ten minutes between appointments, he will pay lightning calls on as many congressional offices as possible. (No telling when the chit will come in handy.) Before appearing on a Sunday morning news show, he puts in three hours of study. "I've never known anyone who mainlines it the way Jimmy Baker does," says one former associate. "The man is methodical. The man is better prepared." He knows how to say no, they say; how to rank his priorities; how to ration his time . . . the more people strain to describe his method, the more it comes to sound like Management 101. In fact, it is Baker's will to perform consistently at this level that sets him apart.

That will is traceable back to his boyhood. Jim Baker's father and mother had been married for thirteen years before Jimmy, their first child, was born in 1930. Previously, the couple had been told they could have no children. "So when I came along, and then my sister eighteen months later, we were something special as far as they were concerned," Baker says. Longtime friends remember the Baker household as a formal one, the older parents as loving but stern. If Baker slept past 7:00—even on a Saturday—his father doused him with cold water.

In 1983, when his son John was undergoing drug-abuse treatment at a New York hospital, Baker and his second wife, Susan, flew up from Washington to go through some counseling with him. The age-old question of paternal discipline arose. "Look, you think you have it bad with me," Jim Baker finally said. "My father was so strict that my friends called him 'the Warden,' growing up."

John also remembers his father showing him letters from the Warden that he received in boarding school. "Letters such as, 'If you don't get your grades up in French, you're not going to go on the tennis tournament tour.' . . . And, 'You're not writing enough. You need to write more letters to your mother.'" He was the kind of father who urged his children off the high dive, whether or not they were scared. "My dad and I had a wonderful relationship," Baker says today. "He spent a lot of time with me, and he and I were really good friends. At the same time, he was a very stern disciplinarian. He held us to high standards." Father and son began hunting together when Baker was six, and spent enough early hours on the tennis court together that Baker earned a state ranking as a junior player.

Baker says that such high expectations were a boon to him. But he will not say the same on his sister's behalf. Bonner Baker, named for their mother, was a very bright, imaginative, but shy child. In Preston Moore's recollection, she often took the prize at the extended family's Sunday dinners, when Captain Baker would offer a dime to the grandchild who could stand and tell him the best story. (Jimmy was more likely to earn the dime he offered the child who could walk around the pitch-dark dining room at night without crying out in fear, as Captain Baker sat listening in the study across the hall.) Through college, she was involved in painting and creative writing. But at Smith College, she "came unhinged," in the words of one relative; another describes her crisis there as a nervous breakdown. She graduated with honors in 1954, but spent much of the next thirty years in and out of institutions. Her chief problem was eventually diagnosed as schizophrenia—a disease she now controls with medication, enabling her to live fairly independently. But her history was complicated by depression, and Baker has told family members he believes that his father's very high expectations, a useful goad to the son, were a devastating burden to the daughter. "No doubt," affirms Susan Baker, "her feeling that she had to achieve was a component."

Jimmy, on the other hand, had no difficulty following his father's path to the Hill School in Pennsylvania and on to college at Princeton, where he majored in history with a minor in classics. The remarks of friends at Princeton suggest that "Bake," as he was known, had already developed a firm sense of destination—and a natural talent for adopting the local camouflage. He was a member of Ivy, the snootiest of Princeton's eating clubs, of its "bicker" committee in charge of reviewing the next class of members, and of two drinking clubs. The only mention of Jim Baker in the four-year class history at the end of the 1952 yearbook is as one whose efforts "kept party spirit alive" through the fall of his junior year.

"The whole trick" to college in that era, says Baker's old friend Stockton Rush, a class behind him, "was to get good grades and look like you never worked." But none of his friends mistook him for a party animal. Says a former roommate, James M. Detmer: "He knew what he was about, and he got where he wanted to go. . . . He was always in control of the situation."

The ability to go gracefully along with his surroundings would also serve him well at the University of Texas, where, like his father, he studied law. Between college and law school he had served a stint in the Marines, married his college sweetheart, and had a son. But in Austin, he pledged the undergraduate fraternity Phi Delta Theta at his father's request. "He felt strongly about it, because it was his old fraternity," Baker says mildly. Uncomplaining, he trudged through hell week with all his eighteen-year-old brothers, choking back the raw eggs and being masked and dropped off in the countryside to find his way home. Uncomplaining, he spent something like a week—he doesn't remember exactly how long—carrying a dead fish on his person at all times, even home to his wife and baby. "But they did a lot more of that kind of thing to the fellas right out of high school," he adds, again mildly.

———

Jim Baker and George Bush met in Houston in the late '50s through Baker's first wife, Mary Stuart McHenry, a fervent Republican from Dayton, Ohio, who grew up across the street from a distant Bush relative. It began as a tennis partnership (with the benefit of Baker's forehand and Bush's backhand, they won two successive club championships), became a friendship, and ended as an alliance. Without Baker, it is said, Bush would not be president. Without Bush, it is likely, Baker would not have entered politics and might not even be a Republican today.

Baker was raised a Democrat in an age when the GOP was almost extinct in Texas, and for years he regarded election days as a chance to go hunting. Through the 1960s, he was single-mindedly absorbed in his legal career. Barred by a new anti-nepotism rule from joining Baker & Botts, he had settled on the old-line firm most closely associated with it, Andrews & Kurth, where he launched into a standard Houston corporate practice: oil and gas clients, some banking law, eventually, as the Texas economy changed, some mergers and acquisitions and securities work. It was Mary Stuart who donned a straw boater to pass out leaflets when Bush ran for the Senate in '64 and for the House in '66 and '68. But Baker was gradually becoming interested. And in 1969, when Bush was planning his second bid for the Senate, he urged Baker to run for the House seat he was vacating. Baker would have done it had his life not suddenly jumped the rails.

Mary Stuart was dying of cancer. She'd been diagnosed with breast cancer in the fall of 1968. The Bakers did not discuss death with each other. According to a family member, Baker did not tell his wife the doctor's prognosis, and later, when it was clear she was dying, she put her thoughts into a letter for him. In the meantime, they went ahead with plans to build a new house on land they had bought far from the center of town, and Baker threw a surprise party at the Bayou Club for his wife's thirty-eighth birthday. She died in February 1970, a few weeks shy of moving into the house she had furnished. Baker was two months short of his fortieth birthday.

Left suddenly with four boys ranging in age from eight to fifteen, Baker grieved by throwing himself that much more completely into his work. "For me," says John, who was almost ten when his mother died, "he was never home, and so that was very difficult." In place of the closeness he was looking for, John remembers his father replicating his father's sternness. "I think he tried to spend more time with us," James A. Baker IV, known as Jamie, told the *Washington Post* in 1985. "But he did it in a way that his father did, and that wasn't necessarily right for us. And that is hunting, getting you out of bed at 5 to stand in the dark, in the cold, at the duck blind."

In 1973 Baker married Susan Garrett Winston, a divorcee who had been one of Mary Stuart's closest friends. Susan's ex-husband, a son of Houston who had also been a friend of Baker's, was an alcoholic who died of acute pancreatitis the year after Susan and Jim Baker married. Merging the children of these two sadly broken families—there were three Winstons, just younger than the Baker kids—proved a recipe for turmoil, and the hard-driving Baker was ill prepared to smooth the way. John, clearly troubled in the wake of his mother's death, was away visiting his maternal grandparents when his father remarried; he remembers learning of the marriage after the fact. "Susan was with my father, and they picked us up" at the airport, he says. "And my dad was like, 'Guess what we did?'" John made up his mind to break up the marriage—and nearly succeeded. "I was just bound and determined to make their life miserable," he says, "because I didn't care about anything else." He got into drugs, beat up his siblings, and—because his father was rarely around—was as nasty to Susan as he could think up ways to be. He and one of his brothers both developed drug problems serious enough to require in-patient hospital treatment. John was arrested in 1982 for selling marijuana to an undercover police officer. He was fined $2,000 and entered drug treatment a short time later.

Susan, who has a friendly manner and the regal prettiness of Maggie Smith, is clearly the glue that eventually bound this family together. Strongly religious, she says easily that she finally solved the problem through prayer, asking God's intercession to make her love her stepson. "And it was just a miracle," she says. "God changed my heart." Today, John and Susan express great affection for each other. What is striking about their two accounts is that Baker clearly played little role in the rapprochement. (Baker told me he would talk about his children only if I agreed not to quote him as the source of the information.)

Bush had urged Baker to pitch in on his Senate campaign as a salve for his grief. Baker was appointed chairman of the effort in Harris County—Houston and the area around it. In 1972 he served as state GOP finance chairman and ran the fourteen Texas Gulf Coast counties for Richard Nixon. Three years later, Bush pressed Baker to the next level of involvement by recommending him to Commerce Secretary Rogers C. B. Morton as an undersecretary. Baker moved to Washington to take the job, and only eight months into it was recruited to follow Morton into President Gerald Ford's foundering 1976 campaign as chief "delegate hunter." Deep into the primary season, Ford and Ronald Reagan remained locked in a tight race, so Ford needed a man with Baker's organizational skills to track and woo the uncommitteds and to keep an iron lock on those already pledged to him. According to political consultant Paul Manafort, Bush also had a hand in this appointment, commending Baker to his old House colleague.

Baker's drive and his exigent sense of detail made him a natural at the delegate job—so much so that, once Ford was nominated, Baker was asked to replace Morton as chief of the still-aimless campaign. A political neophyte, he found himself running an incumbent president's campaign. "For him," says Susan, "it was probably the first time that all of his talents had been demanded at once." Ford came from more than thirty points behind to lose by a hair.

By then, Jim Baker was thoroughly hooked. He came out of that race fired up for a political future of his own, telling Susan that if he could raise enough money and gather enough support from the Republican establishment, he wanted to run for attorney general of Texas in 1978. Asked to recall her feelings about this, Susan says bluntly, "They're not printable." The couple had a daughter of their own, Mary Bonner, who was not yet out of diapers. The family turmoil was only beginning to settle, and Susan was expecting "a nice quiet hiatus," in her words. But she is supportive of her husband's choices. "One smart thing about Jim Baker is that he doesn't waste a lot of time on guilt," she says. "In fact, he doesn't waste any time on it."

The 1978 campaign is an intriguing passage in Baker's life. It was his only bid for a political base independent of George Bush (who reportedly told Baker that attorney general of Texas was an office beneath him). And it was the one arguably quixotic effort of his career. Only one Republican, Sen. John Tower, had won statewide election since Reconstruction. Baker's calculation was that the Democrats would nominate Price Daniel Jr., a liberal, allowing Baker to gather up the conservative Democratic vote. The day after the primaries, however, he found himself facing Mark White, Daniel's more conservative opponent. He ran hard anyway. His law-and-order platform was not far different from the rhetoric of presidential candidate George H. W. Bush a decade later, and about as relevant: in Texas, the attorney general has little to do with criminal law enforcement.

"My opponent, Mark White, says we don't need to change our criminal justice system," ran one television ad featuring a somber and somewhat stiff candidate Baker riffling through purported criminal record files. "Here are the facts: a man convicted of murder gets probation—he's free. A criminal sexually abuses young children—no jail time. A drug pusher sentenced to six years serves one, gets out and repeats the crime. Had enough? I have." A voice-over then intoned: "Jim Baker for attorney general. Because we've had enough."

Baker polled a respectable 45 percent in the general election and never ran for anything again. "I think it took him a long time to get over the anguish of having run for office and lost," says Al Ebert, a partner and old friend at Andrews & Kurth. "I just got the impression that he didn't have a very good taste for actually running himself." Before his run, Baker had set up George Bush's political action committee, the first seed of Bush's long-planned 1980 presidential quest. Bush called the day after Baker's loss to offer him formally the role of campaign chairman—the role that would get him back on the national stage, into the Reagan campaign, and finally into the Reagan White House, where he became chief of staff.

Baker's relationship with Bush began to change dramatically during the 1980 campaign. Sooner or later, all political hands seem to talk about their candidate with a sort of fond contempt, and Baker was no exception. When Bush, on his way to the New Hampshire primary after a surprise Iowa caucus victory, would burble about "the Big Mo" that would carry him through the Granite State, Baker would mutter to reporters, "We'll have to do something about that." As Bush's campaign faltered, Baker took his first drastic step to manipulate his friend. In late May Baker, convinced that Bush no longer had a prayer, was concerned that he would come to be seen as a spoiler and might blow any chance of securing the vice presidency. So Baker quietly sabotaged Bush by telling reporters that the campaign was out of money and would not run seriously in the California primary. Bush was embarrassed to learn on the road, from reporters, that his campaign manager had essentially pulled the plug. In the end, Baker's tactics did help win Bush the vice presidency. Having helped Bush this far, however, Baker clearly made a decision to surpass him. "You just sort of got the sense that if Bush had been on any kind of pedestal," says David Keene, who served as political director in that campaign, "after '80 it was, in Baker's mind, a level playing field."

Once in the White House, Bush and Baker had side-by-side offices down the hall from the Oval Office. Baker, with tenuous ties to the Reagan inner circle, was careful not to show any partiality toward Bush. While Baker partisans have said that he secretly used his position in the White House to make sure Bush was "in the loop," this is news to Bush's first vice presidential chief of staff, Admiral Dan Murphy. "The reason I knew he was close to the vice president was because I read it in the paper," says Murphy. "The evidence of closeness during the Reagan years was minimal—to a surprising extent."

Reams have been written about the finesse with which Baker, the outsider, entered the camp of the Reagan Californians and bested such longtime advisors as presidential counselor Edwin Meese III. But perhaps the best description of Baker's overarching method was written by Baker himself in his senior thesis at Princeton, a study of the postwar British Labour Party. The thesis (dedicated "To Mumo with Love") contrasted the styles of two Labour leaders, pragmatist Ernest Bevin and hard-left socialist Aneurin Bevan. "Bevin was not interested in theories, but in practicalities," Baker wrote admiringly in 1952. "Bevin believed in solving the problems of the present before tackling the problems of the future. The solution of the immediate difficulty outweighed consideration of the long-term goal." Or, as Baker told journalist Taylor Branch in 1982: "I'm not a man of vision. I don't pretend to be. But you don't need one here [in the White House]. Not in my job." In this, too, Jim Baker is a Washington ideal. In the capital, where the greatest accolade is to call someone a pragmatist, he has profited greatly by keeping his convictions unclear. Just how unclear is illustrated by the fact that two of his intimates, in trying to describe his views, assigned him two diametrically opposed opinions on abortion.

"I'm a Texas Republican, in my own mind very conservative," Baker says. But his inclination is to avoid messy factional politics. After the 1976 race, for example, he was the leading candidate to become party chairman, but Ford's loss clearly presaged a major war for control of the party, and Baker opted to stay out of harm's way. He zealously conserves his reputation for "effectiveness," taking on only what he thinks he can win. In May 1981, for example, forecasting heavy political weather for the Office of Management and Budget's proposed cuts in Social Security benefits, Baker insisted the plan be issued by the Department of Health and Human Services instead of the White House. When Congress began squawking, Baker led a quiet retreat. As recorded in former budget director David A. Stockman's memoir, notes summarizing conversations at White House senior staff meetings changed over the course of ten days from "Social Security—need strong efforts to inform people about the President's proposals," to "We're not backing off on this, but the President will not lead," to "Social Security—need to get this off the front page. Only submitted to Hill in response to a request from a Congressional Committee for a position . . . *No Presidential involvement.*"

Even one of Baker's signal achievements at Treasury—passage of the sweeping 1986 tax revision bill—was a crusade he joined reluctantly, and only after it was clear the issue was not going to go away. Once he put his back into the fight, it was more as a legislative challenge than as a campaign for better public policy. "The challenge of tax reform was not because of tax reform," as a former associate put it. Baker "doesn't sit there and think through, 'What is good tax policy for America?' It's the game."

In the process, Baker took none of the risks assumed by the legislators who had to vote to cut special-interest tax preferences (indeed, he was insistent on keeping some of the kinks in the code that benefited men like him, including oil and gas breaks and limits on the "kiddie tax" of income earned on gifts from grandparents to their grandchildren). Nor could Baker have framed the issue in a visionary enough way to get it moving. It was his much-maligned predecessor at Treasury, Donald Regan, who put tax reform on the

map by producing a first plan, known as Treasury I, that rejected political reality entirely in favor of pure reform. Baker's aides and
acolytes insist—probably correctly—that Treasury I was a politically
hopeless document, but fail to acknowledge that, in this case, tax reform champions in Congress would have gotten nowhere without
such a radical opening bid from the Reagan administration.

Few public officials have worked the press as assiduously or as successfully as Baker has, and the Washington press corps has been one
of his firmest allies. Robert Wright of the *New Republic* terms him
"the man who has turned smelling like a rose into a job description."
And a former associate says, "I've never known anyone who studies
his own press more closely than Jim Baker." Reporters like him and
are convinced that he likes them. Over the years, as a result, he has
drawn little substantive criticism. His roles at both the White
House and Treasury, for instance, assigned him some responsibility
for the ballooning federal deficit—a classic example of what the undergraduate Baker waved aside as "the problems of the future." But
the conventional wisdom thanks him for negotiating a tax increase
in 1982 and notes that he urged the president in vain to cut the defense budget—then lets him off the hook for the many occasions
when he led the administration in abandoning a politically difficult
effort to raise revenue or cut spending.

Last year, after stepping in to chair the Bush campaign at its
nadir, he got glowing notices as the maestro who revived Bush's candidacy. At the same time, he eluded almost all blame for what the
press growled was a negative, empty campaign—and one that kept
the media as far as possible from the candidate.

It is all part of Baker's talent for associating himself with success
and divorcing himself from controversy or failure. Says one White
House aide, "The fact that I'm having difficulty thinking of something he fully supported in the White House that went awry maybe
says it all." Jim Baker is known as the man who can walk on water.
You say he only tries in January, when the water is frozen? So much
the better, answers a dazzled Washington; that only proves his
wisdom.

Baker's single apparent vanity is his horror of being thought a politician. If he has parlayed it into a great strength—taking great care, while operating shrewdly, never to seem an operator—it also remains his greatest weakness. For politics is unavoidably the root of his power.

Baker has said over and over again that his role as Ford's delegate hunter was "demeaning," full of pleading and horse trading. And as a candidate himself, he took seriously his stump observation that, "Texas needs a lawyer, not a politician, for attorney general." Shortly before election day, a *Houston Chronicle* reporter heard Baker snap at an aide, "I am a lawyer, not a politician. And don't ever forget it." Asked if he disliked running for office, Baker says, "No, no, no. I enjoyed campaigning. . . . There are some parts of it I don't like. You know, a candidate is the lowest form of human life. You *know* that." He is joking, but he is very animated. "It's true. Candidates are raked over the—." Here he catches himself, to finish in a more deliberate vein: "That's part of the process. But I can't say I didn't like it—I won't say that." His wife will, though. "He never wants to do it again," she says vehemently. "Because it's not only demanding, it's demeaning—the way you have to beg for money. You know?"

Baker had several more shots at a political future. Invited to run for the Senate in 1984 when John Tower left his seat, Baker considered it, and even asked then-White House Political Director Rollins to conduct a poll—but decided he already had climbed well beyond the status of a junior senator. "Look around," he told one group of legislators who urged him to run. "I can walk into the Oval Office any time." Why would he want to give that up to raise $10 million and spend two years campaigning for the Senate, where, he told an associate, "You have to sit on the back bench for six years before anyone will even listen to you"?

His options thus narrowed, he made the one move of his career that openly betrayed his ambition when he swapped jobs with treasury secretary Donald T. Regan at the start of Reagan's second term. Of course, one cannot hold Baker responsible for all his successor's mistakes. But in the face of the president's passivity, Baker effectively picked that successor. And in his desire for the Treasury job, he made sure Don Regan edged out more capable competition. Before Regan broached the switch with Baker, the chief of staff job had essentially been promised to former secretary of transportation Drew Lewis. According to a new book by President Reagan's longtime confidential secretary, Helene von Damm, Lewis, by then in private industry, came to Washington to discuss the prospect with Baker, Meese, deputy chief of staff Michael K. Deaver, and Nancy Reagan. He was told the president knew of the plans and looked forward to his return to Washington. Lewis confirms the story while declining to go into much detail. "I had pretty much agreed to do it until I picked up the *New York Times* and read that Don Regan was going to get the job," he says.

That day, Baker called Lewis to say that the swap "was too good to be true." Tellingly, few of Baker's admirers suggest that Baker couldn't or didn't foresee the result.* Ed Rollins says he believes Baker crossed his fingers and hoped that he had larded the White House staff with enough men of good sense to overcome Regan's deficiencies. "My assessment," Rollins adds, "is that he thought that Don Regan would self-destruct in about six or eight months, and leave, and not do the kind of damage that he did."

Treasury was, for Baker, an important step away from the role of politico and toward the role of statesman. He was therefore deeply reluctant to step down to run the Bush campaign last year. Poised to move from one premier cabinet post to *the* premier cabinet post, he told associates he was concerned that he would once again be perceived as, well, a campaign manager.

He eventually acceded, of course, to the ancient political law that you dance with the one that brung you. But it was the first time his distaste for a political identity came openly into conflict with his

---

*Regan, an impatient and undiplomatic man used to being in charge, fared poorly in the job. The Iran-Contra scandal occurred on his watch, and Regan resigned amid speculation—never substantiated—that he had orchestrated a cover-up.

ambition. In the first four years of the Reagan administration, Jim Baker, as chief of staff, had been a far more powerful figure than George Bush—an outcome that, many observers believe, Bush resented. "I'm sure in Jim Baker's mind today he knows he could be president of the United States," says Rollins. It is the familiar Washington syndrome, known to the greenest aide on Capitol Hill: hey, I could do that.

But as 1988 drew nearer, the positions had inevitably shifted. Baker was again dependent on the political fortunes of Bush. He is too smart to forget this, but also too proud to like it.

Baker's major contribution to the 1988 campaign was in persuading Bush to listen to his hired guns. They offered a deliberate plan to drive up Dukakis's "negatives" by tarring him as a hard-left liberal, soft on crime, and—as the campaign subliminally underlined with the issue of furloughed convict Willie Horton—intent on coddling blacks. Bush, chronically wanting to be nice, had reservations—not strong enough to make him stop, just strong enough that he needed to be prodded on a regular basis. "I heard Baker on the phone lecturing Bush to stick to the scripts," says a former campaign worker. "The way you'd say it to a child: 'Look. Don't change it. . . . No, I don't think it's time to soften the message. Just read it the way we gave it to you. *Thank* you.'" One of Washington's legion of mediators called Baker to offer the support of a certain organization—a group that the Bush campaign was very eager to win over. One of the few things this group wanted in return was a meeting with Baker to hear the standard vague assurances that a Bush administration would be in sympathy with the group's interests. But after first agreeing to the meeting, Baker balked. Margaret Tutwiler, his loyal aide and anxious monitor of his reputation, told the go-between that Baker had become concerned that, as secretary of state, he might one day have to rule on issues affecting this organization. He was determined, Tutwiler said, to avoid any appearance of impropriety. So Baker proposed, through Tutwiler, an alternative: someone less fastidious, more willing to soil his hands in the daily grime of politics. He set up a meeting with the next president of the United States.

Bush, of course, exacted his own revenge for this treatment. According to the journalist Michael Kramer, Baker sometimes rebelled at having to force-feed the candidate. "You call him yourselves," Baker once yelled at media advisor Roger Ailes. "You're not the ones who have to carry that message and have him say, 'If you're so smart, Jimmy, how come I'm the one who's vice president?'"

Throughout the fall, Baker stayed as far out of the public eye as possible, directing the action from an office in Washington. Lee Atwater, handpicked by Baker to be the campaign manager, was hungry for recognition and happy to accept the notoriety that came from the slashing campaign. But even he was sometimes amused by the gentlemanly persona Baker was able to maintain. "Jim Baker, plain and simple, never hesitated at all" in the 1988 campaign, Atwater says.

Baker rejects as "absurd" the widespread conjecture that he would like to run for president in 1996, once George Bush has had his fill. If he is telling the truth, then he has now reached his pinnacle—the premier cabinet job in an administration run by his closest political associate. For a man who has so carefully rationed his political capital through some of the most difficult jobs Washington has to offer, the intriguing question is: Will he now find some worthwhile way to spend it? The answer will determine whether Baker remains for all time a skilled operative who mediated many of the achievements of the Reagan—and possibly the Bush—presidency, or whether he joins the tiny number of cabinet officers who have transcended the crisis of the hour to make their own mark on the age.

Some happily extend Baker the benefit of the doubt. "I think he will go down in the same sense that John Foster Dulles went down in his era, and Harry Hopkins went down in his era, and Daniel Webster went down in his era," says Atwater. "I think he's a titan. He's done more than most people I can think of, and he is just entering the job that will define him." Atwater, a southern pol to the core, says this with the eye-bulging sincerity he brings to all his most hyperbolic statements. But you have to give him that last part: after eight exacting years here, Baker may have to make his reputation all over again.

The question isn't whether Baker can handle the substance of the job. His tenure at Treasury earned him fairly good marks on international finance and was marred by only one obvious boner—his possible role in causing the 1987 stock market crash with tough talk about not letting West Germany "squeeze" the American economy with high interest rates. His notable initiatives include coordinating economic policy with major allies and driving the value of the dollar down in an effort to reduce the trade deficit. He is criticized for not moving more aggressively in some areas—the savings and loan crisis, Third World debt—that are slouching toward some future reckoning. But few seriously argue that he is unqualified to be secretary of state. The question is whether Baker can leave the safety of what has served him best to seek the uncertain rewards of leadership. "The game" is not the same thing as history, however greatly Washington cherishes that illusion. The secretaries of state whom history remembers—the George C. Marshalls, the John Foster Dulleses—are those who have permanently changed, if not the world, then at least America's idea of it. As he moves forward to clinch his transition from lawyer to pol to statesman, Baker is moving ever further into jobs that might be said to require vision.

The evidence so far is that this man of overpowering political skills still lacks a political imagination. "I don't think he would pretend to bring to the job of secretary of state initially the conceptual framework that Henry Kissinger did," says former White House communications director David R. Gergen. "He doesn't see himself in those terms. I do think he'll feel that there are probably two, three, four things he can do as secretary of state . . . and that's what he'll set his mind to do."

Yet four more years, or eight, is a long time to succeed by doing the doable and winning the winnable. Baker is probably accomplished enough to keep it up for as long as he wants to—but at the almost certain expense of any greater claim to fame. If he wants a place at the head of his class, then he has begun the job in which his ambitions must finally go to war with his caution. For the final lesson of success in Washington is that it is, by nature, evanescent. Washington loves the ones who grease its gears. But history only remembers the ones who shift them.*

—*January 1989*

POSTSCRIPT (THREE YEARS LATER): THE STRING TWITCHES AGAIN

If you had to devise a private hell for Jim Baker, you couldn't do better than to pattern it after the events of this past summer. As Bush's polls streaked downward through June and July and into August, it became clear that Bush—who had never won a national election without a vital boost from Baker—would once again need to call on him. Baker, at the age of sixty-two, had thought he was long past this. Yet by the sort of strict pragmatism that had always ruled his career, he was forced to acknowledge that he was less valuable running U.S. foreign policy than he would be in the role of White House chief of staff and unofficial head of the Bush campaign.

As the summer proceeded, Bush and Baker danced the same minuet they had danced four years before. Heated denials. Then a slight

---

*In a 1992 follow-up profile—portions of which I have blended into this earlier piece—Marjorie gave Secretary of State Baker reasonably high marks for "bringing the Arab states, Israel, and the Palestinians together for their first direct negotiations." (The Oslo Accords were negotiated the following year.) But she faulted Baker for being slow to recognize the collapse of the Soviet empire and Saddam Hussein's arms buildup prior to Iraq's 1990 invasion of Kuwait. On this last point, she wrote, "Desert Storm [i.e., the 1991 Gulf War] was a diplomatic failure before it was a military victory, and the responsibility lies squarely with Baker's State Department for failing to understand Hussein's aggressive designs and to give any strong advance signal of U.S. resolve." The postscript that follows is drawn from the 1992 follow-up.

shift, the door left open a crack. A highly publicized fishing trip to Wyoming, and the coy no-comment afterward that definitively confirmed that something was up. This time, though, there was a strange slow-motion quality to the dance. It dragged on, leaving the campaign in limbo; it was all too clear that neither man wanted to face the inevitable.

Until it finally ended, on August 13, when Bush and Baker made back-to-back appearances to announce Baker's shift to the White House. It was one of those rare moments when you can see, beneath the subcutaneous fat of politics, the pulsing flesh of a real human relationship, in all its gory contradictions and dependencies.

Bush came to the White House briefing room and, in the manner of a child eating his spinach, confirmed the decision he had been putting off all summer. It was an extraordinary admission of weakness. Not only would Baker come to take over the White House and the campaign, and not only would he bring along his own group of top managers—an implicit criticism of the crowd with which Bush had heretofore been muddling along—but the entire move was phrased in language that made of Baker a political messiah. Baker's role, the president said, would be to "help me build on what we've started by developing an integrated second-term program of domestic, economic, and foreign policies." If voters didn't like the Bush presidency, ran the subliminal message, maybe they'd like Baker's version better. Bush's appearance, which lasted scarcely more than five minutes, made him seem hurried, grim, blatantly political. "It just proves," said a disgusted caller to C-SPAN during its live coverage, "that George Bush would do anything to get elected."

Baker's appearance, on the other hand, was lofty, high toned—presidential. Instead of speaking to an inquisitive press corps, he addressed an audience of civilian foreign-service officers in the State Department's huge Dean Acheson Auditorium. He delivered a twenty-minute speech that ranged from Bosnia to Cambodia to America's inner cities; it summarized his own achievements and set out the themes of Bush's future campaign. While this speech, too, was obviously political in intent, it was strikingly more ambitious than Bush's, striving to solemnize Baker's move as a gift to generations yet unborn.

It was clear to experienced readers of political semaphore that Baker had extracted the maximum advantage in the manner of the move—above all, in the way the door was left open for his renomination to the State Department after the election. Even as they came together to salvage their political fortunes, there was, between Bush and Baker, that visible tug of competing interests.

Underlying the morning's events, once you peeled away all the layers of politics, was the awesome sight of each man face-to-face with his own shortcomings.

There was Bush, nakedly courting his own humiliation—reduced to acknowledging that he simply can't run for the presidency without Jim Baker's impeccable cynicism to guide him. Over and over, he has shown himself incapable of acting *deliberately* to win the presidency by the means that have worked in the past. He has never seemed to confront, head-on, exactly what moral choices are made in a campaign like the one he ran in 1988. He clings to the self-image of the Greenwich-bred moderate he once was, while he runs as a red-meat conservative who is the heir of Ronald Reagan. He wants the innocence of the former, and the political success of the latter. While he skitters back and forth from one to the other, he has Jim Baker behind him to help override his conscience. No one else but Baker, with his gentleman's pedigree, is able to do this for him.

And on Baker's side: once you cracked open his proud rhetoric, you found the fastidious Baker pacing the prison of his own past methods. In a dozen small ways, he has won his decades-long competition with George Bush. But when the crisis came, it was still Bush's right to call on Baker; it was still Baker's duty to obey. For Baker, at every turn, has chosen the appointive over the elective office. He has excelled at working behind the scenes, through influence and intrigue. Unlike Bush, he has declined to reach for jobs that would have subjected him to repeated referenda by masses of mere voters. As a result, his political fortunes are tied to those of a man less gifted than he, and today he faces the loss of everything he has worked for.

For more than a decade, Baker has been able to mute the tension between his quest for power and his disdain for politics. As he pulled the strings, wrote the attack lines, and lifted the hem of his coat primly from the mire, he could persuade himself he was above the pandering of men like Bush. But every four years comes the inconvenient reminder that power, in a democracy, is distributed by votes. In the painful summer of Baker's sixty-second year, the roots of Baker's power—the *true* roots—were exposed. And when they were seen clearly, without the mediation of his craft and wintry charm, they were seen to be out of his control.*

—*October 1992*

---

*Bush, of course, lost to Bill Clinton. Baker got even with the Democrats— and, arguably, with democracy—in 2000, when he led George W. Bush's successful effort to call the disputed presidential election in his favor. Six years after that, however, the younger Bush spurned the recommendation of a panel cochaired by Baker that the United States take steps to wind down its military occupation of Iraq.

LA BELLE DAME
SANS MERCI

(PATRICIA DUFF)

Welcome to the seventh circle of litigation hell: a cramped, gloomy courtroom on the fifth floor of the Supreme Court building in Lower Manhattan, suffused with brown even on a brilliant May afternoon. Patricia Duff is dressed for court with her trademark simplicity: a tailored navy pantsuit, a simple black Prada bag, her shiny blonde hair unstyled. The severity of it all makes her slim frame look tiny in the high-ceilinged room. To complete the effect, she is limping toward her side of the table that dominates the well of the courtroom, her left foot still in a cast from a spring-vacation stumble.

Justice Eileen Bransten does not seem especially happy to see her. "Man magnet" Duff, as the *New York Post*'s "Page Six" likes to call her, and her ex-husband, the driven billionaire Ronald Perelman, are now nearing their third year of litigation over the future of their four-year-old daughter. And quite a fight it's been, ever since the courtroom was opened to the public, last December, at Duff's insistence. "It's become *The War of the Roses*, where they've both lost sight of what they're doing," says someone who knows them both. "And it just keeps escalating." Perelman has steadily upped his demands in court, criticized Duff's performance as a mother, and made sure the tabloids got word of a court-appointed psychiatrist's conclusion, paraphrased by Perelman's lawyers, that Duff "has a personality disorder with paranoid, narcissistic, passive-aggressive, histrionic and borderline features" and that she is "unable to distinguish her needs from those of the parties' daughter." Duff, in her own filings, has raised what she calls her ex-husband's "utterly false and hypocritical piety, his womanizing, his wayward way of life, his unrelenting punitive behavior to his ex-wives, his children and to anyone who does not bend to his will, and his systematic harassment of me in a multitude of ways."

"Frankly," she says in an interview, "considering what I've gone through, how besieged I've been, I think my ability to hold up and keep my daughter happy and in good shape is pretty extraordinary." The entire lawsuit, she claims, is part of his vindictive drive to control her.

"Hah!" replies Perelman. "The likelihood of any man being in a position to control Patricia is somewhat less than zero."

The case is, among other things, an experiment in what happens when a powerful control freak collides with a woman who sometimes seems to live for the transgression of boundaries. It's also a rare look at divorce in the financial stratosphere, where parents can discuss with straight faces whether $36,000 is an adequate yearly clothing allowance for a four-year-old but cannot get along well enough to make sure the girl has a clean outfit to wear to preschool on the day she shifts households, and where the tumble from life with a billionaire to life as a mere millionaire can seem like the world's most precipitous slide. But at its most arresting, the case is the climactic chapter in the forty-five-year-old Duff's career as a femme fatale.

To this day's dull procedural hearing, the litigants' notoriety has drawn a small knot of reporters and half a dozen activists—from the National Organization for Women, from the National Coalition for Family Justice, from Amicus for Domestic Justice—who have come to murmur their support for Duff's contention that she and her little girl are the butterflies being broken on the wheel of Perelman's wrath. But extensive interviews and a reading of the available records—including police reports in two states—point to a much more complicated conclusion: that Patricia Duff is a woman so intent on seeing herself as a victim that she may, at last, ensure that very result.

Even before the Perelman case spiraled out of control, the four-times-married Duff was a topic of fevered gossip in New York, Los Angeles, and Washington, for she has had a colorful career in each of those cities: as the belle of Carter-era Washington who, in the brief interval between two early marriages, was courted by congressmen; as an aspiring actress and then political doyenne in Hollywood, where, after marrying studio executive Mike Medavoy, she made herself a figure in the nexus where politicians and stars trade cash for cachet; and then in New York, where she arrived in 1994 to live with Perelman, already pregnant with his child. Since her split from Perelman, she has taken up with New Jersey Senator Robert Torricelli, an up-and-coming Democrat who formerly dated Bianca Jagger, and who was recently tagged by *George* magazine as one of the ten biggest publicity hounds in Washington. Careers like this may be common in Hollywood, but it has been at least a generation since Washington or New York has seen a woman with such a penchant for the high-profile relationship. *New Yorker* media critic Hendrik Hertzberg, who has known Duff since the Carter presidency, muses admiringly, "If Jackie O. was Elvis and Pamela Harriman was Jagger, she'd be, what? Tom Petty? Neil Young?" Her legend is so delectable that when I called Warren Beatty for an interview and told him I was writing about Patricia Duff, he laughed. "Congratulations!" he said.

It hasn't softened Duff's notoriety—or the tone of those discussing her—that she is a staggeringly beautiful woman. Photographs don't do her justice: in person she is, in the words of one woman who doesn't even like her, "*uncannily* gorgeous." Her wheaty, shoulder-length hair is pleasantly tousled; her eyes are a rare, disconcerting shade of green, so deep as to be almost olive. The impact of her beauty is completed by her voice. It is soft and sandpapery—too deep to be kittenish, but with a definite help-me hush. Beth Dozoretz, national finance chair of the Democratic National Committee, recalls that on her first meeting with Duff, "I said, 'Excuse me for staring at you, but you're so beautiful.' And you know, she's beautiful in a disarming way—it doesn't seem like it's a lot of effort." Men in Washington still recall her heyday as a political staff worker and social ornament among the Democrats who came to town with Jimmy Carter. "She was one of the most beautiful things I had ever seen, maybe after the Grand Canyon," recalls *Washington Post* columnist Richard Cohen.

Her beauty has not faded over time. Perelman recalls, of the encounter in late 1992 that sparked his relationship with Duff, that "she just captivated me—she looked in my eyes and captivated me. She can be the single most charming human being in the history of the world. She looks at you with those eyes. . . . And she looks great, and she moves great, and she smells great, and she sounds great. And I thought, This is *great!*"

Before her marriage to Perelman, Duff's high-water mark among gossips had been early in the Clinton administration, after she and Medavoy, who had been campaign supporters, took their turn as guests in the Lincoln Bedroom. Back in Los Angeles, Patricia regaled friends with stories of the president's solicitude; the *New York Post* reported that she said he was (nudge, nudge) "one full-service president." She denied having hinted at anything untoward. But the gossip alone was enough to end her easy access to the president. "The president was quite angry about it," recalls a former Clinton staffer. "And then she was kind of cut off. She stopped getting invited to see him in L.A. . . . She just seemed dangerous after that." Most people doubted that she'd actually had an affair with the president. But the talk served to burnish the myth that Duff has worked hard at cultivating, liberally polishing the duller parts, editing and augmenting the less glamorous bits. The higher she has risen, the more careful this editing process has become, excising a husband here, altering a chronology there.

But if Duff has lived the life of a femme fatale, she lacks the flinty self-awareness that marks the genuine article. "For someone who's an insecure person to start with, she's chosen a very challenging life," says a person who worked with her in California. "Patricia is not Pamela Harriman. She's just not as tough." And lately Duff's story has been less the Legend of Cleopatra than the Perils of Pauline. With the implosion of her marriage to Perelman, the tone of the talk about Duff has darkened. She has always had enemies— especially among the women who have watched her rise from millionaire's wife to billionaire's bride. What is striking now is how many erstwhile friends—old and new, in Hollywood and New York—have begun to pull away.

"I've sort of made an effort to sort of not call her much lately," admits an old friend from L.A. "I used to call her and check in to commiserate, and I'd get such an earful, it was all so crazy, that I didn't want to get sucked in by it. . . . I don't quite understand what happened to her life." The model Cheryl Tiegs responded to an interview request by leaving a message on my voice mail, saying, "As much as I think Patricia is a very complicated character, and very interesting to write on . . . , I don't really feel right about betraying what was originally a friendship, and is no longer." In New York, newer friends have sided with Perelman—or with his previous wife, television reporter Claudia Cohen, whose divorce from Perelman, once bitter, has now resolved itself in a close friendship with him. Cohen is a longtime New Yorker who is said to be furious with Duff over her efforts to drag the history of Perelman's last divorce— which was conducted in closed court—into her own litigation. Duff has complained to friends that the glamorous crowd that embraced her upon her arrival in New York, women such as Barbara Walters and Martha Stewart, has now spurned her. Even if some of her new isolation can be explained away by jealousy or opportunism, much is clearly the fruit of her own recent conduct, which has sometimes been decidedly odd. "She's just incredibly, incredibly suspicious of everyone," says a friend. "She's sure that the servants and the nannies are bought off by Ronald. She accuses everyone of stealing things, of sabotaging her scheduling, of making her life difficult on purpose." The speed with which she has hired and fired law firms in her divorce case—sixteen of them, in all, by the count of Perelman's lawyers—is but the clearest symptom of the chaos Duff has ushered into her life. "She's more trouble than she's worth," says an old Hollywood friend. "There's a lot of that sense in the air."

———

The name Duff, which Patricia has held onto through her third and fourth marriages, was earned from her second husband, a Washington attorney named Daniel Duff; before Duff, she was married briefly to Thomas O. Zabrodsky, a high-school sweetheart whom she dated for years and then wedded just before her college graduation in 1976. Before that, friends and family knew her as Patsy Orr. But even that was not her original name. When she was born, in April 1954, it was as Patricia Michelle Hoar.

Duff's father, a former navy pilot who became an executive with Lockheed and, later, Hughes Aircraft, legally changed the family's name to Orr in 1960, reasoning that "Hoar" would make life an uphill struggle for three daughters. Patricia was the third child—behind one sister and a brother, with her second sister born hard on her heels a year and a half later. The Orr children spent their early years in Woodland Hills, in the San Fernando Valley, and then moved to Europe when their father was transferred there. Patricia attended school in Bonn and then at the International School of Brussels. Duff doesn't talk much about her family of origin. Friends describe her as somewhat alienated from her parents and siblings, as nursing a sense that something essential was missing in her passage from childhood to adulthood. Her father traveled almost constantly, the parents' marriage crumbled over time, and "Patsy" seems to have felt lost in her middle place in the small crowd of her siblings. "She did not feel . . . emotionally supported," says a friend. Another person describes the family as "fractured" and says she believes that Duff's relationships with men are an effort "to fill this void. To have this sense of a very strong relationship with somebody." In this view, her succession of marriages has been less a climb up the ladder than a series of lunges in the direction of security. How many other girls who graduated from college in 1976, after all, got married twice before they turned twenty-seven? "She's always escaping from a powerful man into the arms of an even more powerful man," says a veteran Duff-watcher. "This is really who she thinks she is. . . . She's not calculating on the surface; she's a scared little girl looking for sympathy and understanding."

Once out of secondary school, Duff enrolled at Barnard, but later transferred to Georgetown University. There, she has told friends, she was increasingly dominated by Zabrodsky, who had followed her to the States from Europe. Zabrodsky has been depicted, in accounts of her life, as an exotic, somewhat dangerous figure to whom she was in thrall. As she has told the story—a tale that has striking parallels to her version of the Perelman saga—he isolated her from almost every other social contact through college and eventually bullied her into marriage. But Zabrodsky, who today is a high-level executive at the Reynolds Metals Company in Brussels, denies with some heat the version of the marriage that Duff has told. "Some of the things that have been said I consider rather defamatory," he says. "I hold no bitterness toward her. But I have been disturbed by what's said about me in the press." Theirs was, he acknowledges, a "turbulent" union. "There was a battle for dominance within the marriage. Who sets the agenda, and so forth. Just the things that happen when you put two very domineering people in the same marriage. . . . But I don't think I'm a particularly overbearing man. I found that it was a marriage of equals, quite frankly."

In any case, this is the marriage Duff has airbrushed from some versions of her life story. Friends from as late as the early '80s— before her marriage to Medavoy—were aware of it. But as she rose in the world, she began to leave Zabrodsky out of her history, whether talking to friends or to reporters. "She always represented him to me as a boyfriend," says someone who knows Duff very well. Another source says Duff made up her mind that the marriage didn't really count. Because she agreed to it under duress, in her view, it was as if it had never taken place at all. She has described it as lasting only for a few months. But Zabrodsky says they were married for more than a year before they separated, and that the divorce didn't go through for at least two years after that.

Separated from Zabrodsky and armed with a degree in international relations and a change in hair color, from brunette to blonde, Patricia snagged a staff post at the House Select Committee on Assassinations, which had been appointed to investigate the murders of John F. Kennedy and Martin Luther King Jr. This began a period, lasting about six years, that might be called the normal chapter in Duff's life. She worked on the committee mostly as a researcher, a job requiring a top-secret clearance; colleagues thought of her as smart and hardworking. Later she worked for John McLaughlin, the former priest who was then beginning his career in broadcasting; for Pat Caddell, Jimmy Carter's pollster; and for political consultant Bob Squier. Those who knew her through Caddell seem to remember her more vividly as a presence in his swimming pool, in her bikini, than in his office. But when she was hired away by Squier, it was to do the complicated job of buying advertising time for his political clients—far from a cupcake job—and she worked her way up to vice president of the small firm. "I've always said, if she hadn't quit, she'd be a partner today," says Squier. "Of course, she was also a trophy office wife for both" Caddell and Squier, says Hendrik Hertzberg, who was a Carter speechwriter, "but what made her such a valuable trophy was that once she had stunned you with her looks she could then surprise you with her brains."

Friends' memories of this time in her life summon up a Potomac version of Holly Golightly, dating congressmen—notably Christopher Dodd of Connecticut, who was on the Assassinations Committee, and California representative Pete Stark—and befriending senators and White House aides. She was widely liked. "I could name you fifty people about whom I'd sooner have said, 'This person is going to try and push to the top.' Or 'This person is going for the power,'" says someone who became friendly with Patricia during this period. Indeed, she seemed to turn down the more glamorous opportunities that came her way, choosing for her next husband Daniel Duff, a handsome, easygoing government lawyer.

"I guess I'm the odd character in this line of men," says Duff, who is now general counsel for a transportation trade association.

"Maybe I offered what appeared to be security and stability." They met in 1978 and married in 1980. The Duffs lived in a reclaimed town house in the tumbledown neighborhood of Logan Circle; Patricia drove an old Vega that leaked whenever it rained. For a time, this life seemed enough. "She was not supersophisticated at that point," recalls Daniel Duff. "There was still a kind of innocent quality about her." Someone who met her professionally in those years says, "She didn't seem to come from any kind of fancy background. She just sort of seemed to—poof!—appear. She had a lot of poise, and knew a lot of people, but it seemed to be clearly all on her own steam."

Yet few thought of her then as someone truly engaged with politics as a profession. And on the side she had begun to find modeling and acting work—posing on the cover of *Washingtonian* magazine, landing a national TV ad for Freixenet champagne, and commuting to New York to take acting classes. She was invited to Los Angeles to audition for a continuing role on Bruce Paltrow's NBC series, *St. Elsewhere*. And though she didn't get the part, her compass shifted. She moved "temporarily" to Los Angeles, but never really returned to Washington and left Duff for good in 1984.

In the legend according to Patricia, she was sent to L.A. that year by Gary Hart's presidential campaign to organize Hollywood on the candidate's behalf—the founding element in her carefully honed image as the savvy political missionary sent to bring substance to the land of laughs. She did end up working for the campaign, as liaison to the celebrities who supported it. But several sources who knew her at the time, both inside and outside the Hart campaign, remember her shift to Hollywood as the move of an aspiring actress; politics, they say, was an afterthought.

She arrived in Hollywood with an introduction to Mike Medavoy from Chris Dodd. Medavoy, then the production chief of Orion Pictures, a title he had previously held at United Artists, was associated with such hits as *One Flew over the Cuckoo's Nest, Annie Hall,* and *Rocky.* He was also the national finance chair of the Hart campaign. Nine months after meeting Duff, in 1984, he left his wife for her.

In part through Medavoy, Duff continued to get acting roles: bit parts in the TV movies *Fatal Vision* and *Blade in Hong Kong,* and in the feature film *About Last Night . . . ,* in which she plays an anonymous woman who picks up Rob Lowe outside a bar. (She has three lines: "Are you going in?" "I really like you a lot." And "What?!") She also appeared in *Gimme an 'F'* (the second installment in the *T&A Academy* series) and *D.C. Cab,* and had guest roles on the TV shows *Moonlighting* and *Hotel.* But after she became Patricia Duff Medavoy, the role that would increasingly define her was that of Hollywood wife. The couple was married in May 1986 in a huge, star-studded wedding at the former Harold Lloyd estate, where Patricia wore a tight, midriff-baring dress that was the talk of the town. "The phrase 'sprayed on' comes to mind," says someone who attended. Medavoy was heavily involved in Democratic politics, and the couple became significant brokers in the romance between Hollywood and Washington, holding fund-raisers, putting candidates up in their home, making introductions. (Their most fateful political act was taking Gary Hart along as a guest to a party in Aspen, at the home of rocker Don Henley, on New Year's Day 1987. It was there that Hart met Donna Rice, the lissome blonde with whom he would torpedo his political career.) In Clinton's first campaign, they were among his earliest supporters in Hollywood—and were quick to let everyone know it. After Clinton's election, Medavoy was rumored to close an uncanny number of phone calls with a hurried announcement that he had to run—the president was on the other line.

Patricia labored to become a political power in her own right, cofounding, with other refugees from Hart's circle, the Show Coalition, a sort of political-education forum for the film community, which enrolled midlevel Hollywood—writers, actors, aspiring directors—and invited politicians to speak at its functions. In her prime there, Duff was skilled in the subtle art of capitalizing on one power center's awe of, and illusions about, another. Washington readily accepted the idea that this glamorous, moneyed, well-connected woman was someone who had to be cultivated in the Hollywood money chase, just as Hollywood accepted her self-presentation as a former political consultant who was hugely connected in Washington. Shrewder observers of the California political scene scoffed at the idea that "Show Co" was a power to contend with. "It was the most extraordinary example of wasted political energy," says someone well versed in Los Angeles fundraising. "It didn't activate people, nor did it raise money. And she dragged any important politician who could breathe in front of it. And they came!" However, this person adds, with some admiration, "She really knew how to use it as a platform." Duff defends Show Coalition's role as a "catalyst" in persuading film people to get involved in national politics, and also notes that it performed community service in the South-Central neighborhood of L.A. "We weren't just talking about issues in the abstract," she says, "but also about working in our own community." On the national level, "I do think we had an enormous amount of influence on getting people involved, getting them primed to give money."

But gossip was rife over power struggles between Patricia and the other big players in Democratic Hollywood, especially the Hollywood Women's Political Committee and the circle around Tom Hayden and Jane Fonda. Which group could inspire the most assiduous courtship by the most important senators? Who would be invited to serve as liaison between Hollywood celebrities and the party's 1988 convention? "There was just a lot of tension, because she was so concerned that she be seen as the most influential Hollywood political person," recalls one old Democratic associate. Says another, "I'm sure there's some great old MGM movie, *The Snake Pit* or something, that would compare" to the venom of these battles. This was when associates began to notice a suspicious streak in Duff. "She always thought people were out to get her, and she'd turn on people," says a longtime Hollywood Democrat. "She was extremely paranoid. . . . You just never knew on a given day when she would be unbelievably sweet and fun, or when on the next day she would think you were plotting against her." This period was also when friends began noticing a tempestuous quality to Duff's days. "She seemed to thrive on chaos, in a sense," says a friend from this era. "The phone would be constantly ringing: 'You have forty-two messages.'" "It's always just a whirlwind at Patricia's house," says a more recent friend, "of activity and being late and canceled appointments and changed minds, and yelling at the servants because the towels aren't lined up just so." "She thought of herself as being in a gilded cage" and compared herself to Nora, in Ibsen's play *A Doll's House,* says an intimate from her California days. Duff wanted to be something more substantial than a Hollywood wife, and made constant feints in the direction of another career. At one point she and a friend started a corporate-consulting firm that lasted about a year. She produced a movie, *Limit Up,* starring Nancy Allen and Dean Stockwell, but it went straight to video. ("In a man's world," begins the advertising copy on the video's box, "a working girl can use a little magic to get ahead.") She published an article in *Premiere* magazine. Around the time of Clinton's first inaugural she founded a philanthropic organization called the Common Good to promote community service, but it never really got off the ground.

Later, after she took up with Perelman, she would become an editor-at-large at *Premiere,* of which he was by then part owner. She would start a production company, Sojourner, but never use it. She would consider a career in TV news, going to a CBS training facility in Dallas for evaluation and doing a brief stint at a Perelman-controlled station in Monterey. She would talk about entering law school or business school, but never go. She would become president of the Revlon Foundation—a position, in her husband's organization, that ended abruptly along with the marriage. "She was too good-looking for her own good," says a friend from the Medavoy days, "and too smart for her own good. If she'd been less smart, she wouldn't have minded. And if she'd been less good-looking, she would have gotten something else going." As she neared her forties, her major occupation was supervising the construction of the Me-

davoys' $5 million house on Hazen Drive in Beverly Hills. It was de-
scribed in a 1992 story in W, in which Duff spoke of entertaining the
likes of Warren Beatty, Dustin Hoffman, and Richard Dreyfuss. But
she sighed over the trials of building such a vast house. "It took so
much work," she said, "I actually developed chronic fatigue syndrome while I was doing it."

What she really wanted, she told all her friends, was a child; she
felt, according to an intimate, that a child might be "the thing that
would validate her life." Medavoy, who had an adult child from a
previous marriage, didn't flatly refuse, but he dragged his feet. In
1990 he had become chairman of TriStar Pictures, which had just
been bought by Sony, and he was very caught up in work. She complained that he was distant, uncaring, emotionally abusive. And so
she moved out—to send him a message, she told friends, that she
wouldn't wait forever. In the legend according to Patricia, she left
Medavoy in mid-1993; some months later, she was taken to a party
by Melanie Griffith, who was soon to start modeling for Revlon and
who introduced her to Perelman. This decorous version proposes a
decent interval between the rejection of Medavoy and the merger
with Perelman. But in fact she and Perelman had begun a passionate
affair the previous winter. It began when she approached him during
a Revlon charity ball in L.A., and the two discovered what one
source calls "giant chemistry." Medavoy, who declined to be interviewed for this article, was apparently stunned. "She comes and she
says, 'You know what, I'm not happy, I need to have a simple life,'"
says a source close to Medavoy. "She says, 'I'm trying to find myself.
I had to build this house, it made me crazy, I need to go travel more,
I need to not be in your shadow.' He's going, What? *What?*"

Duff moved into the Hotel Bel-Air and began a period of dramatic agonizing about her future. Perelman pressed her to get an immediate divorce and showered her with money and jewelry and
Picasso etchings. "Medavoy found out about [her relationship with
Perelman] after she left and got furious. And she by then wanted to
get back with him, and she was devastated," says a confidante from
that time. "She said it was the worst mistake she ever made in her

life, and so on, and it all just escalated from there. But that's her drama. At the time, I thought it was all real—the kind of tragedies that just happen to people who are living their lives. Later I came to understand that Patricia creates these things." Finally Perelman, who already had five children from two marriages, discerned the true price of the prize he sought: if Patricia wanted a child, she would have one. In fact, he told her, she could have two. To enhance his bid, he packed her off immediately to a fertility doctor in New York and paid for her treatment. "It was kind of like a takeover," says someone who watched the courtship closely.

Throughout 1994, the pull between these two lives seems to have played serious havoc with Duff's equilibrium. She told her friends that Perelman was explosive and domineering, that she was afraid of him. When Medavoy declined to take her back, according to two sources, she went into their old house and defaced close to a dozen pictures of his girlfriend, Irena Ward, who would later become his third wife—drawing horns on her head and arrows through her breasts and attaching Post-it notes bearing angry commentary. Duff furiously denies this story. "I have never marked up anyone's property, never defaced anyone's property, never harmed anyone's property," she says. "I'd love to have someone get on the stand and say that." "During '94, in the spring, she was in tears all the time over Medavoy," says someone who knows her well. "But she was also trying to get pregnant with Ronald. . . . But at the same time, she was complaining that Ronald was abusive. That he had these guards who watched her house in California and shadowed her, and that it was terrible being watched all the time. But then, by July, she was really happy because she was pregnant. So now *this* would make her happy, and make everything OK."

Papers filed in the Medavoy divorce show that Duff hedged her bets financially for as long as she could. In October 1993—the same month she first filed for divorce from Medavoy—Perelman gave her a cash gift of $200,000. Medavoy, knowing nothing about this, gave her $10,000 the same month. The following February, the producer gave his estranged wife $100,000, followed by $20,000 in April and again in May. In a later deposition, Medavoy's attorney asked her whether she had mentioned her lover's subsidy when she asked her husband for money. "No, I did not," she explained. "I did not want to be put in the position of having to use the $200,000 if I really didn't have to." Even after she embarked on fertility treatments with Perelman, she filed a request for support from Medavoy in Los Angeles Superior Court, asking that the court order him to pay her $37,000 a month—plus tax. She was unable to work, she noted in court filings, because of recurrences of her chronic fatigue. Much later, when both marriages had run their courses, Warren Beatty arranged for Medavoy and Perelman to get together. The two men realized, according to sources close to both of them, that in the raw period between her marriages she had been simultaneously telling each man how badly the other treated her—and how furiously the other was pressing her to commit to him.

"Men are dumb," says Ronald Perelman. "Particularly the one sitting across from you." He is a dense bullet of a man, compactly contained in a tightly fitted shirt. As he talks in his plush paneled office, he constantly mouths a huge cigar or squeezes a cheap, multicolored Koosh ball. He does have, as people say, a forceful presence— though maybe that's just a function of all the stories one has heard: about his ruthless business dealings in the 1980s, when his acquisitions of Revlon, the Marvel Entertainment Group, and other companies made him one of the chief leveraged-buyout brigands of that lawless era. Or maybe it's the way that employees in his hushed, strenuously controlled townhouse headquarters go around referring to him by the godly pronoun. As in: He's back from lunch, or He's ready for you now. Or maybe it's just that he has so much money. Lately the stock of Revlon, his biggest holding, has declined, and Perelman has been trying to sell it. But even in a bad year, *Forbes* recently pegged his fortune at $4.2 billion. And he is not one of those men on whom billions are wasted. Perelman spends freely on a lifestyle that includes travel by helicopter, yacht, and private jet, and houses in Palm Beach, New York City, and East Hampton. His fifty-seven-acre estate there on Georgica Pond, "The Creeks," is the scene of lavish weekend house parties. One visitor remembers an-other guest telling her, in awed tones, that he had called to the front gate to ask if there was some way he could make a quick trip to a lo-cal drugstore. Instantly, someone pulled up to his door to offer him the keys to a gleaming Mercedes convertible with less than a hun-dred miles on it. "You get the impression the place is full of toys like that," she says.

Surely the money is one of the reasons for Perelman's success with women; since his breakup with Duff he has dated TV personality Eleanor Mondale and, more recently, Ellen Barkin, whom he appar-ently intends to marry once she has completed her divorce from ac-tor Gabriel Byrne.* He can be gracious, even charming, when he wants to be. "We never should have gotten here," he says of the cus-tody case he and Duff are waging. "It's not a good thing for anyone involved. Both Patricia and I look lousy." Around the edges, though, you can make out the annoyance of a man who, when he buys a thing, expects it to stay bought. He pronounces his ex-wife's name Pa-tree-sha. When Duff finally married him, a few weeks after Caleigh Sophia's birth in December 1994, Perelman turned out not to be the world's best husband material. (Might the prenuptial agree-ment, which she signed between the birth and the wedding, have served as her first clue? It contained a provision that neither party would "make disparaging remarks about the personal, private or fam-ily life" of the other party, "including without limitation the other's family, companions, dates, acquaintances, or future spouses.") Once they married, Duff has told friends, he demanded to know her whereabouts all the time. A friend describes her cadging cell phones so she could make calls he wouldn't be able to find out about, and others remember her sneaking out a side door of Barneys to run se-cret errands—including legal consultations—while her car and driver idled at another door.

"'Domineering' is too small a word" to describe Perelman as a husband, says someone who had a close-up view of the marriage.

---

*Barkin and Perelman married in 2000 and divorced in 2006.

"He thinks if you're nice 80 percent of the time, and you're only berserk 20 percent of the time, it's OK." This might be dismissed as the hyperbole of someone on Duff's side, but there is other testimony about Perelman's rages. Anne Kiley, who was one of Duff's attorneys in her divorce from Medavoy, recalls two furious phone calls from Perelman—who at that time was fuming over the slowness of his lover's divorce. "I would pick up the phone, and he would be screaming about something going on in that case, and while he was yelling at me he would turn from the phone and scream at her. Like, 'Shut up, you bitch.' . . . During the second call he insulted her and screamed at her so much that the next day I called his attorney and said, 'I don't want your client calling me ever again.'" Perelman adamantly denies screaming at Kiley or at Duff during these conversations. "Ronald is a total, total control freak," says someone who knows him through business. "He's quite nuts, in his own way."

Perelman is famously hypervigilant about protecting his family and his business interests, employing a huge security force that includes retired New York City police officers and a former deputy director of the FBI. He requires strict confidentiality agreements from everyone who works for him. "He lets out his temper in huge, fast, quick spurts," says someone who is fond of him. "He'll do it at the driver—'Do you know how to fuckin' drive a car? Do you fuckin' know where you're going?'" Clearly, his intimates get their share of this wrath. When his son was getting married in 1996, and the bride refused to sign the proposed prenup, Perelman boycotted the wedding.

Naturally, Perelman's advocates also describe the Duff-Perelman marriage as a living hell—for him. Where she saw a husband who shadowed and controlled and bullied his wife, he saw a wife who lied constantly, treated his other children badly, and ran around town peddling slander about him. It isn't at all clear who was controlling whom. Someone who knew the couple well believes that Duff played "a cat-and-mouse game," meeting Perelman's efforts at control with a constant attempt to elude him and keep him off-balance. Which only made him more controlling. In its way, it was a perfect relationship: just as paranoids sometimes have real enemies, each had found a mate who fulfilled his or her darkest expectations about the possibilities of love.

At any rate, the union was brief. "Once you had lunch with her, you always said to yourself, Boy, that is measured in days or weeks, that marriage," says an acquaintance. Perelman dumped Duff in a legendary blowup in Chicago, during the 1996 Democratic convention, because he was furious with her for attending, the night before, a party he had asked her not to go to. In the accounts of her friends, it was the classic tantrum of a totally despotic man who was looking for an excuse to punish his wife. In the accounts of his camp, her offense lay not in going to the party but in lying about it; this one, apparently harmless, transgression was the straw that broke the camel's back. She told friends she was astonished. Despite the wildly stormy nature of their marriage, she thought things were settling down; in fact, she'd been trying to get pregnant again with the promised second child. They attempted, several times, to reconcile, but every try ended in a fight. The marriage had lasted for about twenty months.

Under the terms of their prenuptial agreement, Duff made out pretty well: she received $5 million in cash, two houses in Connecticut now worth about $6 million, and roughly $1.2 million a year in maintenance, which will continue until Caleigh's sixteenth birthday, unless Duff remarries before then. In addition, she had accumulated substantial assets through gifts and investments during the courtship and marriage. It wasn't the $80 million that Claudia Cohen got from him, but that marriage had lasted almost nine years. (His first wife, Faith Golding, had received only $8 million—but that was in 1983, and she had entered the marriage with a huge fortune of her own.) Altogether, according to a 1997 statement she filed with the court, Duff left her marriage with assets of close to $30 million—including about $3 million she had won from Medavoy, jewelry worth $4.5 million, and art and antiques valued at $7.5 million. Last September they were officially divorced, setting aside the unresolved issues of custody, visitation, and child support to be decided later.

The custody case has already dragged on so long, and spun off so many small tornadoes of sublitigation, that it's hard to make the simplest generalizations about who's trying to do what to whom. Perelman wanted the case tried in closed court, as is common in celebrity custody cases in New York. Duff, however, went to the state court of appeals to open the courtroom, arguing that it was the only way to prevent Perelman's money and power from corrupting the process. The forensic psychiatrist in the case and Caleigh's court-appointed guardian filed in vehement opposition, arguing, in the guardian's words, that Caleigh would be "traumatized by the repercussions of [her] renown." The move was also opposed by Cohen, who conducted her own divorce from Perelman in secrecy, and who now fears that the terms of that divorce, and the details of her own nine-year-old daughter's life, will be dragged into the light of day. "None of it," says someone in Perelman's camp, "is worth putting your kid on page one of the *New York Post*." But Duff won on this issue. This is why all of New York now knows that Caleigh Perelman's parents can't agree on what age is appropriate for riding lessons (she says four; he says never); that Duff was supposedly cruel to Caleigh's older half-sister Samantha; that a court psychiatrist tagged Duff as a histrionic, paranoid narcissist and said Perelman should have long-term therapy to control his fits of rage.

Along the way, there have been bitter battles over such issues as schooling and religious holidays. Duff converted to Judaism as a condition of her marriage to Perelman, a devout Jew who keeps kosher even at Le Cirque 2000 and talks to his rabbi daily. In court, Perelman has charged that Duff isn't sufficiently observant—she held an Easter-egg hunt last year, for example—and has won the right to supervise his daughter on most of the Jewish holidays. Security has been another major point of conflict. Although experts for both sides testified that Caleigh was at relatively low risk for kidnapping, Perelman successfully argued for round-the-clock security, and Duff now labors under a strict requirement that employees of a $1,000-a-day security service—hired by her but vetted and paid by him—accompany her and the child everywhere, screen all their visitors and repairmen, and live in their home. She is appealing this ruling, as well as numerous others. In turn, Perelman has sued her more than once for violating the confidentiality provision of the prenuptial agreement, which contained a punitive clause specifying that he can withhold $500,000 in support every time she is in breach. He appears close to winning a fine against her on this front.

Although Perelman is technically the plaintiff in the custody case, it was Duff who first requested full custody—allowing Perelman to argue that he had no choice but to sue for full custody himself, since New York law leans against the imposition of joint custody in any case where the parents have not voluntarily agreed on it. In fact, what he now really wants is an arrangement in which physical custody is shared, but he will control such matters as education, medical care, and religious training; this is what the forensic psychiatrist recommended. "For me, it's about protecting my child," he says. "As the process has shown, Patricia cares about, and thinks about, Patricia."

What Duff would settle for is harder to say. "She wants to demolish him, and she's not going to be able to do that," says one of her legion of former attorneys. Duff maintains that Perelman's chief interest in the child is as a means to punish the mother. Claudia Cohen, she argues, received similar treatment during her divorce from Perelman. "I lived through that litigation with Perelman," Duff said in an affidavit. "I saw the way he treated Cohen during the litigation: often purposely leaving her on hold for many, many minutes when she called to speak to Samantha, even though Samantha was right there and available; forcing her to send Samantha to his home for visitation even though he was out of town and she would be left in the care of others . . . withholding money from Cohen just to pressure her and in numerous other ways torturing her and treating her punitively." In court papers that were leaked to the *Daily News* in 1996, Cohen charged that Perelman tried to "exert control over me and my personal life," threatening to disinherit Samantha if Cohen dated New York Senator Alfonse D'Amato. But these days Cohen is firmly on Perelman's side, and she refused to comment for this article. Both Duff and Perelman have friends who attest to their devotion as parents.

Just to complicate matters, after the custody trial was opened to the public last winter, in the middle of Perelman's presentation of his case, Justice Bransten, who was being transferred to a different division of the court, abruptly halted the proceedings and assigned the question of child support alone to another judge; that proceeding, which began in the winter, was in turn stopped when two of Duff's attorneys were disqualified, on the grounds that they had represented Cohen in her divorce from Perelman. Duff has appealed the disqualification, throwing the child-support hearing into hiatus. And now Justice Bransten has temporarily returned from her new assignment, ready to resume the custody trial later this summer. This stop-and-go process, Duff argues, has effectively silenced her, while the judge makes incremental decisions on things such as holiday visitation without the benefit of any evidence from Duff's side. Or, as she puts it, "I waited Gandhi-like for two years of rulings by the judge, until I could put on my case. And then just before it was supposed to start . . . the judge closes it down." There has been, she charges, "an appalling lack of due process that has been part and parcel of this case from day one."

And then there's the money. Perelman's camp claims that Duff is dragging the case out in order to make, in child support, the spectacular score that the prenuptial agreement prevented her from getting in alimony. "The only way to increase your standard of living, if you're her, is child support," says a Perelman ally. "And there isn't a child in the world you can spend that amount of money on, unless you're planning to hang Matisses on the wall of the nursery." "This isn't about money," Duff says. "I don't want anything for myself." For Perelman's side to portray her as a gold digger is, she says, "a cruel joke." "It's only about the kid, for her," affirms Richard Emery, a friend who has also acted as her attorney. "She has a completely pure-hearted belief that the child's only chance at a life with a semblance of normalcy is to be with her."

Yet Duff's side has argued that it's important for Caleigh to live at least as well as her half-sister Samantha—whose mother has a Park Avenue apartment that was worth almost $8 million in 1994, and an 8.5-acre East Hampton estate that cost more than $4 million a decade ago—and, to the extent possible, to see her mother and father as financial equals. "It's about getting what Claudia got—that's really what she has in mind," says someone who has discussed the issue with Duff. "It's clear [in New York State support guidelines] that there should be no great disparity between the [parents'] homes," Duff says. "There's no way I can ever equalize it. But what I don't want it to be is so different that somehow or another she could be, in effect, seduced away from me. At those times in her life, particularly as she reaches puberty, that she sees the difference. She sees it now! She'll say, 'Mommy, can we get a screening room in Connecticut?' Well, I used to have screening rooms in my old life. But that's not something that's an option now. She's well aware that her father has a yacht. She's well aware that in her other house, with her father, there's huge playrooms." She maintains that Perelman should be responsible for the purchase of a fine New York town house—claiming that the court-imposed security regime means that she needs a bigger house than she can afford herself. "No co-op board will accept them," wrote Duff's legal team in one filing. "Only the most unaffordable town-houses can accommodate their space/security needs." (If necessary, Duff notes, Perelman could purchase the house himself and allow her to live there only until Caleigh reaches eighteen.)

And in a filing last summer, Duff indicated that she and Caleigh might be expected to have monthly expenses—not including the Manhattan housing costs—in the neighborhood of $267,000, including $15,000 for vacations (each month), $20,600 for household help (which would, presumably, cover the chef that her legal team claims is in order for Caleigh's care and feeding), $1,750 in beauty-parlor and salon treatments, $15,000 in clothing for herself, and $3,000 in clothing for Caleigh. Pending resolution of the child-support issue, Duff asked for interim support of $60,000 a month, to include rent. At present, she is receiving $12,000 in interim support, with Perelman also paying all fees for nannies, schools, and camps. Until all this is settled, Duff has cast herself and Caleigh into the limbo of a $30,000-a-month suite at the Waldorf-Astoria—and is trying to move up to a bigger suite at $50,000 a month.

"She *wants* the money," says a woman who knows her. "When the separation first started, I said, 'God, Patricia, why don't you just get a divorce and get a job and get on with your life?' She looked at me as if I was talking a foreign language, and said but then her daughter wouldn't live in the same way as his other children. And I said, 'So what?' Her daughter would still be fine. And she looked as if I was talking a different foreign language. To her, it's inconceivable that her daughter won't be as well off as his other children." In the meantime, Duff has been plowing through the cream of the New York matrimonial bar at the average rate of one law firm every two months since her divorce from Perelman began; Perelman's lawyer says she has used sixteen firms in all. "The Duff case could also be called the Lawyers' Full Employment Act," says Stanford Lotwin, who was fifth in line. Duff insists that some of these lawyers have worked in teams, so the numbers look artificially high. "I don't think all the attorneys I've had have necessarily always been on my side," she adds darkly. "She's sure that they've all been bought off by Ronald," says someone who knows her well. "That they're all giving her bad advice, and fooling her, and withholding information, because Ronald has gotten to them. . . . She wants them on twenty-four-hour call, and then she disagrees with everything they tell her. . . . So she calls friends and asks for recommendations because it's an *emergency*, and no one is *helping* her, and you wouldn't *believe* what's happening to her. And then the cycle starts again, with the next one."

But it isn't true that she has fired them all; at least four of them have fired *her*, and a fifth has petitioned to leave the case. Lotwin was one of those who quit. Although he has seen clients through some tempestuous divorces, including Donald Trump in both his splits and Claudia Cohen in Perelman's previous divorce, he couldn't hack this one. "I simply found that it was causing too much stress on myself and members of my staff," he says. "When someone has gone through many lawyers, they haven't just had a lot of bad lawyers. They're a difficult client." Another of Duff's former attorneys complained of "the second-guessing and the criticism and the hysteria. . . . She's just too suspicious, and too difficult to handle."

Then there's the matter of payment. At least six firms, including her current one, claim to have been stiffed by Duff. In February, her former attorney Herman Tarnow sued her for $70,434.85. The following month William Beslow—who represented her for about three months beginning last November—sued her for unpaid fees of $114,009.50. Last November Norman Sheresky—one of the lawyers who quit the case—took her to arbitration over money she owed him. And now one of her current firms, Cohen, Hennessey & Bienstock, has asked to withdraw from the case unless Duff will agree to a schedule of payments and stick to it. Another lawyer has written off the fees she owes as a lost cause, and still another is in the threatening-letter stage of trying to recover some money. As of late May, two more parties had come after Duff for funds: a court reporter who has not been paid by Duff's side for transcripts of the proceedings, and Jo Ann Douglas, the court-appointed guardian who represents Caleigh, who wants to recover $20,000, Duff's unpaid share of her fee. This last one, despite the relatively small sum involved, is really the most astonishing: it would seem self-defeating in the extreme for Duff to be on the bad side of a woman whose recommendations will carry enormous weight in court.

But in Duff's view all these creditors seem to be part of Perelman's vendetta against her. "All these decisions about what's going to happen to my daughter aren't going to be based on her interest. It's going to be based on whether I can stay focused on the litigation when there's other litigation coming from three or four other parties. And I frankly don't think it's just a coincidence." Duff says this in the same way she says everything about her case—fast, but in a calm, normal voice. Watching her pretty face at a time like this, you have the feeling of momentary dislocation that is described by people who've been through earthquakes, a queasy shifting in your sense of reality.

According to people who have talked with Duff about the case, she believes that Perelman is literally trying to drive her crazy, gaslighting her with an elaborate series of small, malicious acts of vandalism and theft performed by her quickly shifting cast of household help. When anything goes wrong—the mail is late, or a storm seems to damage more of her trees than her neighbor's—she sees his machinations at work. Over the past three years, she has called police in Connecticut and New York City at least seven times to report episodes of mischief for which she believes he's responsible. In June 1997, for example, she called the Fairfield police to report a raft of thefts and vandalism, including tampering with her telephone. "Duff located marks on her office door which is always locked indicating it had been removed from the hinges," wrote the responding officer. "The office had cassette tapes of conversations with her husband Perelman. Duff's voice is still on cassette, Perelman's voice was erased." She phoned the police again five months later with a complete list of the items she said had been stolen from her. It included four Hermès belts, a Hermès crocodile handbag that had been whisked from behind another locked door, "Twenty-four Baccarat highball glasses valued at $3,120," six Hermès scarves, and "three Pratesi sheet sets, value $7,500." When another officer followed up two months later, he wrote, "Duff has no suspects but believes any person employed by Perelman after their separation could have been instructed to remove the items from the house."

In September of last year she summoned the police again at almost 10:00 p.m., reporting the theft since May of so much property that it took the responding officer four pages to enumerate it all: twenty-five shirts valued at $10,000, fifteen Ralph Lauren leather belts, and twenty pairs of black pants, valued at $24,000. A cell phone, a photo album, a rug, a cable remote, film containing pictures of Duff, and Duff's notes documenting all the incidents she was reporting to police. This time, Duff named a specific employee as the culprit. "Miss Duff stated the suspect is removing the items to cause an inconvenience to her, a divorce with her husband is pending and all security personnel are employed by him." Two weeks later, Duff called police again to report that two Plexiglas window guards in Caleigh's room had been tampered with. "Mrs. Duff feels that her ex-husband . . . is somehow responsible." Duff is so persuaded, by now, of Perelman's omnipotence that she often makes phone calls from the homes or offices of friends. She has been known to ask people to use pseudonyms when they call her, and she has put combination locks on the doors of her bedroom and bathroom at the Waldorf-Astoria. At some point, she began recording the regular phone calls she makes to Caleigh when the girl is visiting her father; Perelman got a court order to make her stop.

"This is actually a really easy case," says Perelman's lead lawyer, Adria Hillman. "There have been half a dozen serious settlement negotiations. Every time she gets close, she fires her lawyers or finds some other excuse." To be sure, this is what Perelman's lawyer would say—and pretty much the same thing Duff has said about him. "If I could extricate myself from this," she says, "I would, in a minute." But some of her former attorneys concur that it is Duff, more than Perelman, who has kept the fight alive. "She always found an excuse not to resolve it," agrees one of her former attorneys. "When it comes down to it, she'll find an excuse that's meaningless . . . that's her more than him."

"I think he would like to have settled it," says Lotwin. Had they settled the custody question early, when it was framed more as a matter of working out a visitation schedule, the court's presumption would have been mostly in the mother's favor. "As time has gone by, she loses ground," argues one of her former attorneys. "He didn't want as much decision-making power" in the beginning. But in refusing to settle, she opened the way for the appointment of the forensic psychiatrist, whose conclusions about Duff were devastating. This attorney also believes she has alienated Caleigh's court-appointed guardian. And Justice Bransten may well be tired of hearing herself described as Perelman's pawn. He, meanwhile, has moved to press every advantage. "The terms you could have gotten a year ago, you couldn't get today, in the settlement," says the attorney, adding, of Perelman, "You're talking about Mr. Tough. It's not like a normal person." Could Duff lose custody completely if she and Perelman force the trial all the way to a conclusion? "It could happen," says this attorney. "At the beginning of the case, I would have thought that was impossible. But now it's certainly a possibility."

The custody trial is scheduled to start again in early August. In the meantime, Senator Torricelli continues to play the knight-errant, scaring up lawyers for Duff and sitting in on an occasional conference about strategy. They have been seeing each other seriously since spring of last year, when Democratic fund-raiser Beth Dozoretz brokered a date between them. According to a friend, he's hoping desperately that Duff will see the light and settle the case, or that a judge will do more to force a settlement. But apparently the impulse to ride to Duff's rescue is one that few men can resist. At a birthday party he threw for her this year, Torricelli made a toast that elaborately compared Duff, in the wake of her divorce from Perelman, to the survivors of the *Titanic*: "On April 12th, the *Titanic* entered the Atlantic and Patricia entered the world. And at some point in their voyages, the *Titanic* sank, and its survivors swam to a ship that was simply passing in the night unaware," he told thirty guests at Fresco. He described this toast to me proudly in an interview after the fact. "I was making the point that I was that ship, and the survivor swam aboard," he said. "I was comparing myself with the *Carpathia*." But if the past is any measure, he'd do well to watch for icebergs himself. For it's striking, in the end, how much at home Duff seems in the midst of her distress. She is undoubtedly, sincerely miserable, but she is at home.

More than once during our interviews, Duff burst into precipitous tears. "I just think I'm up against impossible circumstances," she said during one such outburst. "The longer I'm in this, the more I see it. I feel as though I'm completely overwhelmed by forces that are just so far beyond the norm." When the tears clear, she looks as radiant as ever, like a garden refreshed by spring rain.*

—*August 1999*

---

*In the end, the judge did indeed grant custody of Caleigh to Perelman. Duff received extensive visitation rights and not quite $150,000 a year in child support, according to *Forbes*. Torricelli retired from the Senate in 2002 after being admonished by the Senate Ethics Committee for accepting gifts from a campaign contributor. He and Duff had long since split up.

MAN OF A
THOUSAND FACES

(GEORGE H. W. BUSH)

It would take a marriage counselor—someone, at any rate, versed in the realm of the irrational—to understand. In the seventeen months since the end of America's war in Iraq,* public opinion about George H. W. Bush has touched not one but two outer edges of the known galaxy of presidential popularity. First, in March of last year, he scored the highest approval ratings of any president since World War II. Then, in June of this year, he plunged to the lowest level of public esteem ever measured, in the same postwar era, for a president late in his first term. (Worse than Ford, that means. *Worse than Carter.*)

First he was the cool customer who had taken on Saddam Hussein; who had banished the ghost of Vietnam; who had restored America's faith in itself. To read the papers or watch TV, you'd have thought that words like "resolve" and "firm" were actually part of his name. He was unbeatable. Now he is, in the words of *Time* magazine, "the incredible shrinking president." Mired in an endless recession, he is widely said to offer no domestic vision, no articulable

---

*The first one, which began on August 2, 1990, and ended on March 3, 1991, after an international military force led by the United States forced the Iraqi army out of Kuwait.

plan for his second term; he is derided, by the conventional wisdom that emanates from inside the Beltway, as a fearful ditherer who hasn't even been able to assemble a competent political campaign. In the definitive formulation of comedian Arsenio Hall, he has become "George Herbert irregular-heart-beating, read-my-line-lipping, slipping-in-the-polls, do-nothing, deficit-raising, make-less-money-than-Millie-the-White-House-dog-last-year, Quayle-loving, sushi-puking Bush!"

Surely there's something crazy about a political culture that can take such a massive shift of perception in stride. Granted, there are identifiable reasons—notably the recession*—why America has soured on its president. But could anyone conceivably deserve *both* these reputations?

It's not as if either of these extremes was the result of a dramatic new development in the character of George Bush. At least since he was nominated to head the Central Intelligence Agency in 1976—in other words, for as long as it has been important to know who George Bush is and what he's really like—he's been pretty much a known quantity. The positive and negative attributes his friends and critics described back then are more or less the same ones voters cite today. These qualities have made their bows, in regular cycles, in 1980, 1984, and 1988, and his behavior in office, for good and ill, has been clearly related to them. It may be comforting to President Bush, from his vantage point down there in the 35 percent approval range, to recall how often he has been written off in the past, only to have his putative virtues rediscovered. But as a comment on our political maturity, it should give the rest of us pause. On the eve of George Bush's final general election campaign, it is worth taking stock of how often and how radically we have changed our minds

---

*The recession of 1990–1991 had been over for more than a year when Marjorie wrote this, but the National Bureau of Economic Research—the country's official arbiter of business cycles—didn't confirm that until after Bush lost the 1992 election.

about this man, rejecting and then discovering, again and again, the same basic reality that has been there all along.

Of course, Bush has given us lots of help in blurring his basic outlines. This son of Greenwich, Connecticut, started out, after all, in the camouflage of a Goldwater conservative, outfitted to blend into the landscape of his adopted Texas. When he ran for the Senate in 1964, he opposed the nuclear test ban treaty, called Medicare "socialized medicine," and hammered Democrat Ralph Yarborough for favoring the public accommodations section of the 1964 Civil Rights Act—positions that got him nicely through a bruising primary. (By the fall campaign, however, when it was clear that the national ticket was going down to epic defeat, the name Goldwater rarely crossed candidate Bush's patrician lips.)

Two years later, running for the House, he eased to the left; he wooed his district's black vote, and in 1968 he cast a vote in favor of open housing. But as a presidential candidate in later years, he would follow the Southern Strategy that Richard Nixon pioneered in 1968—luring white southerners from the Democratic Party by playing on racial tensions, notably with the specter of Willie Horton.

During his four years in Congress, Bush devoted so much time to family planning policy that House Ways and Means Committee chairman Wilbur Mills gave him the nickname "Rubbers." But when Ronald Reagan invited Bush to be his running mate in 1980, Bush's profile as a Planned Parenthood Republican swiftly changed. He was now flatly opposed to abortion rights and in favor of a constitutional amendment to end them.

"I'm not going to get nickel-and-dimed to death with detail," he said, when reporters challenged him on this and other changes of heart. The man who had coined "voodoo economics" to describe Reagan's economic policies now said, "I'm for Mr. Reagan—blindly." And though he had criticized the massive tax cuts Reagan proposed in the 1980 campaign, he would play exactly the same note in his own 1988 campaign, swearing, "Read my lips: no new taxes." By the time he became president, then, George Bush had a long history of inviting us to redefine him. In a sensible world, this inconsistency would have made it easier, rather than harder, for voters to form a constant view of his nature: one that saw his expediency *itself* as the most consistent theme of his career. Why have we have greeted him, again and again, with fresh surprise?

At first he seemed too good to be true, spanning some of the growing fissures in our politics. In a typical comment during Bush's 1970 Senate race, columnists Rowland Evans and Robert Novak wrote, "Bush—young (46), handsome, a Connecticut Yankee turned Houston oilman—is a glittering exponent of the 'modern' school of southern Republicans as contrasted with the 'primitives.'" He was the future of the Texas Republicans—conservative but not too conservative. This was the phase in which journalists called Bush telegenic, even "articulate." Why, if he won a seat in the Senate, there was no telling what he might do. Perhaps Nixon would replace Agnew with him in 1972. . . .

But he never won the Senate seat. And by the time he had done Nixon's and then Gerald Ford's bidding at the United Nations, at the Republican National Committee, and at the U.S. Mission in China, a more quotidian view of Bush had settled in. He was competent and loyal, as far as that went, but he had been passed over thrice for the vice presidency. He seemed to have more titles than achievements to show. "George Bush . . . may have the abilities necessary to bring off a monumentally difficult assignment," wrote the *New Republic*'s John Osborne of Bush's nomination to be CIA director. "If he does, they have escaped the notice of acquaintances who admire him for his amiability and his competence in handling less demanding tasks."

In the 1980 campaign, Bush was rediscovered. He was a fresh face at the level of presidential politics, and his surprise victory in the Iowa caucuses made him, briefly, a media favorite. He called himself a "moderate conservative," whatever that was—but he did seem reassuringly middle-of-the-road in a race that included Ronald Reagan, Phil Crane, John Connally, and Bob Dole. To eastern establishmentarians, he promised a return to sanity after the wild internecine bloodlettings of recent campaigns—an attitude summed up by Michael Kramer, who gushed in *New York* magazine that Bush was "the almost perfect candidate: scholar, athlete, war hero . . . George Bush may be the one Republican for whom Republicans need make no excuse." Kramer wrote that, "George Bush at his best" was "combative, confident, at ease, with a sure sense of himself and a sense of humor, unashamed of doing what he is doing, and, above all, honest."

As winter gave way to spring, however, the press took the inevitable second look. What once seemed a becoming moderation now seemed a refusal to stand for anything; he appeared to hold himself out as the one man elastic enough to appeal to everyone. "What I'm getting in my polling now is that people think he is a lightweight. They don't know where he stands," said an opponent's pollster. Momentum alone, he appeared to think, would carry him through the election, and when "the Big Mo" turned against him, he began to seem kind of . . . plaintive. He talked more about political tactics than about issues, until finally advisors began muttering to reporters about "putting an issues base under him"—very much the way Bush advisors talk today about surrounding their man with a domestic policy. By campaign's end, Bush's image had returned to the workaday truth observed four years earlier by Osborne. A *Washington Post* editorial summarized Bush as "a center-right, traditionalist, establishment-oriented, competent government figure who showed himself to be resilient but not especially presidential in the campaign he ran in the past couple of years."

In the vice presidency his image worsened, reaching its low point in 1984, during the second Reagan-Bush campaign. In part because he was running against a woman, he seemed unnerved, shrill, "testy." He had, reporters wrote knowingly, "a high-strung side." In the words of another *Washington Post* editorial, "he seems to reveal himself, as all viewers of *Dallas* will long since have noticed, as the Cliff Barnes of American politics—blustering, opportunistic, craven and hopelessly ineffective all at once."

Similar language followed him into his presidential race in 1988. He was seen as pathetically deferential to Ronald Reagan; in the vicious formulation of Garry Trudeau, he had placed his manhood in a blind trust. "Fighting the 'Wimp Factor,'" read the famous *Newsweek* cover that appeared the week Bush officially launched his campaign.

By the time of the Republican convention, Democratic nominee Michael Dukakis was up seventeen points in the polls; all Bush offered, said *Time* magazine, was "a resume without a rationale." Polls showed that more than 40 percent of voters had a negative opinion of Bush.

But over the next four months, America's idea of George Bush turned its most astonishing somersault yet. By January he was a new man. Why, in retrospect, he had been a foreordained winner. On Inauguration Day he was seen to be a man of preternatural grace: sire of five fine children, husband to the Silver Fox;* a cool-headed leader come to restore government by the elite; a born president.

Which brings us to the role of the press. Of course, all new presidents are granted honeymoons. The public is eager for vindication of the vote it has just cast, and the press, eager to curry access in a new administration, is happy to oblige. But there is a longer history to the media's fickle treatment of George Bush. The press has long been the chief vehicle by which America has invented and reinvented Bush—mostly for impersonal, even accidental reasons that are ingrained in the mechanics of political journalism.

The main thing is the need for a story. There's no heat in reporting that George Bush is pretty much the same guy he was the last time the reader or viewer checked in, deploying the same skills, acting out the same limitations. The reporter who can discover a new shade of meaning, a shift, is the reporter who has a story; the bigger the shift, the bigger the story. In addition, the conventions of mainstream journalism make it difficult to take a steady bead on a public figure. It would have been hard, in 1988, to find a dozen journalists in Washington who believed George Bush's pledge that he would not raise taxes—not because they could prove any specific intent

---

*See "The Wife" in *The Woman at the Washington Zoo*.

to deceive on his part, but because they knew the math that would confront him once he actually had to govern, and they knew him as a late, unpersuasive convert to the supply-side religion. But mainstream journalism affects a neutrality that forbids pressing an argument—however commonsensical—that a candidate is lying. Finally, George Bush's gyrating reputation is the fruit of a fairly new fad in political journalism: an increasing tolerance for the whole idea of self-transformation.

Consider just a brief period during the 1988 campaign, in which Bush was credited more than once with reinventing himself. The GOP convention, scripted down to the sentence, was greeted by the press as a transformative event in the life of George Bush. The *Washington Post*, in a front-page story, described Bush as "casting aside his old identity as Reagan's vice president." *Post* columnist David S. Broder wrote, "From the moment he arrived here to claim the nomination, he seemed taller, looser, funnier—and more purposeful." At the center of the drama was what all the pundits agreed was his "crucial" acceptance speech. Never mind that all the credit for the themes and language of the speech went to the speechwriter, Peggy Noonan; Bush's delivery was covered as a magnificent act of political reincarnation. The *New York Times* reported that "after eight often trying years, [he] became what he had always claimed he was: his own man." Added a *Times* editorial, "What was most striking about his speech is how firmly he grasped the wimp epithet and turned it inside out. . . . Intimacy and modesty radiated from the TV screen." This was followed, of course, by a slashing fall campaign distinctly lacking in intimacy and modesty. For a few anxious months the press wrung its hands about Bush's tactics—the Willie Horton ads, the flag factories, the stigmatization of what Bush called the *Aaaay-Ceee-Elll-Yoo*. But immediately after Bush won the presidency, he was once again seen to transform himself. He disowned the divisive symbolism that had driven his campaign, and the press greeted the change not as an act of hypocrisy but as the natural move of a statesman. Under the front-page headline "Bush's Metamorphosis: From Loyal Subordinate to Self-Assured Leader," the *Post* observed that Bush had "recast himself as a statesman far removed from the fray of the campaign that had consumed him only days before. . . . Over the next ten weeks, he sustained and embellished this new George Bush, as he soothed his defeated foes and assembled a Cabinet, all with confidence and a grace that startled many of those who had witnessed his campaign ferocity. . . . Such is the metamorphosis of a public man." Press enthusiasm for such narratives of personal renaissance is a recent fashion in our politics. Back in 1968, when reporters and political opponents spoke of the "new Nixon," it was an insult—meant to condemn what was seen as Nixon's calculated bid for a new image. And can anyone imagine, say, LBJ plausibly undergoing a ten-week metamorphosis? Can anyone imagine him *wanting* to?

But it's the voters, in the end, who consume the poses concocted by politicians and served up by the media; who have given Bush his wild ride from a 90 percent approval rating down to 35. This is where diagnosis might best be made by a good marriage counselor, someone accustomed to understanding extreme feelings as part of a larger system. For it is not happenstance that Bush's new record-low popularity was preceded by a record high; the two extremes are part of a single dynamic. It is the common, unspoken dynamic that underlies so many angry marriages, in which each partner invests in the other the responsibility for whatever it is that pains them. When things are going well, the spouse seems omnipotent, larger than life; but when things are going badly, it is all his fault. How much easier to hold unrealistic expectations of one's mate—and then blame him when he fails to meet them—than to examine those expectations closely and give away our fond illusions. The more blindly faith is invested, the more bitter the ultimate blame.

At the altar George Bush told us, like Reagan before him, that he could give us everything we wanted: that we deserved to pay lower taxes and get a constant flow of goodies from the government. And we have shown, again and again, that we would rather marry that sweet lie than act on a true understanding of our situation. But it's not Bush's fault that we bought the con. It was always a sham, and the deficit—which now suffocates so many possible solutions to the

problems that surround us, from the economy to the inner cities—
the deficit is the enormous result of our illusions.* And now that the
lie is crumbling, there is something dishonest about our insistence
on blaming the liar. In reality, George Bush is the same old husband
today that he was a year ago. He'd rather watch a ball game than
clean out the gutters; and he's fabulous at parties, but he's not much
good with the kids. And while he's done his best to obscure these
basic facts of his nature (it takes two to tango, any marriage counselor will tell you), it's not his fault that we've never taken the responsibility of facing up to where we are, and what we need to do,
and to whether he is the man who can partner us in that.

Over the next three months, you may be sure that the Bush campaign will proffer further astonishing shifts in Bush's character and
fortunes; you can bet, too, that he and his handlers will find a willing audience in at least some segments of the media. The only unknown is what use voters will decide to make of George Bush this
time, which idea of him will prove the most satisfying.

We will either find a way to become infatuated with him again,
or else we will apply the age-old remedy for disillusionment, and
throw the bum out. But in the absence of any effort to understand
the sick dynamic of the attraction in the first place—to acknowledge how thoroughly we have been ruled by the fantasy of rescue—
you know how that story ends. We always marry another one just
like him.

—*August 16, 1992*

---

*Continuing the trend of the Reagan years, the federal budget deficit bal-
looned under president George H. W. Bush to an all-time high of $290 bil-
lion in 1992. Bush broke his "no new taxes" pledge in the fall of 1990 in
order to reverse that, but the deficit numbers didn't start going down until
1993, by which time Bush was out of office. President Clinton eliminated
the deficit entirely by the end of 1998, but the budget surpluses he produced
promptly disappeared under George W. Bush, and by 2004 the younger
Bush had surpassed his father in deficit accumulation (even factoring in
inflation).

POSTSCRIPT (EIGHT YEARS LATER):
DUBYA'S SCOWL

You know a campaign issue has traction when a mainstream magazine can capsulize it in a gimmick like *Fortune*'s new "George W.
Bush Suit-O-Meter," which purports, with a pen-and-ink silhouette
topped by the head of the Texas governor, to measure the Republican front-runner's success in allaying fears that he's turning out to
be an empty suit. It's a crude way of summarizing legitimate questions about whether Bush has the intellect to back up his spectacular political performance so far.

But the suddenly widespread concern about Bush's mastery of
substance leaves untouched a question that may be equally important. Is Bush too peevish to be president? Bush's history suggests that
he has struggled for much of his life with a kind of defensive anger—
an anger more subtle, but perhaps more corrosive, than the temper
tantrums of which his rival John McCain has been accused. Beneath the winning optimism of his politics he sometimes shows,
even today, a curious air of resentment, which is all the more puzzling for its place in a life so touched by advantage.

He shows it in the way he discusses his years at Yale and Harvard
Business School, when he looked around at classmates protesting
war and racism and found cause for indignation only in the fact that
his peers dared to question their lives at the top of the heap. He has
repeatedly fumed, in interviews, about how "arrogant" and "right-
eous" his fellow Yalies were, huffing, "These are the ones who felt so
guilty that they had been given so many blessings in life—that they
felt they should overcompensate by trying to give everyone else in
life the same thing." In his twenties and thirties, he was legendarily
short fused, especially when drinking. At twenty-six he challenged
his father to a fight after the elder Bush reprimanded him for driving
drunk with his fifteen-year-old brother in the car. And as the *Washington Post* reported last year, he once berated and swore at journalist
Al Hunt, in front of Hunt's small children, for the capital sin of pre-
dicting that then–Vice President Bush would lose the 1988 campaign for president.

What accounts for these flashes of petulance in such a lucky man? Most people explain the darker strains in his character by citing his high-pressure patrimony. It could indeed be a grinding burden to have your father presented, all your life, as both a man of unattainable grace and accomplishment and the model you must match in all things. But even more puzzling than where his resentment came from is the question of where (or more accurately, whether) it went. In Bush's account of his life, his rough edges were a function of youth and his fondness for drink; they were sanded smooth, he attests, by his 1986 decision to quit drinking and by his increasing religious devotion. Yet these changes in his life preceded his performances as Sonny Corleone in his father's 1988 and 1992 campaigns.

Today, watching his breezy confidence on the campaign trail, it's often possible to credit what his friends say: that he has disciplined himself, and in making his own mark on the world has grown, or mellowed, out of his sullen streak. But then, suddenly, there it is— the flash of testiness; the grudging, pugilistic response, especially to questions about his intellect. He reads four newspapers a day, he told moderator Brit Hume in answer to a question during a recent debate. And then he couldn't resist adding, with the shadow of a sneer, "I'm not so sure I get a lot of knowledge out of them, but I read them every day."

This surly edge isn't by any means the dominant note in Bush's public persona. But neither is it something his fans can wish away. Especially disturbing was his interview last summer with *Talk* magazine, in which he ridiculed Karla Faye Tucker, a murderer who was executed in Texas in 1998. Writer Tucker Carlson reported that Bush snapped at him for asking about the many pleas for clemency that had flooded into the governor's office and then mimicked the repentant prisoner's own pleas for mercy: "Please," Bush whimpers, his lips pursed in mock desperation, "don't kill me." He actually seemed to bear the dead woman a grudge for the political headaches she had caused him.

Petty angers like this, strangely, may be more worrisome in a candidate than the booming temper of which McCain stands accused. At least those who give voice to their tantrums, LBJ-like, tend to reach tranquility on the other side. But in a president, sins of small-mindedness are rarely small flaws. Our most resentful recent leaders, surely, have been Richard Nixon and Bill Clinton. Clinton's legacy will be forever tarred by the mulish self-pity and blame laying with which he helped to extend and worsen the impeachment drama. Nixon was, and Clinton is, among the smartest presidents we've had—a distinction that did little to spare either from the ruinous weight of the chip on his shoulder.

—*January 2000*

TRISTAN & ISOLDE, LLC
(JAMES CARVILLE AND MARY MATALIN)

James and Mary are a continent apart, talking on the phone. She is at home in Washington; he is in Los Angeles, in the bowels of the Bonaventure hotel, waiting to speak to hundreds of delegates to the California Democratic Convention. The vice president of the United States is onstage at the moment, but James Carville has taken refuge among the grim amenities of the windowless VIP room to avoid the mauling to which he is subject anytime he shows his famous face among the party faithful.

"You're right," he is telling his wife. "We've got to get this thing under control. We *will*."

"This thing" is the monster enterprise their marriage has become. Ever since their introduction to America in the 1992 presidential campaign as the Romeo and Juliet, the Hatfield and McCoy, the Tracy and Hepburn, of American politics—in short, as God's gift to feature writers everywhere—James Carville and Mary Matalin have been the media couple of the moment, their improbable bipartisan romance giving exponential boosts to their separate and joint careers. Carville, the eccentric Clinton campaign strategist, is now raking in money on the lecture circuit while sporadically advising the White House. And Matalin, the pugilistic deputy manager of the Bush campaign, has become celebrated as host of the weirdly appealing CNBC cable show *Equal Time* and as the Republican political pundit on the *Today* show. Together they snagged almost a

119

million dollars for their joint memoir, to be published late this summer, of the 1992 campaign. And along the way they overcame a certain amount of cynicism about their romance—how too impossibly high concept it was—by actually getting married last Thanksgiving.

But success, they have discovered, is time consuming. "They're terrific together," says a friend of the couple's. "But I don't think they have any ongoing life. I don't know when they see each other." In the past nine days, Mary has been to Texas, then New York, then Arizona, and back to New York. James was with her in Texas and Arizona, but then went to Louisiana; in the next few days, he is doing gigs here in California and then in Oklahoma. The day after *he* gets home, *she* has to go away again for three days, taping a special series of shows for *Equal Time*. The day after *she* gets home, they're going to the White House Correspondents' Dinner, an intimate Saturday evening with more than 2,000 of their closest friends. And then the day after *that*, James is leaving town again. On Tuesday they will get together for lunch—along with 200 or so executives of Prudential Asset Management, to whom they will give one of their rollicking, lucrative, self-satirizing joint speeches. And this is typical. It is rare for James to spend an entire week in Washington. Small wonder that Mary has told me, "I've learned more about him reading profiles than talking to him."

On this fine Saturday morning, then—it is clear and cool here in L.A. and also, Mary has glumly told James, back in Washington— James hangs up and sighs. "Mary's got to work on the book all day long," he explains. "And it's a beautiful day in Washington, and she hasn't done any, like, grocery shopping in weeks, and she's just mad 'cause I'm out here." He has mustered a weary patience for his own ordeal today, although nothing is going as planned: "If God had wanted us to be on time," he says philosophically, "He wouldn't have made us Democrats." The workshop he was supposed to give at 10:30 is scrapped, then rescheduled, then gradually creeps later and later as Carville sits and waits in a second, even grimmer holding room. Which leaves him ample time to call Mary again, an hour after their first conversation. He listens for a while, scrunching up that low-set forehead, bobbing in the constant motion that is his hallmark, nodding, murmuring. Then: "You've got to do a show in New York on *Friday, too?*" A pause. "We have lost control," he says.

Later, he will talk at length about how tough this life is. "Our lack of time we get to spend together is getting to be a problem," he will say. He will diagnose the disease, saying, "We're both scheduling sluts. We just get talked into anything. . . . If we don't just get serious about trying to have more time together, like I say, I'm making all this money to pay for a house I never see and a baby I'm never going to have." He will prescribe a solution: "We just need to just say, 'We're going to the mountain house for a week.' [But] the phone rings incessantly. And the fax machine, you have no idea how much noise that makes, as soon as we walk in. . . . Once people know you're out there, that's it—you're toast," he will complain. "But if we don't do something about this schedule, it's going to wear. I don't *like* being away from her." But that is later. For now, he has other calls to make. He dials his mother in Louisiana. "Mama, it's me," he says. And: "Well, I have some good news. Baton Rouge is on the book tour!"

As a couple, Matalin and Carville are powerful reminders of the truth that all of life is basically a magnified version of high school. He is the smart, chronically underachieving, faintly dangerous bad boy. She is the good girl who is also, secretly, the bad girl—the prom queen who yearns not for the football captain but for the leader of the pack. And somehow their coming together, in the moist, overgrown soil of Washington's media culture, gave them the perishable glamour that we remember from adolescence—that air of being stars for just this moment in time.

Matalin is perhaps the only person involved in the 1992 Bush campaign whose star has risen since that election. Familiar to political junkies as one of candidate Clinton's most vitriolic attackers ("We've never said to the press that he's a philandering, pot-smoking draft dodger," she sweetly told the *New York Times*), she has created a new profile since the May 1993 debut of *Equal Time*, becoming what Rush Limbaugh has termed "a hot info-babe." And certainly Carville has a larger-than-life quality: from his Louisiana roots and gumbo-thick accent to his ranting style of political discourse, he is an original. "Carville is a wild man," says Chicago media consultant Marilyn Katz, who got to know him ten years ago in a Senate campaign. "He is probably the most intense human being I have ever encountered in my life." Most people say that his persona includes a large element of public shtick; one of Carville's attractive qualities is that he's perfectly happy to concede this point.

But it was their relationship that pushed Matalin and Carville across the membrane between political recognition and true celebrity. Both of them, media-savvy to their fingertips, have incorporated this knowledge into their acts. Carville often introduces himself in speeches as "Mary Matalin's husband." And the set of Matalin's show resembles a girls' dormitory in its celebration of Carville's stardom: a poster from the Clinton-campaign documentary *The War Room* dominates one wall, while Carville's face, superimposed on the body of a dog, is the logo that closes the show each Friday. "Serpenthead," as Matalin calls Carville, in tribute to his odd face, constantly mentioned on the show, like a talisman of *Equal Times*'s coolness. By making us a part of their marriage, Carville and Matalin create the spurious intimacy with their audience that is the signature of modern celebrity.

While much has been made of their supposed incompatibility, their pairing seems in some ways inevitable. Both have the very specialized intensity of the campaign rat; neither is introspective. Both have the intimate acquaintance with reality that comes from a blue-collar background, and both belong to the more populist elements of their parties. "They both breathe fire," says a friend. "And they both like to live on the edge, and do what they're not supposed to do." And while they have different marital histories—Carville never married before meeting Matalin, while Matalin had two very brief marriages before Carville came into her life—they seem to have lived similar emotional lives, moving through relationships and campaign cycles without much baggage until finding the fateful match.

"I never would have thought . . . that I'd ever see the day when James would settle down with a woman, or maintain anything like a marriage," says Bill Zimmerman, a California media consultant. "It seemed to me he never was willing to take the time to develop that deep a relationship with someone."

"James is like the first man who wasn't fawning over Mary," says Matalin's sister, Renie O'Brien, in recalling her first impressions of Carville. "Mary can be a really strong person. But he'd dish it right back. He was more of an equal than the other men she's been with—which is what Mary has needed all these years."

It was Matalin's strong will that brought the couple together. She saw an article about James in the *Wall Street Journal* in 1990, just before he broke into the big time as a consultant, and asked an acquaintance to introduce them. James was receptive, and they had their first date in early 1991. "Back when I was single," he explains, "I really liked blind dates. I don't want to go pick women up in a bar; I'm too ugly for that." Her first impression of him: "I thought he was really different. And funny, and snappy, and a demagogue. . . . We just started fighting right from the beginning, arguing, debating, and screaming at each other. It was a very exhausting experience just to have a conversation." His first impression of her: "Honestly? She was a lot better lookin' than I thought she would be."

No one who knows them believes that their marriage is *only* a public artifact. But even their friends marvel at how thoroughly Carville and Matalin have capitalized on their romance. "Ugh! Not another one," groaned GOP lobbyist Roger Stone when I called him for this story. Jim Pinkerton, a senior fellow at the Manhattan Institute who worked with Mary on Bush's presidential campaigns, said, "This is the American Dream, circa 1994. If Charles Manson can sell T-shirts, I guess this is nothing." In joint appearances, says a longtime friend of Mary's, "she stands up and ranks on him, and he stands up and ranks on her. It's nauseating. It's showbiz." And their friends tend to discuss even their private moments in tellingly public terms. "They're back and forth at each other when they're together," says presidential pollster Stan Greenberg, fondly. "It's a bit of a TV show, all the time."

In the midst of their fame, there is something inevitably competitive about this marriage. In talking about himself, for example,

Carville acknowledges that his marriage has "added to the persona." He pauses. "Given the show that Mary does, she's at least—she's probably as well known as I am." Another pause. "Just about." On Mary's side, there is still enough hurt left from the 1992 campaign that as of April she had not seen *The War Room*.

Some old friends are disappointed by how obviously Carville and Matalin have taken to the rewards of fame: the dinner parties with Sam Donaldson; the new intimacy with the likes of Bob Woodward and Katharine Graham; the Oscar-week party at Spago in honor of Carville and some political cohorts. "In the past," says Bill Greener, a friend of fourteen years in Republican politics, "Mary would be one of the ones who would poke holes in all that stuff." "I never thought I'd see the day when James would join the Sally Quinn dinner-party circuit," echoes one of James's old friends. Certainly the capital social scene runs counter to the Carville persona, which specializes in smiting the vested interests of Washington. Among the many elites he attacks in his speeches, one of Carville's favorite villains is "the hot-air boys, the pontificators, on the Sunday-morning shows." But of course Carville and Matalin are the media's creatures, as surely as the media are theirs. And after two years of profit from conducting their love affair in such a public way, the couple may be bumping up against a corollary: the price.

I had mixed feelings about getting on a plane with Carville for the five-hour flight from Washington to Los Angeles. One reporter I know, after riding in a van for two hours with Carville during the New York primary—on a day that found Carville in his most full-throated, ranting anger at anyone wearing a press pass—said afterward, "I almost had a nervous breakdown."* Matt Cooper, who

---

*That was me. It was the day Clinton admitted (to CBS's New York TV station) that when he was a student at Oxford he tried marijuana, but "I didn't inhale." Stuck in heavy traffic on the Cross-Bronx Expressway with Carville and a couple of other reporters, there was no escaping his manufactured fury over how we jackals of the press were sure to fixate on this ludicrously hedged revelation.

covers the White House for *U.S. News & World Report*, adds, "When he's in overdrive, he can get that up-in-the-bell-tower-with-a-long gun look." So I am surprised by the friendly, only moderately jumpy guy my companion turns out to be. His calm may have something to do with what appears to be his basic travel strategy: self-anesthesia. Carville begins with the glass of champagne that is offered to first-class passengers on takeoff; moves on to two Chivas and sodas on the rocks (actually, the first one is—to Carville's disgust—a Chivas and Sprite, proffered by a flight attendant who couldn't quite make out his order through his thick Cajun accent, but he drinks it anyway); then accepts a shot of chilled vodka from the cart that passes the pre-dinner caviar; and, over the course of the flight, downs seven glasses of red wine. Drinking is a subject that comes up a lot in conversation with Carville and Matalin—especially wine. "Our biggest weakness is good wines," Carville explains at 39,000 feet. "Northern Rhones—the Côte-Rôtie wines. We both like these real big, fleshy wines." But even the laid-back Carville is a fairly antic fellow. About halfway through the flight, well into our interview, an attendant approaches. "I don't mean to be rude," she says, "but a passenger on the other side has asked if I could ask you to keep your voices down. Apparently he can't hear the movie."

Carville's oddities are, of course, legend—which is just the way he likes it. There are the legends of James not changing his under-wear during the last week of a campaign, swallowing a half-bottle of Maalox every day, wearing gloves indoors on election day on the chance that it might enhance his karma. And then there are the legends of James and Women. For years and years, notes one old po-litical friend dryly, James's girlfriends "trended younger." The friend says, "For many, many women that he dated that I know, he was like a father-figure type. Why else would twenty-two-year-old women date a forty-five-year-old guy who looked like an eel?" Finally, there is his legendary twitchiness. "James does have the concentration span of a hummingbird," says Matalin. Writing a book—even one for which someone else was hired to do the actual writing—was, therefore, a trial. "I could do it about a half hour," Carville says of his conversations with the ghostwriter, "and then I'd have to get up and open a bottle of champagne and shoot my rifle off the front porch of the house." It's all part of the eccentricity that makes Carville the only pol in America who flaunts the fact that he often cries in public. "James is one of the most bizarre combinations of immaturity and maturity you'll ever meet in you life," says a campaign colleague. "He has this life experience that makes him very much tuned in to what people think. And then he acts like a child: he has to be the center of attention, he has to get his way in most cases, or he'll pout."

The day after our flight, I have a chance to witness his famous impatience. After a long day at the California Democrats' convention, where James has given his all in the way of stem-winding speechmaking, he is taken down to the hotel's lower level for one more thing: a series of handshakes and photographs with big party donors. In a small lounge area, a few members of the State Senate step to a microphone to make brief remarks. But one of them is not so brief: Bill Lockyer, the president pro tem of the State Senate, goes on for five minutes, ten minutes . . . .

James passes me a note. "HOW DULL? 1–10," it asks. He has come all the way across the country to help out at this convention. And he has put up with a lot, in a fairly gracious way. But he can't stomach even a few more minutes of this boredom. He pens another note, soberly counting out letters to pose this query: "IS THIS M- - - - - - - - -R GOING TO SHUT UP?"

Carville and his partner, Paul Begala, are working on two statewide races this year, both for prior clients: Pennsylvania Senator Harris Wofford's reelection effort and that of Georgia Governor Zell Miller. From each client, they get a retainer of roughly $25,000 to $30,000 a month. In addition, they have a $300,000-a-year contract with the Democratic National Committee, primarily to offer political advice to the White House. But Carville spends the vast majority of his time giving speeches: some unpaid ones, such as his weekend with the California Democrats, and many paid ones, to Seagram and Citicorp, the National Association of Home Builders, and the American Hospital Association. For these, he is reported to get from $15,000 to $20,000 a pop. Ironically, because his talk schedule is skewed toward the business-oriented groups that can afford his fees, he spends most of his time talking to Republicans. "He's really straightforward about it," says an old friend. "He's said he's going to get out there and give as many speeches as he can, and get as rich as he can. Because he struck gold, and you only strike gold once."

"He certainly is getting rich," says Begala. "But there's rich and there's rich. All he had to do was turn this into a lobbying firm if he wanted to get really rich. . . . We make a lot of money, but we've turned down millions and millions and millions and millions and millions of dollars' worth of work in corporate PR work and lobbying."

For a populist, Carville has expensive tastes. "My populism don't extend to my choice of hotels," he is fond of saying. He loves the Crillon in Paris ("towels *this* thick everywhere you look"); he loves room service, and great food, and even—his signature blue jeans notwithstanding—good clothes. At the end of the 1992 campaign, Matalin and Carville bought and renovated a house in the Blue Ridge Mountains near Front Royal, Virginia. It has a treadmill and a StairMaster, a satellite dish and a steam room. He can't be accused of hypocrisy, though. For one thing, he holds the deeply American view that there's nothing wrong with money; it's social class that's insidious. For another thing, he did his time as an underdog. "You can't begrudge him a thing," says presidential advisor George Stephanopoulos, "because he worked for twenty years for this, and did it all himself."

"In that business, you're either a hero or a schmuck," notes Marilyn Katz succinctly. "James was a schmuck for a long time." After a college career at Louisiana State University that took seven years, interrupted by a stint in the Marines and a year teaching grade-school science, Carville went to LSU law school and launched a desultory career as a Baton Rouge attorney. It wasn't until he was in his midthirties that he decided to try politics, joining a local consulting firm. And it wasn't until 1982 that he was hired to run a statewide campaign. He lost that effort, Dick Davis's bid for a Virginia Senate seat, and in 1984 he lost heavily with Texan Lloyd Doggett's campaign for the U.S. Senate. "Doggett was the biggest, worst defeat a Democrat had ever suffered in Texas," says Begala. "It was the worst ass whipping you could get." Carville's career was in such poor shape that he was still filing a 1040-EZ tax form. "It is a searing thing, to be forty and broke," he says. "Someone did a piece and suggested I embellish that to build up the James Carville persona. Not true. I was on the goddamned edge of being a colossal failure. The difference between being the guy who has run the most losing campaigns ever and being probably the most famous political consultant ever is *that* far." He holds up a thumb and finger less than a centimeter apart. "*That* much. It's 70,000 votes somewhere in Pennsylvania."

Those 70,000 votes came in the 1986 victory of Pennsylvania governor Robert Casey. Casey, then known as "the three-time loss from Holy Cross," was making his fourth run for the governorship; few strategists were interested in taking the campaign's helm. "James and Casey each got basically the only person who would have him," says Begala. When Casey beat William Scranton III, Begala continues, "it was *everything*." From that race, Carville went on to a winning streak, culminating in Harris Wofford's victorious 1991 Senate campaign against former attorney general Dick Thornburgh. Because Thornburgh was closely associated with the Bush administration, his defeat—largely over the issue of health care—was seen as an important harbinger for the 1992 presidential campaign. Suddenly, Carville and Begala were the hot consultants to have, sought by Clinton and two other contenders for the Democratic nomination.

Carville believes that he was able to persist, through all those years of failure, because of his upbringing. Born Chester James Carville Jr., he is the oldest of eight children raised twenty miles from Baton Rouge in Carville, Louisiana, where his father and grandfather were postmasters, and his father ran a general store. "My mother always made me the center of attention," says Carville. "There is some bond between a mother and her oldest male child.

She just always instilled so much confidence in me. . . . Everything we had, we were taught that we had *the best*. Our folks said, 'We are *so* lucky; God has been *so* good to us.' I thought I had the most charmed life that a kid could have." His father was an important influence in a different way. "My daddy was a very kind, almost conflict-averse person," he says. "My mother was more aggressive than my father. She drove faster, for instance. My sense of him was he was very sort of *pleased* with his station in life." Carville's tone indicates this is not a good thing to be. "He was not aggressive. I think that's what made me aggressive in campaigns." His roots in Louisiana contribute to Carville's gut empathy with middle-class voters. Beyond this instinct, people say over and over, his political talent is twofold: a gift for leadership and a capacity to focus. On the first count, says Stephanopoulos, "all those kids in the campaign loved him. . . . It was amazing, because he would just *sit* there. But somehow he motivated them."

As for focus, his most famous contribution to any campaign is, of course, the Clinton mantra, posted on the wall of the War Room: "[It's] the economy, stupid." Says a Democratic consultant who has worked with him, "He is not, in most campaigns, the person who finds the focus, or finds the message. It is that he demands that there be one. His big contribution to Clinton was not that he figured out the economy was the way you should run against Bush; anyone could have done that. It was that he demanded they stay focused on that." One of his chief tools is a sort of strategic rage. *Washington Post* reporter Martha Sherrill learned this when she was briefly in negotiations with Carville and Matalin to ghostwrite their book. (In the end, they hired Peter Knobler, who had rendered similar services for Texas governor Ann Richards and for Kareem Abdul-Jabbar.) Matalin, Sherrill relates, took her to the "Bat Cave," the basement apartment where Carville used to live. "We all sat down and started yelling. We fought for three solid hours," Sherrill recalls. "That was how they sniffed me out. James, especially. Within thirty seconds of coming in, I was sucked into this screaming match. It went:

"'Fuck you!'

"'Fuck you!'

"'Well, fuck you!'

"'Well, fuck you!'

"And Mary would say, 'James, fuck you—leave her alone.'"

Carville has a disconcerting way of stepping in and out of this anger, as if it were a costume. "A lot of things, half of it is me doing a shtick, defending the president. And half of it is really at the heart of me," he says. "So a question I really love is when someone stands up and says, '*Jim?*'" He inflects the speaker's familiar use of a nickname—one Carville himself eschews—with a wonderful tone of snottiness. "'Jim? The president, with his tax increases, is taxing the most productive people in the country.' I just love that question. I say, '*Let me tell you something:* My *daddy* worked thirty *years* at the post office, and my *mama* sold *encyclopedias* door-to-door. And today I can walk into the White House. But *never* think that I think for a *day* that I'm more productive than she is.'" The rhythm of his voice has changed; its pitch is higher. Passion and anger infuse every word. Until suddenly he pauses, comes back to earth. "But I can do it a lot better than I just did it," he says. "If I'm giving a talk at 12:30 tomorrow, at 12:29 I'll get pissed off again. . . . I always get afraid it won't be there anymore. But I get up, and there it is."

In daily life, it helps a lot to have a normal alter ego. While it is Carville's partnership with Matalin that has drawn all the limelight, it is his partnership with Begala that has been crucial to his success. Says Stephanopoulos, "Paul tethers James. Much more than me, Paul has the same feel James has. But he's not crazy like James."

"Look, in their relationship, Paul does the work, not James," says a White House official. "On the other hand, this is what you pay James for: you pay James to work a twenty-hour week, or a forty-hour week, or whatever, and you pay him for the two hours in which he has brilliant ideas. And the other eighteen hours, he lies around on a couch and scratches his testicles."

Curiously, Carville now talks down his skills as a strategist. "There was a time in my life when I could say, if I were running for office, I would hire me to manage the campaign. That time is probably not right now. . . . I'm clearly not the best political consultant in the country right now." At first this seems a shockingly uncharacter-istic bit of modesty. But, of course, he's playing the expectations game—just as he would do for a candidate before a big debate. Carville has already lost an important race since Clinton's election, New Jersey governor Jim Florio's reelection bid. And he is now em-broiled in two tough races—Wofford's and Miller's—for which he will get not much credit if he wins and lots of blame if he loses.*

Carville clearly thinks a great deal about how easily success can turn into failure. He is quite certain, he says, that had he succeeded any sooner he would have destroyed himself. "I'm consumed by the idea that I might pull the trigger on myself, get consumed by this." He gives Matalin a lot of credit for grounding him. But in the next breath, he seems a little baffled that just as he became a pop-culture star he also settled down. "At the same time as I become a caricature, a persona, I acquire a house, a wife, a car," he muses. "I am monoga-mous, when I could be fucking starlets. . . . I always wanted to get into the candy store. When I would run, I would dream of being this big, important, famous guy. And finally someone lets me into the candy store, and I order a plate of meat loaf and mashed potatoes."

Some of Mary's friends believe that part of James's appeal to her is a resemblance to Lee Atwater,** who was her boss and mentor at the Republican National Committee until his death from a brain tumor the same year she began dating Carville. "She'd say, 'He re-minds me of Lee so much,' over and over again," says a longtime as-sociate. One can see some similarities: the radical intensity; the passionate, almost unbalanced dedication to politics; the boyish self-absorption. But it's a parallel that Matalin rejects, saying, "It ir-ritates me. It totally irritates me. It's such a obvious, clichéd, super-ficial thing to think. Implicit in it is that I was similarly attracted to them, and there's a psycho-weirdness in that that I object to."

---

*Miller won; Wofford lost.

**See "The Story of a Bad Boy," page 205.

My interview with Mary takes place over the phone; it's all she has time for. When I begin by reminding her that I spent the previous weekend in California with her husband, she wisecracks, "Oh. How is he?" They haven't spent a weekend together, she says, in six or eight weeks.

Matalin's new career as a talk-show star is a more accidental development than Carville's long climb to the top. She had done her own long march in Republican politics. But her strongest attachment was always to the fortunes of George H. W. Bush. And in the wake of Bush's 1992 loss, "I was very, very depressed," she says. Martha Sherrill says of the time when Carville and Matalin were planning their book, "He was the king of the mountain, running around doing speaking engagements—everything. And Mary was dragging around. . . . She was really *lost*, really down. She had *nothing*—no gig at all. They weren't engaged yet. They were [renovating] their house in Front Royal, and Mary was doing it all, choosing everything, making all the decisions. She started to sound like one of those housewives who can't get their husbands involved." But then CNBC approached her with a weird little format for a new talk show. And like her husband, Mary found a way of taking her own basic personality and simply projecting it onto a vastly larger screen. That persona is the one that used to appear at morning campaign meetings—in the presence of men like James A. Baker III and Bush pal Robert Mosbacher—in pink foam curlers and work her way through the strategy chat with her eyelash curler poised for action; the same Midwestern woman who uses terms like "goofy," "loopy," and "hissy fit."

On *Equal Time*, she has the wisecracking, worldly air of a gun moll, almost too weary to move her jaw when she speaks. She has a real but imperfect beauty that makes her seem sisterly; she's still evolving, before her viewers' eyes, from a shaggy haircut and gem-studded cowgirl shirts to a smooth, businesslike bob and a power-anchor wardrobe. Her voice is pitched low, with flat Chicago vowels and an ever-present suggestion of sarcasm; her delivery is a combination of tough-gal political commentary and ditsy stream of consciousness. Political opponents are "Darth Vaders," while male guests bring on a "Cute-Guy Alert." *Equal Time* has been aptly described as *Wayne's World* for girls. During the commercial break of one show last spring, when Jane Wallace was still her cohost, Matalin engaged in girl talk with guest Lani Guinier, Clinton's spurned nominee to head the Justice Department's Civil Rights Division. "You're so pretty, and so composed, and you have such cool clothes," said Mary to Lani. "I always thought they should just hire you to be a television personality." Afterward, marveling over Guinier's lack of bitterness at Bill and Hillary Clinton's treatment of her, Matalin remarked to Wallace, "Isn't she an inspiration? We get our periods and we're a wreck."

Since Wallace left the show in early April—reportedly over CNBC's refusal to raise her salary—the cable company has been puzzling over how to replace her, filling in with a series of guest hosts. "I'm not sure it can be replicated," Mary says of their partnership. The team had a successful chemistry—perhaps because of one's distinct impression that Matalin and Wallace didn't much like each other. It gave the show a faint edge of danger.*

There is something beguiling about *Equal Time*'s insistence on bringing a feminine sensibility to bear on the heavily masculine arena of public policy. But its version of femininity is determinedly superficial. Of Guinier's book, Matalin said on the air, "It's very scholarly and academic, and I don't pretend to be able to understand it."

Because she is so flippant, it's hard to know how smart Mary Matalin really is. On the one hand, she's quick witted, talking fast and with conviction, rat-a-tat-tat, about political subjects. But her combative tactics in the Bush campaign sometimes seemed flat-footed. The Clinton campaign was able to milk several news cycles of anti-Bush coverage out of a Matalin "attack fax" that was headlined

---

*Wallace was eventually replaced by former Clinton press spokeswoman Dee Dee Myers. Matalin herself would be replaced by Bay Buchanan in 1996.

"Sniveling Hypocritical Democrats: Stand Up and Be Counted." And on the show, when discussing serious issues—especially foreign policy—she speaks with a tense, frowning concentration, as if afraid that she might at any moment mispronounce "Gorazde."* One understands that fearful look a little better when Matalin's little sister, Renie O'Brien, confides that "we had this thing growing up, that Mary was the pretty one and I was the smart one. Although she was very intelligent—it was just how it went in the family."

She was raised on the far south side of Chicago, the daughter of a steelworker and a beautician. Her father, the son of Croat immigrants, worked a night shift at U.S. Steel and studied for an engineering degree during the day, making his way up the ladder from machinist to superintendent; her mother, who stayed home when Mary was a baby, later taught at the local Don Roberts Beauty Schools, eventually buying into the franchise. Taking her turn behind the counter at the school, Mary learned before she was an adolescent what it meant to work. "I'm the product of ethnic Americans," Mary says. "And to the extent that they came here with nothing and made a life, I was raised with a real lot of indoctrination: individual initiative, hustle, self-improvement." When she was growing up, almost all the kids in the neighborhood were boys, so Mary was a tomboy. At T. F. North High School in Calumet City, she was both the pretty, "good" girl—homecoming queen and pompom girl—and also the family rebel who dated boys in black leather. She was distinctly a girl of her generation: one who learned early the double-edged art of attracting, while also emulating, the boys.

She went to college at Western Illinois University, but, like her future husband, took about seven years to finish, dropping in and out of school and hopping from major to major. As stopgaps, she worked a series of jobs—in her mother's schools, at U.S. Steel, and in a store that sold day-old baked goods. She also married a fellow student; they divorced about a year later. "She was still bouncing

---

*A city in eastern Bosnia that was besieged by Serbs during the Bosnian war (1992–1995).

around coming up on thirty," recalls Renie. "My parents wrung their hands a lot." When Mary finally hit on politics, as a paid staffer in the 1980 Illinois Senate campaign of one David O'Neal, she knew right away she had found a home. "Instantly. *Instantly.* Because I really had worked since I was eleven years old," she says. "I had so many points of reference to know what working was and how boring it could be. . . . So to me, that first day, opening mail, was the most exciting thing."

From that campaign she was referred to the Republican National Committee in Washington, and started out as a foot soldier in the political-education office. There she was spotted by Rich Bond, a Bush advisor who in 1982 went to the RNC as deputy chairman and hired Mary as his executive assistant. For the next seven years Bond was her chief mentor as she moved through a series of positions that gave her a full education in the mechanics of national politics. By 1988 she was Midwest field director of Bush's primary campaign. And after Bush's election, campaign strategist Atwater tapped Matalin to be his chief of staff—a role that made her de facto party leader when Atwater fell ill. From there, it was a natural step to a prominent job in Bush's reelection effort, and she was named deputy manager of his campaign. Hers has been a professional, brass-tacks field career: not quite the dashing, high-risk life of the consultant, but a series of jobs that placed Matalin in rooms traditionally few women have entered.

In 1983 she married a fellow RNC staffer, Art Arnold. In a brief bid for more respectable credentials, she left the RNC to go to law school at Hofstra, but hated it, and fled both marriage and law school to return to politics. "I got married in college, which didn't last," Mary says dismissively. "And I got married in law school, which didn't last. So it was some scholastic distraction thing. . . . I've just never felt like I've been married; I now feel like I'm married."

Introspection is not a useful companion in a life or a career such as Matalin's. Witness the way she discusses a horrible experience of her midtwenties, when she was a trainee at U.S. Steel. On her way to the company's Gary, Indiana, plant one day, she got lost and was pulled from her car by a group of young men. "And they had knives, and they cut me up, and cut my clothes up, and beat me up. Lord knows where they were going next—well, I know where they were going next—but some decrepit old guy just came up and started yelling at them to stop." Mary's sister first told me this story, solemnly, and with the proviso that I could write about it only with Mary's permission. "It really messed her up for a while," said Renie. But when I asked Mary about it, she dismissed its impact. "It hasn't affected my life in any way, other than I changed jobs," she said. "I think it bothered my family that I didn't want to dwell on it, I didn't want to go get counseling; I'm surprised my sister even mentioned it. They kind of followed my lead, and we never talk about it. It's not like I haven't dealt with it; there's nothing to deal with."

Matalin may have a big future. Friends hazard guesses that she will go on to a career in television production or corporate-board work. Carville thinks she could have a career in radio.* What she might not have is a big future in the kind of hands-on politics she loves. For it's hard to imagine Carville and Matalin sustaining the balancing act they pulled off in the 1992 presidential campaign. To the extent that either of them suffered for it, it was probably Mary more than James. For one thing, she was a less senior member of the Bush campaign than Carville was of the Clinton circle. For another, her party is the underdog in national politics for the time being, and losers aren't as forgiving as winners. And for a third, a woman probably faces more sexist assumptions about pillow talk than does a man.** Mary's friends say no one within the Bush campaign ever seriously

---

*Matalin subsequently hosted *The Mary Matalin Show* on CBS radio from 1996 to 1998. Later she was hired by the book publisher Simon & Schuster to run Threshold, a conservative imprint.

**Matalin was forced to give up a senior role in Bob Dole's unsuccessful 1996 Republican challenge to Clinton because some Republican leaders were discomforted by her marriage to Carville. In 2001, though, Matalin became counselor to vice president Dick Cheney. She left the White House in 2003 but remained an informal advisor.

questioned her motives. But some of the more conservative state party chairmen, for example—true believers who were already inclined to see the Bush administration as a captive of moderate, big-government thinking—were revolted by her romance, according to a party activist in D.C. "Here it was hip and interesting," he says. "Out there it was a sign of everything wrong in Washington." Even this past April, Matalin says, when she sat in as guest host on Rush Limbaugh's radio show, she got faxes from angry conservatives assailing her marriage.

The balancing act may have fallen apart last fall, when Republican strategist Ed Rollins boasted to reporters that the campaign of New Jersey gubernatorial candidate Christine Todd Whitman, his client, had bought off some of the state's black vote—and then promptly recanted the boast. Because Whitman's win had meant a high-profile loss for Carville's candidate, eyebrows were raised when Matalin—an old friend of Rollins's—told the press that he had made the same boast in conversation with her. Events got still more tangled by the fact that Rollins hired as his lawyer Michael Carvin, the man with whom Matalin had lived before she started dating Carville. (Not to mention that after NBC dumped Rollins as the *Today* show's Republican political pundit during the fracas, Matalin was the person hired to replace him.) By now, Matalin and Rollins have made up, and both say they want to let bygones be bygones. But the whole affair may have increased the common impression among Republicans that Matalin's relationship with Carville makes her a potentially dangerous colleague.

It may turn out to be a real problem for Matalin, who still loves politics with a rare fervor: "Never in my wildest dreams did I ever think I would be doing what I'm doing now," she says. "And I still don't think I'm doing it. Someone wakes me up in the middle of the night, I don't think, Hey, I'm on TV. I think, I'm a politician. . . . The minute any conversation turns to politics—flat-out politics—I just get a feeling like I don't have about anything else."

This is the passion that lies at the heart of her marriage to Carville. Which leads, finally, to the $64,000 question: How do two partisans, joined by their love of politics but divided by their actual politics, get along? One possibility is that their politics aren't actually that far apart. Carville's beliefs, for all his fire-breathing populist rhetoric, bow to the basic conservatism of the middle class on social issues. And Matalin, for all her new visibility as a GOP poster girl, is actually a moderate Republican whose chief ideology has been her great personal loyalty to George Bush. To the extent Carville and Matalin have serious disagreements, they say, they tend to be about economic policy. "If we start talking about Reaganomics, that'll get to blowup," says Carville. "I basically think those people ran off and looted the country. *That'll* get us going. So we just stay away from it." Matalin agrees they do best when they avoid certain topics. "You know when we had our least screamy conversations? Was during the campaign. Because we couldn't talk about what we were doing. . . . You do this in all marriages, stay away from the topics that make the other guy's hair catch on fire."

But this agreement tends to obscure the fact that the conflict these two people played out so publicly, all through 1992, was a real one, and one that actually mattered to a great many people. The mystery at the heart of this marriage is perhaps best expressed by Bill Zimmerman, the Democratic media consultant who has known Carville for about a decade. "If your politics are part of the core of your life, and part of the values that guide your life, it's very hard to put them aside in the formation of friendship. And I don't see how a friendship could be profound enough to be the basis of a marriage if that friendship contains such a big contradiction to the core of your values."

There are two possible answers to this mystery. The obvious one is that people like Matalin and Carville—even when they believe in their candidates—are always more interested in process than in ideals. They are the technicians of politics, drawn less by the chance to change the world than by the adrenaline high, the instant "family" of co-workers, the escape from the ordinary that is the inside of a political campaign. The other answer—a supplement to the first— is surprisingly simple: it seems likely that sheer *motion* mutes the potential conflicts between Carville and Matalin. Again and again, in describing their marriage, Mary notes passages in which some possible bone of contention was resolved or, more often, avoided by their lack of time to talk about it. She first learned he was going to work for Clinton from a reporter, during dinner at a restaurant. Hearing it this way was, she says, "kind of cheesy. But looking back on it, he hadn't been home [from the Wofford race] for very long, and I was in a transition, and there wasn't, like, time to talk about it. I picked him up the night he came in and took him to *Nightline*, and every day was something like that. It was a whirlwind."

It's an easy out for a pair of campaign rats who have always been drawn by the intensity of the game, by the need for total focus on externals. But it's not a great recipe for intimacy. To the same extent their attraction was based on a shared culture of action and extroversion, it's hard to see who brings the glue to this marriage. I ask James and Mary, separately, if they're considering starting a family. Carville says, "That's a good question. We talk about it a lot. I'll be fifty in October. And Mary's forty. I worry about how long I'll be healthy."*

"Sometimes yes, sometimes no," says Matalin. "That goes back to the question, Are you ever going to have a normal life? I wouldn't want to try to squeeze a family into the life we have now. . . . I have no resistance to changing our lives, but I don't really see a way to do it right now." In a sense, though, Carville and Matalin already have a baby, or at least a voracious, all-demanding equivalent to which they have surrendered every bit as much control as an infant demands. Their image is their baby, and they feed it morning, noon, and night.

At the Tuesday luncheon of Prudential Asset Management, a predominantly male crowd assembled in a banquet room of Washington's Capital Hilton, Mary speaks first, opening her act with a

---

*A year after this was written, Carville and Matalin had a daughter, Matalin "Matty" Carville. A second daughter, Emerson "Emma" Carville, was born in 1998.

string of James Carville jokes. In the course of her speech, she refers to him as "serpenthead," "the demagogue," and, in reference to his baldness, "my folically challenged darling." Hearing this, one can't help wondering if a toll is exacted by this constant self-satire before strangers. They are even willing to do for money what they forbear doing to each other in private: fight about politics. John Shakow, a former assistant of Carville's, says, "They won't be baited into it" in their personal life, but "sometimes they'll do it for pay. . . . But it always really costs them. It rarely becomes acidic. But when it does, both of them pay for it."

I ask Carville if his marriage, like his own persona, doesn't have an element of shtick. He bridles: "If we're in public, we're onstage. But in private, it's like *boom*—it's *gone*," he says. "In every sense imaginable, our marriage is very, very real." But can anything as intimate as marriage be so insistently used without wearing out? There is only one way to understand their willingness to spend so lightly something so hard won. An old friend of Mary's says, "She's complicated, because anyone who comes out of the blue-collar roots she does and runs in the environment they run in today has to question themselves: 'How am I here? Why am I here? Do I deserve to be here?' If you were a hairdresser sixteen years ago, and now you run with presidents—there's plenty of insecurity there." And Paul Begala says of Carville, "You gotta understand what he comes from— and in his mind how close he is to going back to those days, when he couldn't get a job, he didn't have any money, and he had to borrow against his life insurance. I think he carries that with him."

It is Friday night, the week after James's trip to California. Now Mary is back from New York, and James is back from Oklahoma, and he has come to see her tape an *Equal Time* interview with radio personality Don Imus, which will run Monday, and at last they have some time together. At the show's close, Mary opens a bottle of wine; then she and James head off to the restaurant where they eat almost every night after her show if James is in town. An alley's walk away from the studio on 20th Street, the Palm is a high-end steak joint where caricatures of Washington personalities cover the walls.

With them tonight are Ann Klenk, the producer of the show; Imus and his fiancée, Deirdre Coleman; Martha Sherrill, who is working on a profile of Imus; Tony Kornheiser, the *Washington Post's* sports and humor columnist, who was Matalin's guest cohost for the Imus interview; two executives of WTEM, the Washington radio station that airs Imus's show, one accompanied by his wife; Anna Perez, the former spokeswoman for Barbara Bush, who now works for Creative Artists Agency, who is friendly with Matalin and with Sherrill, and who happened to have no plans for tonight; and me. Just a romantic dinner for twelve at the Palm.

Mary is sitting on James's left as four simultaneous conversations start and grow and atomize and restart. Several $40 bottles of wine make their way around the table. She looks about and puts her strong, well-manicured hands flat on the table. "This is my life," she says, to no one in particular.

—July 1994

MOTHER'S MILK

(TERRY MCAULIFFE)

"You probably know," says Terry McAuliffe, thumping the arms of his chair at the Oval Room, a restaurant two blocks north of the White House, "I come here a lot. This used to be George's table." He's sitting in the see-and-be-seen chair, the one everyone has to pass on the way into the main dining room. He doesn't have to spell out that he's referring to George Stephanopoulos, former media favorite and advisor to President Clinton, who became a White House pariah last year after publishing a political memoir. "Yeah," he says, in case you missed the point. "Old George is kind of out of favor now, and I'm in." So this is the first clue to how a man becomes what vice president Al Gore has called "the greatest fundraiser in the history of the universe." It's not about subtlety.

"I'm one of the few fighters in the party," McAuliffe likes to say. "I think that's one of the reasons the president loves me. I'm the only one around with any you-know-what." He can afford to crow. After two decades at the slippery peak of a pursuit most men tire of after two or three election cycles, McAuliffe is the acknowledged master at separating political donors from their money. He is, at forty-two, a self-made multimillionaire, with a fortune that may reach into nine digits. And, icing on the cake, he has achieved the official role of First Friend to the president, a status sealed during the fall when he posted collateral of $1.35 million in cash to help the Clintons buy their new house in Chappaqua, New York.

The Clintons' reliance on a private benefactor, especially one as controversial as McAuliffe, raised so many questions that they went on to arrange a different form of financing, without McAuliffe's help. But the home-financing deal was, in the scheme of things, a drop in the bucket of Bill Clinton's debt to McAuliffe, the culmination of one of those instructive Washington symbioses: between a man who calls himself "the king of money" and a man whose flirtations with personal and political disaster have made him more financially needy than any other president in memory. "The feeling I had is, the one guy, if he did this, that they couldn't criticize [by saying] he was going to get something out of it was me," says McAuliffe. "Because I was so far into everything. I mean, what's the president going to do, give me another round of golf?" The "everything" that McAuliffe has been "into" has included leading the fund-raising effort for Clinton's 1996 campaign, at a time when many other Democrats were writing him off as a one-term president; chairing (and raising money for) his 1997 inaugural; raising nearly $7 million for the president's legal defense fund ("I am *the* fund-raiser for it. I raise all the big checks," he says); raising money for Hillary Clinton's Senate campaign ("I put her whole money team together. . . . I made fifty calls for her this week-end. . . . I love old Hillary!"); raising money for the president's future library, budgeted to cost more than $125 million; and rounding up corporate sponsors for the administration's planned millennium cele-bration on the Mall. And, when he has time left over, raising money for the president's vice president.

It says something about Clinton that McAuliffe is his last best friend as the final year of his presidency begins. Clinton came to Washington, seven years ago, surrounded by longtime policy com-rades like Lani Guinier, Robert Reich, and Peter and Marian Wright Edelman. Their politics were embraced by some and loathed by oth-ers, but at least they *had* politics; Clinton has since chewed through or cast off or triangulated away most of those old friends, the friends who belonged to whatever part of him came to Washington wanting more than the eternal survival of Bill Clinton. The last man standing is the one whose chief commitment has been to save Clinton's political skin. McAuliffe's career offers an illuminating map of the by-ways between money and politics. A Georgetown University–trained lawyer and an entrepreneur who has prospered in more than half a dozen industries, he has done a brilliant job of exploiting his connec-tions while avoiding the traps that lie in wait for the incautiously greedy. People on the other end of some McAuliffe transactions have a funny way of winding up with lawsuits, grievances, or even indict-ments. But McAuliffe has had a genius for evading harm in the in-vestigations that have dogged his career. McAuliffe's personal history makes him the perfect poster boy for his party at the turn of the mil-lennium. His life—from his Irish Catholic roots in middle-class Syra-cuse, New York, where he was steeped in Democratic politics as a child, through his climb to the top of Bill Clinton's Washington—closely tracks the evolution of the party; he was present at every important stage in the growth of the cash heliotropism that has in-creasingly inclined the Democrats toward the wealthy sources of their sunshine. "These people—the Rolodex kings—are the party now," says a mournful Democratic politician. "And they're all nice people, naturally."

The First Lady is on the speakerphone from Bratislava. Here in Washington, in the borrowed fourth-floor conference room of the Edison Electric Institute, it is nine in the morning, and it is only seventeen days until a birthday salute, at the Capital Hilton, that is budgeted to raise half a million dollars for Hillary Rodham Clinton's not-yet-announced Senate campaign.* The First Lady delivers some general remarks of thanks to the twenty-two benefactors seated around the burnished table—a group typical of big-ticket political donors, which is to say that they are mostly white men. But the real purpose of this meeting comes when Terry McAuliffe rises to "warm up" the audience, who have all agreed to hit up friends, acquain-tances, and business associates to donate to the coming event. "This

---

*Hillary Clinton was elected New York's junior senator in 2000 and won re-election in 2006. In 2008 McAuliffe chaired her unsuccessful presidential bid.

is going to be the main Washington event for the First Lady," McAuliffe explains to them. "So our plan is for everyone here to bring in ten." He means $10,000, in contributions of no more than the federally allowed $2,000 per person, with a thousand counting toward the primary campaign and a thousand toward the general election. Fund-raisers rarely use the word "thousand." They speak of "tens" and "twenty-fives" and—when they get up into the higher reaches of "soft money" fund-raising, in which big donors and companies are asked for large checks that go to the more loosely regulated party committees—of "fifties" and "hundreds" and even "two hundred fifties."

"Is there anyone here who couldn't do it?"

(McAuliffe always asks this question during warm-ups, he has told me. "No one's going to put their hand up in front of all their peers" and say no.)

"So we're all committed for ten," he says. "So all you need is two and a half couples. So I want you to make five calls every day. . . . Stop people on the street. Tackle 'em, and grab their checkbooks! This is IT. . . . Please, folks, *please.* Please make your calls every day." McAuliffe is physically striking—tall, though thickening at the middle, with a dense mop of chestnut hair, a glowing Irish complexion, and a ready smile. His right eye is blue; his left eye is a dark greenish brown. You notice this in one-on-one conversation, because McAuliffe focuses on you as if both your lives depended on unbroken eye contact. He uses your name earnestly and often, proffering it between respectful commas. He's the kind of guy who says "gosh" and "golly" and "goodness gracious!" Who describes his wife, Dorothy, as "a load of fun." Who constantly uses the phrase "to be honest with you," especially when he's about to pitch you a really shameless bit of spin. He conveys, with every restless gesture, that he is Just Terry, the Macker, a sunny Irish Catholic boy, the luckiest mother's son ever to rise out of the middle class in upstate New York.

"There are people that are hard to say no to because they're relentless. And there are people that are hard to say no to because they're likable. And he's in the latter camp," says Steven Rattner, deputy chairman of Lazard Frères and a reliable Democratic donor. The persona on display to Hillary's donors is at once the real Terry McAuliffe and a slightly sly parody of the type; part of his allure, people admit, is the way he can both inhabit this charming persona and also seem faintly hip to it. "Occasionally I'll see him in a restaurant, like the Oval Room," says Charles Lewis, executive director of the Center for Public Integrity—one of the watchdog groups that keep a critical eye on the Terry McAuliffes of the world. "He's always a little bit like Eddie Haskell. Like, 'Hello, Charles, and how are you today? And how is Integrity?' It's hard not to smile when you see him."

"You can't not like the guy," says a reporter who has tried. "And he's Machiavellian with the press. He really dishes, and so you don't want to alienate him."

McAuliffe wears his useful niceness everywhere he goes. When, for example, he gave a deposition to the Senate committee that in 1997 investigated campaign finance abuses, he was closely questioned by committee counsel Gus Puryear about his involvement in instigating the "coffees" that shuttled donors through the White House. To Puryear's astonishment, McAuliffe addressed him, throughout the day, by his first name. The word "Gus" appears four dozen times in the deposition transcript. "It's almost like someone who took a Dale Carnegie course and then walked in to give a deposition," Puryear says. "It had just never happened to me before."

At first glance, this Haskellism might seem so exaggerated as to be counterproductive. But notice that McAuliffe was never called as a witness during the committee's televised hearings. Republicans initially had hoped to use him as their opening witness, to establish the overall craving for cash that had led the Democrats into soaking up illegal foreign donations and selling the Lincoln Bedroom. But after his performance in deposition, they grew wary that his cheerful boosterism might make him an impregnable witness, the Oliver North of the fund-raising inquiry. Other campaign staffers became the public face of the scandal, while McAuliffe portrayed himself as uninvolved. "People who deal with Terry know that's the downside," says someone who has worked with him. "There are never any flies on Terry at the end."

"Most of fund-raising is personality," says Laura Hartigan, who served as finance director under McAuliffe in the 1996 Clinton-Gore campaign. Watching him stroke the First Lady's donors, one gets a sharp sense of McAuliffe's value to his party and his president; of why the president and the vice president both attended his fortieth birthday party; of why House minority leader Richard Gephardt, another beneficiary of McAuliffe's skills, once bought the McAuliffe family a golden retriever puppy, house-trained it for two months, and bathed it himself, in his bathtub, before delivering it on Christmas morning.

For one thing, McAuliffe is legendary for his refusal to hear "No." Once he staked out a business executive's lawn at 6:00 a.m. after the man failed to deliver on the last $5,000 of a $25,000 pledge and then stopped taking McAuliffe's calls. To get rid of McAuliffe, the embarrassed man wrote a $1,000 check on the spot, got his wife to do the same, and then knocked on three neighbors' doors to shake them down for $1,000 each. Another time—as McAuliffe loves to tell you—he wrestled an alligator, on a dare by a Florida Seminole tribe, in exchange for a $15,000 gift to the Democratic Party. McAuliffe has a Rolodex about four thousand strong. ("I do have the best Rolodex in the country," he boasts.) For years he kept up his network by sending out dime-store valentines each February. It's safe to guess that these were the only five-cent valentines Pamela Harriman received each year, but his real targets were the secretaries who controlled access to the executives he wanted to dun. "Where most people fall off the wagon is having the appetite to spend as much time doing it as he does," says a prominent Democratic fund-raiser. "I can do it for an hour or two a day, at some times. . . . I suspect he averages eight hours a day. I don't know how anybody can bear it."

In fact, McAuliffe makes roughly five hundred phone calls a week. In big election years, he has spent as many as three hundred days on the road. This past November, he hosted a fund-raiser at his house for Gore. He scheduled another event, at home, for Hillary

Clinton the first week in December. The week after that, the president was slated to headline an event there for House Democrats. This schedule seems even more staggering when you consider that the McAuliffes have four children under the age of nine, including a baby delivered at the end of October. Dorothy McAuliffe went into the hospital the evening of October 28, and the baby arrived early the next morning. In between, Terry could be found on the ninth floor of the *Washington Post* building, buoyantly networking at a party for the paper's gossip columnist, Lloyd Grove. "I hope you give a good plug to Dorothy," a friend of the couple's told me, "just for the shit she puts up with."* Another friend notes that back in McAuliffe's bachelor days, after a night of barhopping, "at 6:00 a.m., Macker would be in the shower singing 'God Bless America.' . . . He has an energy level that is beyond most people's comprehension."

But even more than his toil, McAuliffe's chief value is the cleansing effervescence he lends to the sea of money washing through his party. There is, today, a subtle tension involved in the very act of gathering to talk about political money. McAuliffe, with his air of wholesome joy, is a genius at cutting this tension. "Don't worry, you'll only get a couple of subpoenas," he cracks to the First Lady's check harvesters, reaping nervous laughter. And when he's asked whether children can attend the event, which will be held at the awkward hour of 11:00 a.m. on a Saturday, he says sure, but adds a semi-serious reminder: "We don't want kids writing checks. That's all we need. Next thing you know, we'll be doin' people's cats and dogs."

Toward the end of the Oval Room's busy lunch period, as the restaurant is beginning to clear out, the hostess comes to McAuliffe's

---

*In his 2007 memoir, *What A Party!* (St. Martin's Press), McAuliffe reports unself-consciously that he prowled Dorothy's hospital room ("I am not one to sit still for long") until Dorothy said, "Go! You're like a caged animal here." McAuliffe "went flying out the door" to the party, where he "ran into Marjorie Williams," who was reporting this profile. "She was shocked to see me at the party. . . . Marjorie just couldn't understand how I could have left Dorothy alone."

table. "Alecia is on the phone," she says, meaning McAuliffe's long-time assistant, Alecia Dyer. "The president is calling." McAuliffe jumps up, a flush of pleasure suffusing his cheeks. "This really wasn't a setup," he says, and hurries to the front of the restaurant. For the next ten minutes I can hear him up there, roaring his big laugh into Bill Clinton's ear. HA! HA-HA! McAuliffe entered Clinton's circle relatively late, in 1994, when the Democrats had just suffered their staggering midterm loss of the House of Representatives. Drafted to begin raising money for Clinton's reelection, McAuliffe faced a president who was being written off as a failure, certain to be challenged by others in his party. But McAuliffe raised the entire amount that a primary candidate is allowed to spend, $37.1 million before federal matching funds, in only seven months. More important, his show of muscle tied up all the money that might conceivably have funded a challenger. "You know, I wouldn't be in this office if it were not for your son," Clinton told McAuliffe's parents when they visited the White House last spring.

By most accounts, the friendship went from being a professional one to being a truly social one around the time the Monica Lewinsky scandal broke—the same time, in other words, that Clinton's previous No. 1 golfing buddy, Vernon Jordan, was suddenly off-limits because of his role as a witness in the Starr investigation. (It was Jordan's part in helping Lewinsky get a job in New York that had allowed Kenneth Starr to investigate the affair in the first place.)* McAuliffe replaced Jordan as Clinton's most frequent golf partner, playing with him as often as once a week at the Army-Navy Club. He became the person Clinton is apt to summon to a movie at the White House on nights when the First Lady is out of town. He's been on two vacations with the First Family—though, notably, neither

---

*In 1998 it was revealed that Clinton had had an affair with a White House intern named Monica Lewinsky. The scandal, and the fact that Clinton lied about it under oath in an unrelated lawsuit, led the House to impeach him later that year. The Senate then failed to convict him, allowing Clinton to serve out his term.

was the kind of vacation on which his own family was invited along. Clinton and McAuliffe speak by phone almost daily, either in the afternoon or, more often, late at night, when Clinton talks to unwind. "Terry is one of those safe harbors for him," says senior advisor to the president Doug Sosnik. "He doesn't have to worry about what he says to Terry, because he knows Terry's only agenda is friendship."

But it's hard not to see utilitarian underpinnings in that friendship. Its very existence, because it advertises the fund-raiser's closeness to The Man, makes raising the money the president needs even easier for McAuliffe. "To a large degree, Clinton's friendships are circumstantial," says a former administration official. "Terry's both a very affable, very capable guy and very useful." One friend says that McAuliffe genuinely believed the president's early assurances, in 1998, that he'd never had a sexual relationship with Lewinsky. "He did lie to Terry directly," says this friend. When McAuliffe learned the truth, "he was just crushed. It took even old Mack a while to get over it."

But as always McAuliffe managed to find a way to see this glass as half-full. "I think at the end of the day, the president was trying to protect me," he says now. "Starr knew how much we had talked. We've got a very special relationship. He would never want to put me in harm's way."

McAuliffe was born to Jack and Millie McAuliffe in 1957 and named for the Notre Dame halfback Terry Brennan. (Brennan, Millie McAuliffe explains, ran a kickoff back ninety-seven yards for a touchdown during the Notre Dame–Army game on November 8, 1947. She remembers this clearly because her husband took her to the game on their wedding day.) The family's home was on the far west side of Syracuse, a neighborhood of the flourishing middle class. Jack McAuliffe made a good living developing commercial real estate, but one modest enough that Terry had to put himself through college and law school. It was the last gasp of the cozy, all-encompassing urban Catholic world of the 1960s: parochial school at St. Ann's elementary and then Bishop Ludden High School, where Terry was president of his class for three years, and of the student body his senior year. ("Most Likely to Succeed," his yearbook said, noting that he "dislikes nothing.") Interviews turn up the clear suggestion that Terry, the youngest of four sons, was his mother's favorite. "He is just the apple of his mother's eye," says Dorothy McAuliffe. "When he came in the house, it all kind of lit up a little," recalls Millie McAuliffe. "He just brightened the landscape."

Terry came by his politics early in life: his father was active in the Onondaga County Democratic Party, becoming its treasurer when Terry was thirteen. Terry loved to man the door at party dinners, selling $25 tickets to his father's friends. You might say the McAuliffe family offers a capsule history of the postwar Democratic Party. In the father's day, the party was everything: the arbiter of who might run, the chief source of funding for candidates vetted by the party elders. By the time the son rose to the top of the party hierarchy, politics was mediated almost entirely by television, and therefore by the moneymen who could deal aspirants into the cash needed to stoke ad campaigns.

And as much as Terry seemed to savor politics, he also demonstrated early on that he had a way with money. Scarcely into high school, he started a business sealing driveways and parking lots around Syracuse. In one of the five scrapbooks his mother made to chronicle his career are the founding documents of McAuliffe Driveway Maintenance, including the earnest letter young Terry sent around to drum up business:

Dear Local Businessman:
McAuliffe Driveway Maintenance is just the company for which you have been looking. We are the sealing and repair specialists of Central New York. Your parking area reflects YOU. Your beauty is a big business asset and making your parking area beautiful is our business.

He was fourteen at the time. When winter came, he invested some of his profits in a huge snowblower and rose every snowy morning at four to go around the neighborhood clearing driveways. He would be home by eight, he remembers, pockets stuffed with as much as $200 in cash. And when he got home, he would iron the money on Millie's ironing board in an upstairs bedroom. "You couldn't take 'em to the bank. They were all crumbled and jammed in my pocket," he says. One by one, he ironed the bills, just so, even adding spray starch to get them crisp, until he had a nice, flatly satisfying pile.

He would, he decided, be a millionaire by thirty.

McAuliffe got his start in fund-raising when a college friend lured him to the Carter campaign in 1979, the same year he graduated from Catholic University (as "Outstanding Senior," of course). Here was a career where hustle paid off in huge, readily grasped measures of accomplishment. The campaign sent him out to organize events around the country, often with nothing but the name of a single friendly local businessman in his pocket. It was, however, always a potent name, for this was the reelection campaign of an incumbent president: a name such as that of real estate developer Walter Shorenstein in San Francisco, or the legendary MCA chairman Lew Wasserman in Los Angeles. By the time of the general-election campaign, he had done so well he was sent over to the Democratic National Committee as the top finance staffer. He was only twenty-three, so he added five years to his age and wore glasses with clear lenses to lend himself a bit of dignity. In 1983 he was hired by Tony Coelho, then a California congressman, to raise money for the Democratic Congressional Campaign Committee (DCCC).

This was where he began to have a big impact on the party. Before Coelho, the DCCC had been a desultory little shop, wanly raising money at a single dinner each year. Together, Coelho and McAuliffe courted business money as never before. Their crucial insight was that corporations' political action committees could be sold, as a simple matter of business, on the advantages of supporting the incumbent party (or of, as fund-raisers like to say, "becoming part of the process"). They made the DCCC a powerful machine to perpetuate the party's control of the House, then the only part of government the Republicans had not won in Reagan's revolution. Just as the House Democrats were becoming the most important force in the party, McAuliffe and Coelho were making them more beholden to business than ever before.

In the meantime, McAuliffe had sped through law school, opened a law firm (which is to say a lobbying firm), and joined the board of a local bank, of which he would be made chairman before he turned thirty. "When Terry was in, like, his late twenties, he already cut a figure about how rich he'd gotten, very quickly," says a former colleague. "He had this aura." His practice of law was noteworthy for what it said about his shrewdness. He himself never actually lobbied, and he maintained a virginal ignorance about the workings of the legislative process. "In all the times I spoke to him, I don't think he ever wanted to talk about policy," recalls CNN's Brooks Jackson, the dean of the money-and-politics beat, who spent two years watching Coelho and McAuliffe for his influential 1988 book, *Honest Graft: Big Money and the American Political Process*. "In fact, he very much didn't want to talk about policy. He was kind of a policy eunuch, in a way."

By keeping his distance from questions of policy, McAuliffe remained free to vacuum up cash for the DCCC without creating any unseemly connection between the sources of the cash and the results it bought. That was Coelho's end of the business, as richly documented in Jackson's book. Coelho ultimately paid for the perceived connection between his power brokering and his own financial struggles, quitting Congress in 1989 after it was revealed that he had accepted an unusually favorable loan from a California savings and loan and a sweetheart arrangement enabling him to invest in one of Michael Milken's junk-bond deals. McAuliffe avoided such problems by keeping his personal gain at arm's length, merely steering the people he met through politics to his partners—who did the lobbying for his firm. "Terry just knew so many people," says his former partner, lobbyist John Raffaelli. "And people asked him, 'I got a problem, who do you recommend I use?'"

McAuliffe's conversations are heavily laced with rhetorical paeans to the working man. But if he has any actual politics of his own, they're of the middle-of-the-road, pro-business sort. "People who are too left, too right—they just don't accomplish anything. I'm not a partisan Democrat," he says, in the eternally pacific voice of the deal maker. "I have been successful in life because I stay positive." "He has no political convictions I'm aware of," says a Democratic observer. "I think he'd tell you he's an institutional party man. But what that boils down to is, as long as the Democrats remain in power, he's in the catbird seat. It means new ventures, new sources of business, new avenues of personal advancement."

After his stint at the DCCC, McAuliffe raised money for the presidential campaigns of Richard Gephardt (in 1988) and Sen. Tom Harkin (in 1992). Both these candidates drew heavily on labor support and the more liberal elements of the party. But when Clinton won in 1992, McAuliffe had no trouble changing to a more centrist horse. He quickly entered the graces of the new administration by chairing the Democratic National Committee's business council. In under two years he increased from about 150 to 750 the circle of business donors who paid $10,000 annually to belong. Clinton had come into office talking of campaign finance reform and expanding the party's small-donor base. But by 1994 he had come to see the wisdom of the McAuliffe method: early that year, he tapped McAuliffe to become finance chairman of the entire DNC. McAuliffe quit his law firm to take the post. But his own fortune continued to grow, from a skein of endeavors that have included, over time, banking, real estate, investment counseling, insurance, credit-card marketing, homebuilding, telecommunications, venture capital, and some canny investing of profits. "He's involved in so many different things," says his elder brother John McAuliffe. "I talked to him a couple of years ago about what he did, and he told me all about it, and I walked away saying, 'I'm still not quite sure what you do, Terry.'"

When McAuliffe posted the $1.35 million to help the Clintons win the contract on their house, he lost a measure of his useful camouflage. Everyone in politics knew McAuliffe was rich, but the house deal revealed him as being a different kind of rich—the kind that can raise a million in cash without batting an eye. "It exposed me as being very wealthy, which I don't like," says McAuliffe. "Listen, my parents had no idea. My brothers had no idea." He refuses to comment on friends' reports that peg his fortune at close to, possibly slightly over, $100 million. Even his wife, he says, still doesn't know how much money the couple has. "She's got a great life. Listen, her credit cards are always paid and all that. She knows I do very well. But she has no idea. Myself and my accountants are the only people who know." Hearing him talk, it is odd to remember that Dorothy McAuliffe, thirty-six, is also a Georgetown-trained lawyer who worked for some years in banking law before becoming a full-time mother to their children, Dori, Jack, Mary, and the newborn Sally. A down-to-earth brunette who seems to roll easily with the demands of life with McAuliffe, she clearly knew what she was getting into. The couple met in 1979 when Dorothy was only sixteen and her father was the Florida finance chairman for Jimmy Carter's reelection campaign. She and McAuliffe started dating three years later, when she was in college at Catholic University, and eventually married in 1988.

Terry McAuliffe obviously savors money as a scorekeeper, but he's not into displays of wealth. He still drives the white Jeep convertible, with no air-conditioning, that he bought nine years ago. And while the McAuliffes do have a lovely old house in McLean, a posh Virginia suburb, which they bought in the early '90s for almost $1.2 million, their usual summer vacation is to rent a house in the slightly raffish town of Dewey Beach, on the Delaware shore. One reason for McAuliffe's horror of showing his wealth is that he seems genuinely to care about maintaining his connections to family and old friends. But another, clearly, has been the usefulness of blending in. The fewer people who knew that he was very rich, the fewer would be asking questions about how he got that way.

The bulk of McAuliffe's fortune comes from some shrewd investments he has made over the past four or so years in high-technology stocks. ("To be honest with you," he says amiably, "if you could not have made money in the market in the last four years, you are an idiot.") In addition to playing the market, McAuliffe describes himself as a traditional entrepreneur, seeding new companies with venture capital. "I have probably been an investor and backer and supporter of over one hundred companies," he says. But the most striking element of McAuliffe's business life is the way it has paralleled his political work, benefiting at every turn from the contacts he has made through fund-raising. McAuliffe portrays himself as a sort of political philanthropist, graciously taking time off from his businesses to "give some back" by supporting politicians who believe in the common man. But the truth is that everything in his life—right down to his wife—has flowed from the headwaters of his work in politics.

Begin with his father-in-law, Richard Swann, whom he met during his first assignment with the Carter campaign. Swann, whose Orlando-based Pioneer Savings & Loan went bust in 1990, is now in business with McAuliffe in a cluster of real estate companies and spin-off concerns (title insurance, home financing) based in central Florida. Another political contact was Carl Lindner, the head of Chiquita and the financial conglomerate American Financial Group, in Cincinnati. Lindner and some associates invested with McAuliffe four years ago in a Florida-based homebuilding business, American Heritage Homes. With McAuliffe as its chairman, it has grown to have the largest sales volume of any homebuilder in central Florida, putting up modest houses (average price, $130,000) in developments with names like Lake Steer Pointe and Deer Pointe at Falcon Trace. Still another valuable connection was with Martin Davis, a political consultant. Together they successfully persuaded the thirteen-million-member AFL-CIO to shift its credit-card business to their client, Household International Corp., which hired the pair in early 1996, when McAuliffe was widely known as Clinton's top fund-raiser. McAuliffe and Davis reportedly split commissions worth several million dollars. Later that year, through an old political colleague, McAuliffe met a former Drexel Burnham Lambert bond trader named Gary Winnick. As the *Wall Street Journal* recently reported, McAuliffe made his biggest score yet when Winnick invited him to participate in a transatlantic-cable endeavor called Global Crossing. McAuliffe's initial investment of $100,000 is worth at least $18 million today, he says, and he bought more shares as the price of the stock rocketed.

There is nothing remotely illegal about making such sterling connections through politics. McAuliffe says, "The [criticism] is, 'He met people through politics and has done well.' Well, I'll plead guilty to that. . . . My point always is, if I didn't do what I do today [in fundraising], I'd probably be a billionaire." Yet McAuliffe's career has taken him fairly often to the outskirts of legal difficulty. Last May, for example, the U.S. Department of Labor sued the two trustees of a union pension fund that had invested heavily with McAuliffe in some real estate ventures he designed. The suit alleges that the fund trustees, who invested the pensions of two electricians' unions, made a series of risky deals that gave the unions' working men and women a lower-than-reasonable return. McAuliffe, who had put up only $100 of his own money, earned at least $2.4 million on the deals. But he was not the person accountable for the funds. So while his former partners are explaining themselves in U.S. District Court, McAuliffe has borne none of the penalties for the arrangements he made.

His closest shave came in the 1996 Clinton campaign. The most scandalous elements of the president's fund-raising—the Buddhist temple affair,* the illegal foreign contributions rustled up by DNC fund-raiser John Huang, the wholesale dealing in White House perks such as coffees and sleepovers—were technically violations by the Democratic National Committee, not the Clinton-Gore campaign. As McAuliffe is fond of pointing out, the Clinton-Gore campaign itself, for which he chaired the fund-raising, was not accused of illegalities. But as Sen. Fred Thompson's investigation demonstrated, the distinction between the Clinton White House and the DNC was a

---

*In 1996 the Hsi Lai Buddhist Temple in Los Angeles raised nearly $65,000 for the DNC at an event attended by vice president Al Gore. The temple reimbursed the individual donors, which was illegal. Gore maintained that he never knew it was a fund-raiser.

thin fiction. While there is no evidence connecting McAuliffe to any foreign funds, he was certainly aware of the overall strategy by which Clinton was circumventing the law limiting expenditures in presidential campaigns. Briefly, the DNC spent $44 million on "issue ads" funded largely by unregulated soft-money donations to the party, but closely supervised by the White House. To pay for these ads, the party abandoned almost all restraint on its fund-raising practices.

McAuliffe was the author of a famous memo asking the president to meet with top donors, on which Clinton scribbled a note urging his staff to set up more overnights, and other such White House perks, at $50,000 and $100,000 a pop. McAuliffe initiated the White House coffees that the DNC eventually adopted, overturning a long-standing prohibition on raising money on the premises. These weren't fund-raisers, the administration firmly insisted; they were "donor-maintenance events," for which no *specific* amount was solicited to attend that *specific* event. It was a total coincidence that 92 percent of the people attending these events gave to the party in 1995 or 1996 $26.4 million altogether. By 1996, McAuliffe had far transcended the kind of nuts-and-bolts work that would have assigned him any line responsibility for the inner workings of the DNC. This, too, is part of his method. When unpleasant management tasks arise, says a former McAuliffe staffer, "his big thing, always, was, 'Hey, that's a staff issue. That's yours.'" In his depositions with Thompson committee lawyers, he sought to portray himself both as the all-knowing King of Money and, where it was convenient, as a distant figurehead who was out of the loop.

McAuliffe came nearest to serious trouble over a byzantine scheme between the DNC and the reelection campaign of Ron Carey, who was then president of the Teamsters Union. Three people connected with the Teamsters have pleaded guilty to acts that included agreeing to swap contributions with the DNC. They would give the Democrats a million dollars in Teamsters' political funds, they proposed in the summer of '96, if the DNC would in turn steer a $100,000 contribution to Carey's campaign. The deal was brokered by campaign consultant Martin Davis, McAuliffe's former partner in the AFL-CIO credit-card deal. McAuliffe denied knowing anything about the swap scheme, saying that Davis—one of those who pleaded guilty in the case—had simply offered to steer a Teamsters donation to the DNC, and that he had referred Davis to colleagues at the DNC. He couldn't even remember ("to be honest with you") when Davis had approached him. But two witnesses told Senate investigators that McAuliffe had urged them to try to find a donor for Carey's campaign, and Davis identified him in his plea as the Clinton operative who had agreed to the swap. During the November trial of a Teamsters official, former DNC finance director Richard Sullivan testified that McAuliffe had explicitly urged him to find a donor for the Carey campaign in order to get a Teamsters donation in return. Yet federal prosecutors apparently decided not to pursue anyone on the DNC end of the scheme. In part because its half of the bargain was never fulfilled, there was no legal violation as obvious as the one on the Teamsters' end, where the actors were proposing to use Teamsters' funds illegally to strengthen Carey's control of the union. McAuliffe was extensively questioned about the case, but says, "I was never a target, never a subject" of the investigation. He seems likely to suffer nothing worse than a slap on the wrist that was delivered in the Thompson committee's report.

Of all the stories McAuliffe tells about his amazing life, one is, hands down, the most extraordinary. It is an August night in Skaneateles, New York. The president and First Lady have just won the contract on their new house in New York, after a frantic effort to find a rich friend willing to post collateral for the mortgage. They have been turned down by old friends like Erskine Bowles and Thomas "Mack" McLarty, but finally bailed out by the kindness of their good friend Terry McAuliffe. Now, near dinnertime, Clinton and McAuliffe are riding in the presidential motorcade, talking about what to eat. The president turns to the benefactor who has just coughed up more than a million dollars in cash.

"He says, 'Terry, why don't you figure out how we can get a couple of pies to bring back to the house? A couple of pizzas?' I say, 'What do you want on it, Mr. President?'"

In addition to the bushels of money McAuliffe has already raised for the Clintons, it would be astonishing if the president didn't turn to McAuliffe, once he leaves office, for a piece of the action. If you were leaving office at the age of fifty-four and wanted to earn some serious money for the first time in your life, you couldn't ask for a better tutor than Terry McAuliffe.* But for McAuliffe success has carried its own punishment. He has taken on every task the Clintons have asked of him, and most of his friends say he is overextended. "He's got way too many things going," says John Raffaelli, McAuliffe's friend and former partner. "I think Clinton has totally seduced the sonofabitch." Another friend observes, "If he has one big problem, it's that he can't say no to the Democratic Party or the Clintons. He gets wrapped up in everything the Clintons do." McAuliffe's friends agree that he would like at some point to move away from his identity as the party's cash machine and be seen as a more substantive figure. He planned to make this move after Clinton's reelection; it was generally understood that he was in line to be secretary of commerce in the second term. But when the fundraising scandals broke, it was instantly apparent that he couldn't make it past the Senate. He was, friends say, deeply disappointed. "The paradox is that he wants more than anything else to parlay the money into some other form of respectability. And in the end it always comes back to the money. He can't get away from it," says one McAuliffe-watcher. Commerce secretaries are a dime a dozen compared with men of McAuliffe's gifts and loyalty.

Does he ever chafe at how much more useful he is to the president in his current role? One former Clinton staffer says bluntly that, "Clinton has sold out all his friends, in the end. . . . It would be interesting to find out how Terry sees it. Because that's the best way to have a relationship with Clinton—to see what's in it for you, without any illusions." Clearly, one thing that's in it for McAuliffe is

---

*Clinton instead chose Ron Burkle, a billionaire investor based in Los Angeles. The Clintons, who were broke when they left the White House, had by 2008 earned $109 million. About $15 million of this came through Bill Clinton's partnerships with Burkle.

the pure, alpha-male satisfaction of knowing how badly the president needs him. And, clearly, it's not bad for business. But beyond that, cynics should probably tread with care. For there's no getting around the fact that McAuliffe is thrilled to the cleats of his golf shoes simply to be hanging out with the president. "I lo-o-o-o-ve the action," he says. "I love it. Just bein' with the president, and flyin' all over the country, and ridin' around with him. I'm just *in* the action." Lingering in the restaurant following the president's phone call, he confides, "He said, 'Terry, I love you. You're a great American.' That's what he just said to me."

Terry McAuliffe is, more than anything, a greatly magnified embodiment of everyone who gives money to politicians. Many people donate for the darkest reasons we imagine, with at least the hope of buying policy or access. Others donate because they really believe in the promise of the party or person they're supporting. But lots of people—even, in many cases, those same people, dark or fervent—give for more human reasons. They do it because they want face time; they do it for a photograph; they do it because they want to be part of the crowd that hangs with the president, or the vice president, or the congressman or the speaker or the mayor. They do it because someone they know, or feel vaguely obligated to, asks them to do it. They do it because it feels great to know there is someone in Washington whose job it is to remember their birthday. Sometimes they do it because that is what men of their social circle or business set or peer group do. They do it because—whether they're good for $1,000 in exchange for a signed photograph of themselves with the vice president, or $50,000 for a night in the Lincoln bedroom—it makes them feel important.

This is the strange kernel of sociability at the core of our system. Almost everyone in Washington would secretly admit that money is a moral lesion on the heart of American politics, and that it is one of the reasons most citizens have such a brittle connection to their government. Yet no one in Washington holds his buddies responsible, because everyone's just playing by the rules. And it's hard to change the rules when, after all, they're just part of the scenery, and the scenery is peopled by such nice guys. The folks who raise and give the money—an already unprecedented crop for the coming election—aren't the fat oligarchs of popular imagining, chuckling over bags of cash. They are pleasant men like Terry McAuliffe, going about the frictionless business of their lives.

—January 2000

THE STORY OF A GOOD GIRL

(ANNA QUINDLEN)

When the twenty-four-year-old Anna Quindlen first interviewed for a job at the *New York Times*, she followed a simple strategy: she told them what they wanted to hear. Specifically, when managing editor Seymour Topping asked her what her ultimate ambition was, she told him that she hoped to be a foreign correspondent—preferably with a posting to Germany. And when she reached the office of executive editor Abe Rosenthal, she said she yearned to cover Poland. Topping, she had learned from reading up on him, had been a correspondent in Berlin, and Rosenthal had won a Pulitzer Prize for his dispatches from Warsaw. This classic bit of apple polishing paid off well. Today, as the only woman to write a regular column for the *Times'* editorial pages—and only the third woman ever to be assigned that plum*—Quindlen is among the paper's stars, and one of a handful of candidates to manage the newspaper of record into the next century. She is also a successful novelist, whose 1991 coming-of-age novel, *Object Lessons*, was a best seller, and whose second novel, *One True Thing*, is to be published this month by Random

---

*Quindlen was preceded by Anne O'Hare McCormick and Flora Lewis. Two women have since followed her: Maureen Dowd and Gail Collins.

House. Along the way, she earned a legion of fans through her earlier column "Life in the 30s," in which she wrote, from 1986 through 1988, about the everyday epiphanies that grew out of her private life as the mother of small children, a working woman, and the wife of trial attorney Gerald Krovatin.

After moving onto the op-ed page, Quindlen won the 1992 Pulitzer Prize for her "soft" take on American life and politics. "Public & Private," which runs every Wednesday and Saturday, is highly personal and pointillistic, and was consciously conceived as the work of a female voice; often praised as a refreshing contrast to the *Times'* all-male stable of opinion-mongers, it embodies what Quindlen once called "a world view largely shaped by gender." Quindlen's singularity as a female tribune marks her as one of the most interesting symbols of the new *New York Times* presided over by Arthur O. Sulzberger Jr. She is perhaps the most visible manifestation of the young publisher's controversial efforts to create a more liberal, more "diverse" *Times* than the paper he inherited, almost three years ago, from his father. By extension, Quindlen's starring role at the *Times*, and its reward from the traditionalists who judge the Pulitzer Prizes, says a good deal about how three decades of feminism have crystallized in the mainstream culture. It is true that women are still woefully underrepresented at the top ranks of news and opinion journalism. But it is telling that Quindlen is the *Times's* answer to this problem. For she is an incorrigible nice girl: a powerful sixtyish white man's idea of a feminist writer.

A woman's voice, Quindlen's work suggests, is ladylike. Tidy. *Careful*. It is necessarily, in Quindlen's world, a liberal voice. Harsh, "masculine" subjects such as war and foreign policy call forth a pretty ambivalence; women have no need to conquer this territory, when they already occupy the moral high ground. "She's of the I-was-upset-I-had-no-shoes-until-I-met-a-man-who-had-no-feet school," says one New York wag, perfectly summarizing the column's brand of conspicuous compassion. Thus the story of Quindlen's first job interview, though she has told it on herself, has what is surely an unintended resonance; it might as well be a description of her modus operandi as a columnist. After a brilliant career of climbing the ladder at the *Times*, the forty-one-year-old Quindlen has the journalistic equivalent of tenure at Harvard or a seat on the Supreme Court: she can now say anything she pleases. Why, then, is her voice still so often pitched to tell others what they want to hear?

As any nice girl can tell you, being a nice girl in America is not a matter of passivity. It is about masking normal aggression with femininity, covering ambition with sweetness. Quindlen's friends and associates describe her as a woman of formidable will who has always known what she wanted and gone after it. "When she sets out to accomplish something," says *Times* Moscow correspondent Michael Specter, a close friend, "you should get out of the way." Kathy Slobogin, a friend and former colleague, recalls Quindlen saying, of her Catholic upbringing, that "when other little girls wanted to be a nun, she wanted to be a saint." Quindlen has memorably satirized her own persona, in a column about the character revelations that can be found in a girl's choice of Favorite Beatle. She was, inevitably, a Paul girl; McCartney, she wrote, "got the little ladies like me. . . . Over the years I've sometimes tried to escape being a Paul girl, but it's never worked for long." Quindlen has an open face, straight brown hair with bangs, and a girl-next-door air of friendliness. How many other *New York Times* reporters use adjectives such as "bang-up" and "crackerjack"? But she has used her Paul-girl persona to advantage. "She's very astute," says Slobogin. "She's always said that the men [at the *Times*] see her as a sister rather than a potential date."

Born in 1953, the oldest of five children, Quindlen has Italian lineage from her mother and Irish lineage from her father, a middle-class management consultant whose firm moved the family from Drexel Hill, Pennsylvania, to Wheeling, West Virginia, and then finally to suburban Kendall Park, New Jersey. Quindlen has described herself as "a little girl raised as his oldest son by a man who swore his firstborn would be a boy and never changed his mind." Also as "a textbook-case eldest child—a leader, a doer, a convincing veneer of personality and confidence atop a bottomless pit of insecurity and need." Asked to describe Anna as a child, her brother Bob thinks for no more than a second before locating the right adjective. "She was very *focused*." As a teenager in the '60s, she thought her mother's life as a homemaker looked like hell. "I figured either life was going to be considerably different for me than it was for my mother, or I was going to be angry all the time," she later wrote.

It was a conviction reinforced by family tragedy. During Anna's freshman year at Barnard, her mother became fatally ill, at forty, with ovarian cancer. Anna went home to Kendall Park to nurse her mother through her last days and to become a mother to her little brother and sisters. "There she was in college, getting ready to be successful, have a different life," says a friend, "and she got yanked back to New Jersey to change diapers and make macaroni and cheese. I think it scared the shit out of her." When she emerged from this ordeal, it was with a terrible sense of urgency. "We all know the clock is ticking," says *Times* film critic Janet Maslin, Quindlen's best friend, "but she *really* knows it." On returning to Barnard, Quindlen pored through the college's files of babysitting requests, applying to attend the tykes whose parents happened to be influential journalists. She had, friends say, an extraordinary early sense of how careers were developed and who could help her. "She's like a heat-seeking missile," says one. "She is directed in a way that takes my breath away."

Hired in 1977 after two years at the *New York Post,* Quindlen began her *Times* career as a general-assignment and city-hall reporter on the metropolitan staff. Editors, from the imperious Abe Rosenthal on down, quickly recognized that rarity in the newspaper business: a reporter who combined a genuine passion for news with a writer's flair. They rewarded her with one of the best jobs on the paper, the "About New York" column, which gave her license to turn out short features on any aspect of life in the city. But the *Times* was grooming her for even greater things. At the time Quindlen was hired, the newsroom was in the throes of a bitter equal opportunity lawsuit by women on the staff. As the paper dragged its feet toward settlement, its editors were increasingly aware that they needed women in the pipeline to management. They made Quindlen the deputy metropolitan editor, with clear indications that she was on track to be the next metro editor. But by this time Quindlen was ready to embrace some of the domestic life she had run from so far and so fast. Pregnant with her second child, she quit the paper to create more family time. And Rosenthal, desperate to keep her, devised "Life in the 30s" as a way for her to have it both ways, working part-time at home. Three years later, tired of turning every aspect of her life into fodder for her column, Quindlen again decided to leave the *Times*—and again the *Times* sweetened the pot, offering her what no woman her age had ever had, a berth on the op-ed page.

Her unorthodox career path is one of the things that have earned Quindlen a devoted following among women. It is sweet indeed to watch a woman force a Fortune 500 company to accommodate her children's mealtimes. The paper hasn't always been happy about Quindlen's choices: former managing editor Arthur Gelb still terms it "puzzling and a little disappointing" that she didn't jump at the chance to be metropolitan editor. But Quindlen seems deeply grounded in her passion for her kids. To preserve her family focus, she turns down a majority of the speaking invitations that pour into her office. (It was on these grounds, too, that she refused to take time over the summer months to be interviewed for this story.) And despite being eagerly sought by television producers, she has simply declined the electronic fame that many, if not most, columnists pursue. This detachment, however, doesn't detract from her shrewd sense of *Times* politics. Several people pointed out how striking it was that Quindlen had thrived under both dispensations that have run the modern *Times:* the autocratic rule of Rosenthal, and the more easygoing regimes of his successors, Max Frankel and Joseph Lelyveld, who have taken their cues from young Sulzberger. "She's very good at charming the people who matter most," says a former colleague. "And no one matters more than the publisher, and he's been *very* charmed by her." She is, today, a social friend of Sulzberger and his wife, the artist Gail Gregg. "It's so deeply ingrained in her—her instinct to curry favor with those in power," says another former colleague. "It's part of her very fiber." Quindlen's professional poise is matched in private life by what friends describe as a seamless competence. "It can be a little frustrating to be her friend sometimes, because she does everything so well," says Kathy Slobogin. "It's a good thing she's so nice, otherwise I'd hate her!"

Quindlen married a man she met when she was a freshman in college; she doesn't drink, and eschews the literary party circuit in favor of dinners at home in Hoboken, New Jersey, with her children, and weekends at the family's country house in Stroudsburg, Pennsylvania. The settled existence described in "Life in the 30's" is strenuously perfect, in the accounts of friends. "If Anna wants to learn about gardening, then she's going to know everything there ever was to know about a rose," says Michael Specter. "And if she wants to make veal, she's going to know at what age it's best to butcher the animal." According to Maslin, Quindlen cooks eggs Benedict for her husband every Sunday morning. "She bakes the *ham!*" Maslin moans.

Friends describe a woman who is always there in a crunch. But she is not a woman who often needs the favor returned. "She is not, in the end, someone who feels comfortable leaning on people," says Specter. "I think a lot of people sort of look at Anna and say, 'Where's the crack?' Like, 'Where's the hole in the foundation?' And I think it's just not there." Others believe that Quindlen works with zeal at creating this picture of Superwoman. Someone who has known her for years says, "Anna has engaged in a more concerted effort, consciously or subconsciously, toward mythmaking than anybody I've ever met" of her generation. "She gives these interviews that make other working mothers want to shoot themselves. . . . It's like Martha Stewart hell." Quindlen's priorities in life, say some of her closest friends, represent a circling back to the legacy of her mother. "To the extent that you can bring people back by becoming them, she's done it," says Maslin. "What's astounding about her is that she's assimilated a kind of 1950s ideal of motherhood with a big career." Specter says, "If her mother's looking down from somewhere—and Anna is someone who believes she is—I think she wants her mother to say, 'You're doing it as well as I did it.'"

It is interesting, then, that Quindlen's new novel revolves around a maternal legacy. On the surface, it is a story about the timely issue of mercy killing, in which a daughter is arrested on charges of over-dosing her cancer-ridden mother with morphine. But the book's true subject is the narrator's choice between her mother's and her fa-ther's models of life. The father, a contemptuous, brittle professor of English literature, pushes his daughter much as Robert Quindlen may have pushed Anna; the mother, a homemaker who devotes all her time to the spinning of domestic comforts, is seen by her daugh-ter at the novel's start as owning "a life I had always viewed with something even more dismissive than contempt, a life I had viewed as though it were a feature in *National Geographic*, the anachronistic traditions of a distant tribe." By the novel's end, Ellen Gulden has of course come to see her father as the weaker of her two parents, the mother as the "one true thing" in her young life.

Despite a somewhat schematic plot and a twenty-four-year-old heroine who seems improbably articulate, *One True Thing* is an ac-complished, sometimes gripping book. But as a dialectic about women's possibilities, it seems starkly Manichaean. The father and his intellect are cold; the mother, in her domesticity, is warm. "My father . . . divided women into two groups, although in his case it was not the body-and-soul dichotomy of the madonna and the whore but the intellectual twins, the woman of the mind and the one of the heart," says the narrator. "I had the misfortune to be des-ignated the heartless one, my mother the mindless one. It was a dis-service to us both but, on balance, I think she got the better deal." There is Quindlen's problem in a nutshell: picking the heart over the mind every time—even, alas, when she isn't really required to choose. "I've never been very good at looking at the big picture, tak-ing the global view," Quindlen once wrote in "Life in the 30's"; her stock-in-trade is the vignette, the personal anecdote that illumines a larger truth. It was this approach that made "About New York" and "Life in the 30's" such successful columns. At her best, Quind-len has brought into the *Times'* gray pages a sense of vivid life, or lives—including her own. She can be tart and funny, and while

"Life in the 30's" had both ardent fans and passionate detractors, Quindlen deserves credit for finding a way to bring into the once bloodless pages of the *Times* her appreciation of children and domestic life and all the "personal" stuff that is not officially news.

But now that she occupies the high-visibility, "masculine" real estate of the op-ed page, she is no longer content to take these truths at their human size. She now mines giant lessons in social policy with her miniaturist's tools. While there is validity to Quindlen's view that our media culture devalues the heart in favor of the mind, her solution is to ignore the mind entirely, bringing only her heart to questions that one simply can't feel one's way through. "Think about what it's like when you get to the checkout and you don't have enough money to pay for what you've bought," she admonished President Clinton in a May 1993 column chiding him for avoiding promised cuts in federal spending. "You put back the things you don't absolutely positively need. Maybe that sounds simplistic. But it's how the people who employ you live day to day. And maybe simplistic, or at least simple, is what you're missing right now." Or maybe the political choices required to cut federal spending aren't simple. Similarly, on Bosnia, she has made the tough call that Clinton should . . . do something. Because "stopping the slaughter, foiling genocide is the right thing." But actually determining *how* the United States should intervene—that's one of those brute details she leaves to the men to figure out.

Quindlen deliberately eschews the detached, Olympian language of most op-ed writers; what she didn't want, she once wrote, was to be "a woman doing a bad imitation of a man twice a week on the Op-Ed page." But for some reason this leaves her not with the more tactile or concrete language one can imagine a columnist claiming as the adult woman's discourse—the kind of language at which Barbara Ehrenreich, for example, excels—but with the verbal tics of the perky A student she once was. "Oh, pooh," she writes, and "Phooey, boys and girls."

Beneath Quindlen's breezy insistence that she brings a different lens to the great issues of the day, one can make out the presence of that A student working very, very hard to get it right. Her columns tend to build toward neat, homiletic conclusions:

"As much as laws, it's love that does it," she writes, in urging tolerance of homosexuality.

"Knowledge comes from discussion," she hazards, in condemning Republican rhetoric in the 1992 campaign, "not conclusion and exclusion."

"Ideas should be freely exchanged," she ventures, approving the First Amendment, "because you can learn a lot of good stuff from bad stuff."

Because of this tentative quality, "Public & Private" falls especially short in areas that call for true opinions, as opposed to the exploration of emotions or attitudes. During the Persian Gulf War, for example, Quindlen wrote about national self-esteem and the feelings of soldiers and their loved ones. She wrote, ad nauseam, about her own and the nation's ambivalence. Her collection of op-ed columns includes, all told, eleven vaguely pacifist columns on the war, but not one of them actually argues that the United States should not have waged it. Her column shows an airy, almost Reaganesque disdain for the realm of facts. ("Certain truths," she told one newspaper interviewer, "cannot be told simply by fact.") About welfare, for example, she writes, "The percentage of whites on public assistance is almost identical with the percentage of blacks." If one charitably assumes this is a mistake rather than a lie—probably she meant to say that the percentage of welfare recipients who are white is almost the same as the percentage who are black—one can still grant the legitimacy of the point she is trying to make, that welfare is not a program that serves only or primarily blacks. But it remains a pretty elementary mistake.

In a shrewd dissection of Quindlen's methods, Karen Lehrman has written in the New Republic that, "Quindlen can't seem to strike a balance between empathy and analysis. Instead she self-consciously refuses to discuss the issues, abstract and practical, at stake in the debate, and assumes that bringing her sensibility to bear on the thoughts and the feelings of the central character is revelation enough." But despite her faith in the telling specific, the personal story that illuminates the large public issue, her vignettes tend to obscure rather than clarify. While heaping appropriate scorn on conservative stereotypes such as the shiftless woman who breeds to stay on welfare, she meets those canards with images of equal simplicity. All her welfare recipients are beatific moms stymied only by the difficulty of finding affordable child care; her abortion seekers are almost invariably thoughtful, rueful victims of forces beyond their control.

To be sure, any good opinion writer is grounded in a coherent intellectual stance. But the interesting ones don't shrink from offending fans when their thinking yields conclusions at variance with liberal or conservative dogma. Thus Michael Kinsley, though liberal and pro-abortion rights, argues that *Roe v. Wade* is bad law, and William Safire has a broad libertarian streak that often puts him in the company of the ACLU. But Quindlen almost never strays from liberal orthodoxy. Indeed, she seems to pick the topics that are matters of most settled opinion among liberals, the ones that hold the least threat of provoking a new thought in writer or reader. Condoms in the schools, tolerance for gays, jobs for the inner city are good; homelessness, bigotry, and date rape are bad. Even within these orthodoxies, it is at least theoretically possible for a columnist to draw blood. When Quindlen sounds a satisfying note, it tends to be when she gives voice to a more unruly feminism. In one of her best (and best-known) columns, she excoriated her own paper for its bizarrely shoddy profile of the woman who alleged that William Kennedy Smith had raped her in Palm Beach. But on most days, in offering up her work as an exemplar of the Woman's View, Quindlen advances the depressing proposition that the female voice combines a ringing moral certainty with a stunning intellectual timidity.

Quindlen's prominence at the *Times*—both within the paper and as the jewel in its multicultural crown—represents the triumph of one strand in a long-running debate: between "equity" feminism (the camp that has sought a gender-neutral world, focusing on such concrete issues as equal pay and legal rights) and the more Utopian "difference" feminists (who argue from a belief that women and men are profoundly different creatures, and that one of feminism's missions is to bring women's finer mode of moral reasoning to the cold climate of male achievement). This summary does violence to the subtleties of the debate. But to the extent that this conflict is being thrashed out in organs of middlebrow culture such as American newsrooms, it is on just such a simplistic level. And one side—the side represented by Quindlen's fond visions of female superiority—is clearly winning.

This kind of feminism has its counterpart in debates over newsroom representation of African Americans and other minorities. In this view, it is important to hire and advance women and minority members, not for the inherent fairness of opening up the workplace but so that each of those groups can represent its own at the councils of power, so that women can write about women, blacks can sensitize their editors to the concerns of blacks, and so on. Ever since Arthur Sulzberger Jr. became publisher of the *New York Times* in January 1992, this whole constellation of "diversity" issues has obsessed the newspaper of record. Sulzberger, forty-two, hopes to make his mark on the *Times* by bringing democracy to its newsroom and cultural sensitivity to its pages, saying, "We can no longer offer our readers a predominantly white, straight, male vision of events and say that we, as journalists, are doing our jobs."

At its best, Sulzberger's new broom has meant a long-overdue recognition that white men shouldn't take all the prizes. He has tied management bonuses to minority recruitment and has placed a clear priority on lessening the climate of fear and autocracy in the newsroom. But at its worst, "diversity" has led to the plague of political correctness in the paper's coverage of certain issues relating to race, sexual orientation, and gender. Internally, one longtime staffer says, Sulzberger's touchy-feely philosophy has "made things worse and more strange than they've ever been." Editors are summoned to sensitivity seminars, including a five-day session last year for which the required homework included reading *Volunteer Slavery*, Jill Nelson's angry account of her experiences as a black woman at the *Washington Post*. Even business-side employees are urged, in memos from president and general manager Russell Lewis, to cultivate "Leadership Competencies" such as "Nurturing" and "Self-Improvement." "There's a lot of hugging at the *New York Times* now," says one manager. "I've been hugged by people I don't even want to shake hands with."

The problem with the *Times'* new concept of the newsroom as a representative government is its inherent condescension toward the system's component parts. If women are hired, implicitly, to bring to the newsroom a finer moral discernment or more humane style of working, then the long journey of feminism has brought us full circle back to the Nice Girl, charged with civilizing the men around her. To Anna Quindlen, whose future at the *Times* now seems limitless.

Given Sulzberger's clear determination to boost more women into senior management, Quindlen is constantly mentioned as a candidate to become managing editor or even executive editor someday. "There's to some degree an atmosphere around the newsroom of waiting for Anna," says an editor. "Waiting to see what she decides to do." Quindlen's logical opening would come in about three years, when Gene Roberts, the managing editor recently hired from outside the *Times* as a placeholder, retires. But most students of *Times* politics believe that, because of Quindlen's unconventional career path, she would probably have to accept another editing job in the interim, in the range of posts just below the level of managing editor. Which means Anna Quindlen may have to face the conflict she has so successfully finessed all these years. Can she be the mother she wants to be to three kids, the youngest of them now five, while doing a job that for most people lasts until at least seven or eight o'clock at night? Many of Quindlen's friends believe that were it not for this dilemma she would relish the chance to be the first woman to hold one of the two top jobs at the *New York Times*. "There is not a scintilla of doubt in my mind that she would like to do that," says a friend. "It's the big brass ring."

Quindlen would certainly be a controversial choice. She has never been a foreign correspondent, never worked in the *Times'* Washington bureau; she spent just two years as a deputy metropolitan editor. She might also serve as a lightning rod for all the paper's internal turmoil over diversity. "Anna is a big champion of that— 'Take Our Daughters to Work Day' and so on," says one editor.

"That is really gagging a lot of people here, and she'd have to transcend all that." But even some of Quindlen's detractors believe she could be a very good editor. "To be bluntly honest, I don't like Anna very much, but I think it would probably be a pretty good thing for the paper if she became managing editor," says one. "Because I think she's smart, and she's talented."

Her colleagues point out that before she became the legendary Anna Quindlen, Woman Columnist, she was admired by her peers as a reporter—tenacious, competitive, with an inborn sense of story— and widely liked as an editor.

"She's a good newspaper person," summarizes a colleague. This, in a newsroom, is the ultimate praise. Tellingly, it is a term with no gender.*

—*September 1994*

---

*Shortly after this article appeared, Quindlen gave up her *Times* column to write fiction full-time. She later became a columnist for *Newsweek*. Although Quindlen never climbed onto the management track at the *Times*, another woman—Jill Abramson—subsequently rose to the number-two position at the *Times*, sharing that status, and the title "managing editor," with a man (John Geddes).

THE END OF THE AFFAIR

(LAWRENCE WALSH)

He looked older than usual this Christmas Eve, greeting midnight not at home with the wife he had spent so much time away from but in the studios of Oklahoma City's ABC affiliate, KOCO-TV. Most days, buttoned into the vest of one of his gray or navy suits, he seemed far younger than his eighty-one years. But on this night, the rigidly contained man who had led the Iran-Contra investigation for more than six years had shed his vest, and with it, somehow, a portion of his crisp self-control. President George H. W. Bush had just pardoned former secretary of defense Caspar W. Weinberger less than two weeks before Weinberger's trial was to have started, along with five other men convicted or indicted for their roles in the Iran-Contra affair, wiping out with one gesture all of the independent counsel's pending cases.* Lawrence Walsh was ready to let loose, on

---

*For reasons discussed in this piece, the country's collective memory of Iran-Contra tends to be sketchy. The following précis is as short as I can manage.

The Iran-Contra scandal, which came to light at the end of 1986, involved a series of secret arms deals engineered by the Reagan White House. Anti-tank and anti-aircraft missiles were sold, via Israel, to Iran in exchange for the release of American hostages held by the Iranian-supported terrorist group Hezbollah in Lebanon. The money the White House raised from the arms sales was then diverted to support the Contras, a guerrilla army bent on overthrowing the Marxist Sandinista government of Nicaragua. Both transactions

Nightline, some of the passionate anger he had concealed so carefully for so long. In response to the pardoned man's complaints that Walsh had abused his powers, Walsh said they demonstrated that Weinberger "lied just as readily to the media as he lied to Congress. He's making it quite clear that his first line of defense when he has a troublesome problem is to lie."

This was inflammatory language, the voice of fury, not the calm voice of the prosecutor who must never seem too eager to wield the wrath of the state. Earlier in the day Walsh had revealed that President Bush, like Weinberger, had made notes at the time of Iran-Contra that had only recently been turned over to the independent counsel. Walsh had referred to Bush's "own misconduct"—an explosive phrase coming from a federal prosecutor conducting an open investigation—and had hinted darkly that Bush might soon find himself targeted for investigation. When Ted Koppel asked him why he thought the White House had revealed the notes now, after waiting so long, Walsh snapped, "Well, my first cynical thought was, 'It's after the election.'"

---

violated federal law. The first may have sped the release of three hostages, but three additional Americans were taken hostage shortly thereafter. The second was eventually mooted when Congress voted to resume the Contra funding it had earlier prohibited. Although the Contras never achieved military victory, war-weary Nicaraguan voters turned out the Sandinista government in 1990. Sixteen years later they voted the Sandinistas back in. By then the Contras had disbanded for good.

The scandal's principal figures were Oliver North, a charismatic National Security Council aide, and the two national security advisors he served under, Robert McFarlane and John Poindexter. North and Poindexter received criminal convictions in connection with the scandal, but both convictions were later overturned on procedural grounds. McFarlane was convicted and then pardoned (along with Weinberger) by president George H. W. Bush. President Reagan, who approved the arms sales and possibly the diversion, emerged relatively unscathed from the scandal, largely by projecting an elderly man's air of mental confusion. (This was eight years before Reagan's Alzheimer's diagnosis.)

To some of Walsh's admirers, this performance—and an equally blistering appearance earlier in the day on the *MacNeil/Lehrer NewsHour*—represented a justified sense of outrage and perhaps a principled decision to fight fire with fire: to answer a palpably political pardon with a calculatedly political denunciation. To his critics, on the other hand, this was the smoking gun—proof positive that Walsh was, as Senate minority leader Bob Dole has long argued, "completely out of control," an angry, stubborn old man bent only on producing an important scalp to vindicate his $39 million investigation. But in most viewers who watched him with an open mind, Walsh's responses on that day probably evoked conflicting feelings. A certain amount of outrage seemed not only understandable but appropriate, given that Bush was abruptly aborting an investigation that Walsh had painstakingly developed over so many years. Yet there was, as there has been before, something discomfiting in Walsh's manner. Was it a hint of self-righteousness? A slightly Old Testament tone of retribution? Watching it, one couldn't escape the feeling that Walsh perceived himself as the Last Virtuous Man. Welcome to one of the deeper mysteries of Iran-Contra: the character of Lawrence Edward Walsh.

When Walsh was appointed independent counsel on December 19, 1986, he was an acclaimed choice. For one thing, he had a distinguished career history. He had been a fighter in the squeaky-clean prosecutorial army of New York racket-buster Thomas E. Dewey in the 1930s and later a key aide to Dewey in the governor's mansion; a federal judge and the second-in-command of Eisenhower's Justice Department; a president of the American Bar Association and for twenty years a senior litigator at one of Wall Street's most august law firms—a role in which he lost only a single case at trial. His profile as a faithful Republican, combined with what all of his former colleagues described as a disciplined, almost Victorian sense of duty, made him seem the ideal man to untangle the nation's gravest constitutional crisis since Watergate. But the longer his investigation has gone on, the more Walsh has come under fire. In six years, he has sent only one man to prison. He secured eleven convictions, seven through plea bargains. But his two most important convictions were reversed on appeal; six other figures in his investigation—four already convicted of crimes—were pardoned by President Bush on Christmas Eve. In all this time, he has never been able to submit to a jury's scrutiny the central misdeeds of Iran-Contra—the sale of arms to Iran in violation of the Arms Export Control Act and the violation of the Boland Amendment forbidding covert assistance to the Contras—only the bits and subparts and subsequent efforts by the defendants to cover up those deeds.

Most of this bleak result is not Walsh's fault. He has labored under the burdens of congressional weakness, of outright stalling and subtle obstruction by two Republican administrations, of allegedly false testimony by the key figures in the investigation, and of unlucky breaks in the appeals courts. But still there is debate over the choices Walsh has made in meeting these burdens. And the most interesting debate is not the one that rages between partisan critics and passionate defenders, but the one that quietly occupies the minds of his friends, admirers, and former colleagues from the counsel's office—those who believe, with Walsh, that Iran-Contra represented genuine threats to America's way of governing itself, who would still like to see Walsh meet some definition of success yet who acknowledge wondering whether he has pursued his investigation past the point of reason. Their debate always runs aground, eventually, on an unrecognized subtext: that Walsh's was inevitably an impossible job. Although he was appointed only to pursue the criminal dimension of the Iran-Contra affair, he was subtly assigned, too, a responsibility for policing its far murkier moral and political dimensions. As the years spun by, Walsh's investigation became the repository for all the leftover grievances and expectations roiled by Iran-Contra. Walsh became the designated conscience for America's inability to come to a common understanding of what Iran-Contra was and whether it mattered. As long as he has still been out there, furrowing his distinguished brow over all those details the rest of us have long forgotten, then we haven't had to acknowledge how content we have been to see the whole business slide, unresolved, into the misty past.

It is not Walsh's fault that we have given him this burden. But extensive interviews with people who know him well suggest that he was tragically well suited for the job, the perfect candidate to bear such a burden in the heaviest possible way. He brought to Washington a quirky, rigidly thorough approach to the law; an outsize faith in his own vision of how government should work and in his own moral standing to enforce it; and an otherworldly stamina that has always blurred the boundary, in his life, between duty and obsession. He has been compared to Shakespeare's King Lear; to Victor Hugo's Inspector Javert; to Captains Ahab and Queeg. The seafarers make tempting, if unfair, comparisons, for if Lawrence Edward Walsh has any passion beyond the gray lure of the law, it is a love of the sea. But the most apt analogy for him is not Ahab, hunting his great white whale, or Queeg, bent on searching out a culprit who doesn't exist. It is the Ancient Mariner of the Coleridge poem: a man condemned forever to collar reluctant passersby, without resting, and tell them of the horrific journey from which he has just barely returned. Perhaps only Walsh could have summoned the drive to pursue Iran-Contra so far. And only Iran-Contra could have made Walsh's virtues seem indistinguishable from his flaws. When the granite nature of this man met the amorphous fog of Iran-Contra and all the political confusion it swathed in its mist, it was almost inevitable that Walsh would come out the loser.

Walsh's critics have made much of his "posh" offices in a fancy downtown office building, one of the enormous faux-marble behemoths built during Washington's building boom of the 1980s. "Just ignore the chandeliers," says a caustic Mary Belcher, the office's spokeswoman, as she escorts a visitor through the office. In fact, everything about these quarters has the air of the backwater. Once upon a time, young lawyers by the dozen pulled every string they had developed from their Ivy League law schools and their federal court clerkships to earn a spot on Walsh's team. Now the legal staff has been whittled to eight. Though they talk desultorily of completing their "ongoing investigation" into Bush's failure to turn over earlier his vice-presidential notes about Iran-Contra, little remains for Walsh but to craft a final report summing up his long, frustrating job.

A visitor approaching the office of the independent counsel must first stop at a dingy reception room, where a uniformed member of the Federal Protective Service is shuffling his D.C. Lottery entries for the day. The airless room, featuring nothing more welcoming than a dirty tan carpet and a run-down couch, is cramped by stacks of Xerox paper and miscellaneous brown packing boxes. Behind the door that sets off the "Sensitive Compartmented Information Facility" in which the staff is sequestered, a slightly cleaner drabness prevails. But the greatest surprise in the office is Walsh himself. His greeting makes him seem gentle, self-effacing, and as warm as a very shy man can manage to be. Can this nice old gent really be the brooding inquisitor of Bob Dole's broadsides? He has the diffident man's awkward, somewhat apologetic laugh, especially when he talks about himself; from time to time, he actually blushes. In photographs, the angular planes of his face and his deep-set green eyes give him the imposing, Old Testament look of the man his young colleagues all call "Judge Walsh." In person, he is the man his friends know as "Ed," a slight fellow with a smile charmingly flawed by an asymmetry in the lengths of his front teeth.

"You begin to wonder," he explains mildly, in the odd second-person form that seems the only way he can speak comfortably about himself, "is there any way you can make your critics understand the enormity of the job, and why you can't control the timing? You're at the mercy of the people who produce the records. You're at the mercy of the witnesses who take their time in deciding to tell you all the facts, and you're at the mercy of the courts who schedule your cases, and who schedule your appeals. But how do you explain all this, particularly if somebody doesn't want to listen?"

His disarming manner is especially startling to someone who has spent weeks interviewing former colleagues of Walsh's, from both this office and earlier days. With a few exceptions, the sad fact is that people who have worked for Walsh like him far less than people who have not. As a litigator, he is seen—usually approvingly—as relentless and tough; as a man, he is almost universally described with words like *cold* and *aloof*. "He was not the kind of guy you'd want to spend the weekend with," says one former associate counsel. "I think he's endured far more abuse than he deserves, but he's not a cozy guy." "There were people of his generation from whom he sought advice, from time to time," says another former colleague. "But I never thought he had friends. I was very sorry for him, frankly."

He has almost never lunched with colleagues who have rotated through the office—most of whom were, in any case, forty or fifty years his junior. He has a sandwich every day at his desk, alone. Though he has five children, his office contains no personal mementos of any kind. He had been in Washington for six or eight months, according to Walsh associate Jim Wieghart, before he had dinner with a daughter who was then living there. More than one former colleague on the investigation described his or her essential memory of Walsh as a mental photograph of the former judge standing alone, behind his desk, brooding. Wieghart, a former spokesman for the office who now serves it as a consultant, is one of the colleagues who knows and likes Walsh best. "It's very difficult to penetrate the personal Lawrence Walsh," he says. "I think he just limits that part of his life." When Walsh is in Washington, he trudges a steady path from the Watergate Hotel, where he stays, to the Office of Independent Counsel on 13th Street, where he works, and then back to the Watergate, where he works some more. He does not go out to dinner with any of the eminent acquaintances he has made in Washington in the course of his long career. He does not go to the pool and swim laps, as he would at home. He orders room service. One lawyer who worked for Walsh in the earliest stages of the Iran-Contra investigation remembers dropping off papers for him at the hotel, late at night. "And he was still working—in a coat and tie, at the little hotel desk, as though this was what everybody does at eleven o'clock at night when they're seventy-five years old." That, of course, was six years ago; now Walsh is eighty-one. Yet in the morning, he rises to two or three more hours' work before he heads back to the office. These days, with his investigation winding down, he can spend every second or third week at his home in Oklahoma City. But for most of this time he has been a weekend commuter. Of his monkish existence in Washington, he says, "I've always done that when I've worked out of town. It saves—I was going to say, 'It saves you from thinking.' If you're just thinking about the case, it saves you a lot of trouble."

Though he may be given to simple, plain-as-a-board observations, Walsh is hardly a simple man. His young associates on the Iran-Contra case learned early that Walsh has a quirky, stiff-necked pickiness about his surroundings. Once a colleague brought in a box of doughnuts to enliven one of the long staff meetings that Walsh favored. As recounted in *Opening Arguments,* a book by former associate counsel Jeffrey Toobin, "When Walsh walked in and saw the box, he growled, 'Get rid of those.'" Walsh's judgments on people can be swift and merciless. He referred habitually to a certain defendant's lawyer as "that hopeless windbag," according to one attorney. And for reasons none of his associates could understand, he took a particular dislike to Albert Hakim, one of the middlemen in the Iran-Contra transactions, above all the other defendants the office prosecuted.* So fixed was this prejudice that it was on display in a recent interview, when Walsh raised his name with an expression of particular distaste, then waved it away with a flushed face and a dismissive gesture.

Walsh's temper is legendary. Wieghart describes it as "his occasional wild moodiness," while others talk of receiving a withering glare for a fact unmentioned or a question unasked. When various federal agencies would drag their feet in producing the documents Walsh needed, he would suggest—with apparent seriousness—that the office prosecute the government employee he saw as responsible. "There would be a bureaucratic logjam or something, and he'd say, 'We ought to indict the guy,'" recalls Bryan Blaney, a former associate counsel. "It was like a goblin came out in the conference room," says another of Walsh's former colleagues. Walsh seemed so serious

---

*An Iranian-born businessman, Hakim acted as interpreter and handled various aspects of both the arms sales and the diversion for North. He pled guilty to a misdemeanor charge involving the building of a security fence for North's Virginia home and was fined $5,000. Hakim died in 2003.

that lawyers new to the office found themselves deeply disturbed by these episodes. But more experienced colleagues had learned to take them in stride. Everyone who described Walsh's temper to me stressed that the office never did, in the end, indict any of the people whose names came up in this fashion. "We never did anything close to that wacky," says one lawyer. "But we had to spend considerable time talking him out of it."

In fact, a more common complaint among Walsh's former associates is that he was *too* deliberative in pondering the office's indictments, supervising endless debates among the staff and putting off decisions for as long as possible. "He had a hard time making up his mind. About a lot of things—very important things," says one former prosecutor who witnessed the office's lengthy debate over when and on what grounds to indict Oliver North. "Your reaction might be, those are all important issues. Absolutely, and they deserve to be thoroughly discussed. But I think a lot of people in that office think they were discussed ad nauseam, again and again and again and again—without ever pushing the ball down the field toward an answer." Wieghart acknowledges that some of Walsh's indictment decisions have dragged on, and says, "I almost went mad" over the North indictment. "Practically every lawyer in this office has gotten to the point of coming in and putting a knife to his own chest and saying, 'If we don't do it today I'm going to end it all.'"

It is as if these two sides of Judge Walsh—the infinitely careful senior statesman and the volcanically impulsive man who reveals himself among his trusted aides—exist in perfect balance.

Another facet of Walsh's character that is mentioned by a majority of former associates from both the Iran-Contra era and his earlier work at New York's Davis Polk & Wardwell is his marked, rather cruel perfectionism. "He's absolutely unforgiving as a taskmaster," says one former associate from the law firm. "No amount of work is too great. No mistakes are permitted. Everyone is expected to work around the clock. Before we filed a brief, he would hold it up to the light and make sure the lines all began in relatively the same place on the page, so it wouldn't be too distracting to the eye, to find a

different starting place on each new page." In one incident that became legend at Davis Polk, Walsh asked an associate to postpone his
honeymoon so that he could appear as a witness in a side proceeding
related to a case then at trial. When the young lawyer pleaded to be
excused, Walsh asked the judge for a court order compelling his colleague to appear. This plan was derailed only when the opposing
counsel told the judge what Walsh was up to.

But even many of those least fond of Walsh agree on one virtue:
that his essential motivations are good ones. "In some respects, because of his perfectionism, he's easy to demonize," says a former
Davis Polk colleague. "But he always struck me as an extremely
straight arrow. . . . I guess you can argue about his means in some instances, and maybe you can argue that he was too sure he was right
in some instances, but he would never, ever do something he didn't
think was right on the merits." Walsh was brought up in the Eastern
Establishment party tradition that favored economic conservatism
but had a quasi-liberal faith in the possibilities of good government.
Thomas E. Dewey, whose gubernatorial administration biographer
Richard Norton Smith described as having a "slightly gray tint of
excellence," set Walsh an example of rectitude in public office. He
carried it into service on various state boards, including a commis-
sion appointed to end corruption on New York City's waterfront;
onto the federal bench, to which Eisenhower appointed him in
1954; and into the Justice Department, where he became the officer
chiefly responsible for, among other things, guiding the infant Civil
Rights Division. Walsh is, of course, a man of the world. He has
never been above string pulling—using the sterling connections of a
former deputy attorney general, for example—on behalf of his
clients. In the early 1970s he was able to help ITT Corp., a Davis
Polk client, settle a major antitrust suit by the Justice Department
on advantageous terms, in part through a famous "Dear Dick" letter
to deputy attorney general Richard Kleindienst. But such contacts
fall within the mores of the old-fashioned Republican gentlemen's
club, a very different matter from lying to Congress, in Walsh's
mind, or from any of the other extravagantly ideological shenani-
gans of the Reagan era. The material of Iran-Contra deeply engaged

and even shocked this man, who still refers to himself unblushingly as "a Dewey Republican."

Some of those who know Walsh charge that his moral clarity borders on moral arrogance. "He has a certainty of rightness about him," says Chesterfield Smith, a Miami attorney who, like Walsh, is a past president of the ABA. "He believes that his motives are pure, and he questions judgments that are inconsistent with his. Therefore . . . he respects his own opinions far more than he does anybody else's." Others characterize his clarity as a kind of innocence. "I think that what was most impressive to me was that he was a man of great moral uprightness," says one former associate counsel, "but also a man of some simplicity. The core issues weren't complex: the core issue was that these people had lied, when they were in a position to tell the truth. . . . They just lied outright. That was incomprehensible to him."

If Walsh judges others harshly, it is apparently no more than he does to himself. Colleagues remember with a degree of puzzlement how burdened—even tormented—he seemed by his responsibilities. "He seemed a tortured man, to me," says one former colleague. "Tortured in a good way, if there is such a thing. He wanted to do the right thing. He wanted to do the responsible thing. He wanted to do the correct thing." This sense of duty was especially keen, former colleagues say, when Walsh contemplated the elderly men he saw as his peers on the legal scene. Men such as the three judges of the U.S. Court of Appeals who appointed him, and men like the late judge Gerhard Gesell, who tried the case of Lt. Col. Oliver North.

"I don't think I ever saw him enjoy it," says a former associate counsel, of Walsh's tenure in the office. "He was appointed to do a duty that was a very important duty, and he was going to do it if it killed him. But I can't think of a single day when he enjoyed it."

It pays to remember that Walsh is a man for whom duty and gratification are indistinguishable, conflated years ago as he grew to manhood. Walsh was born in Nova Scotia, in the small town of Port Maitland at the mouth of the Bay of Fundy, a scene he remembers with a vibrant specificity. "It's a fishing hamlet, actually, it's not even a village. A school and two general stores and a post office." The sea was in his blood. His maternal grandfather—one of the most important figures in his life, according to a friend—was a sea captain whose service dated back to the age of square-rigged ships. Though the family moved away from Canada when Walsh was only two, he returned every summer until he was twelve to stay with his grandparents.

Walsh's father was a small-town doctor who relocated to Queens in New York to study ear, eye, nose, and throat medicine as a specialty, and then stayed to establish a practice there. So Walsh was raised in Flushing, when it was more like a village than a part of New York City. He remembers a happy boyhood, with parents who "weren't harsh, but they were strict." And yet, his self-descriptions yield a theme of financial peril. Soon after Walsh turned fifteen, his father died suddenly, leaving him, his mother, and his sister with a shaky financial foundation. Lawrence worked his way through college and law school at Columbia University, clerking in a bookstore, doing Christmas duty at the post office, earning his meals by working two hours every day in the cafeteria. Summers he put out to sea—to Germany, Puerto Rico, Buenos Aires, Manila, mostly on steamships, working as everything from a bellboy to a seaman. He was supposed to be an engineer, he says; that's what his father had wanted. But "I didn't do very well in math, so I couldn't be an engineer." Instead he switched, during his undergraduate years, to prelaw.

Walsh wasn't looking for the high-wire career he has had. He was only hoping, he says, for a career in trusts and estates law. This remark is typical of the humility that runs through all his conversation about himself. This is not the blithe self-deprecation that marks many accomplished people, but a powerful, seemingly unconscious belief that in his life he has only narrowly escaped failure. "I wasn't a good student in either place," he says of college and law school. "I was good enough to get into college, but in college I really became much more interested in extracurricular activities than I should have." (Chiefly swimming and rowing, at which he was, he says, "hopelessly outclassed.") "Law school was a lot more serious than college," he continues, "and my first year at law school I did not do well." He graduated from law school in 1935, while the Depression dragged on, "and it took a long time to find a job." Again and again, he alludes to the harsh lessons he learned in the Depression. His most vivid, most personal language recounts his anxiety of these earliest years, when his future seemed, in his word, "gloomy." When he did find a job, as a special assistant attorney general on a Brooklyn bribery investigation, he worried constantly about losing it. He determined to become the hardest-working young lawyer in the city.

At one point in his early career—even after his first marriage, to Maxine Winton, a year out of law school—"I remember figuring out to myself that if I had one night at home a week, it was better than average," he says. As he rose through his series of impressive jobs, he became no more gentle with himself. It was all very well to have a federal judgeship; to become chairman of the ABA; to be elected to Columbia's board of trustees; to be appointed to the second chair at the negotiating table in the Paris peace talks, as Walsh was in 1969. Even after he became a senior litigator at Davis Polk, doggedness remained the keynote of his legal style. From 1961 to 1981, when the firm's standard retirement policy forced him to leave, Walsh did civil litigation for corporate clients such as AT&T, R. J. Reynolds, General Motors, and the chemical firm Richardson-Merrell. A large corporation that hired him typically had a very important case, with a very large potential stake or liability; the kind of case in which time and money were no objects in pursuit of victory. Walsh was famous for researching and pondering every possible question or document or wrinkle that might arise at trial. While he was capable of very imaginative argument, former colleagues say, the essence of his style was his thoroughness, his insistence on 100 percent certainty. "A lot of lawyers believe . . . that improvisation is the core of litigation," says a former colleague from the law firm. "But Judge Walsh is entirely the opposite. A lot of lawyers would think Judge Walsh is from another planet."

Another former Davis Polk colleague says, "I'm not sure he ever had the confidence to say, 'This is the direction we're going to go, and we've done enough to get there.' . . . Some people are confident enough to make a decision after looking at three-quarters or seven-eighths of the facts, and are willing to live with the risk of knowing that there's a one-eighth still out there. He was not a man who ever liked making judgments of that kind." This person observes that the habits Walsh has brought to Iran-Contra are the habits of a lifetime. "I'm not surprised at a single thing," he says. "I'm not surprised that he dug in, that it took him a long, long time, that he spent a lot of money, that he has chased everything to the end. It doesn't surprise me a bit. That's the way he litigates. . . . He did it with every case he ever had here."

Walsh admits that, well into his sixties, his memories of the Depression pushed him to take on more cases than a normal man could quite handle. "It never is a perfect balance," he says. "As between being light and being overloaded, there was a certain amount of comfort being overloaded. . . . I go back to the Depression, that reaching for security that is there, and it becomes instinctive." Naturally, other parts of life fell by the wayside. He has, however, always kept up his exercise, and for years he sailed small boats in the summer, off Cape Cod. The year after Walsh's first wife died of cancer, in 1964, he married his second, Mary Alma Porter. But beyond these scant facts, even close friends and colleagues tend to be stumped for information about Walsh's life outside the office. "I've never seen another part of his life that he's interested in, or that occupies him in any positive way," recalls a former colleague from the independent counsel's office. But is Walsh's pattern so different from the life of any very successful, hard-driving man? Only in the clarity with which he lets you know that his drive is rooted not in arrogance and ego, but in an early sense of inadequacy. Walsh suggests this answer most starkly when he is asked about his reputation for aloofness. "I blame it all on law school," he says, without missing a beat. "When you waste your opportunities in law school, you have to work extra hard for the rest of your life." He pinkens, laughs a little, as he so bluntly reduces his life story to this simple calculus of crime and punishment. But then he rushes on, with the eagerness of the un-introspective man stumbling on self-knowledge. "That started out as a joke," he says, "and now I begin to wonder if there's some truth to it."

It's an interesting comment on the puzzle of Iran-Contra that among Walsh's most thoughtful critics, there are diametrically opposed opinions about where he might have gone wrong. He should have indicted Lt. Col. Oliver North and former national security advisor John Poindexter earlier than he did (some say), before Congress could ruin his case by granting them immunity in exchange for their testimony at congressional hearings in the summer of 1987. No (say others), the important point is that he should have insisted on prosecuting a broad conspiracy charge, as he initially tried to do. No, he should never have tried to prosecute the conspiracy at all. He should have stuck with charging perjury and other obstructions of congressional investigations, and then called it a day.

He shouldn't have given a plea bargain to Robert C. "Bud" Mc-Farlane, who, though a chief participant in both the arms-for-hostages sales and the secret funding of the Contras, was allowed to plead guilty only to four misdemeanors (and who, despite his promises of cooperation, later helped to torpedo Walsh's case against North).

He should have given immunity to Albert Hakim . . . .

He should have given immunity to Joseph Fernandez* . . . .

Behind each one of these opinions is a valid strategic argument, for anyone intrepid enough to follow it through the twisty maze of the case. But almost from its first rumblings, Iran-Contra developed an arcane quality, making it the exclusive property of a small gang of initiates, conspiracy buffs, and professional Iran-Contraologists. It involved so many countries, so many different operations, so many

---

*CIA station chief in Costa Rica and a key North contact with the Contras. Fernandez was indicted for conspiracy, obstruction, and making false statements. A judge dismissed the indictment, upholding Fernandez's claim that his defense would require disclosure of classified information.

layers of untruth laid down, first in the course of the arms-for-hostages and funds-for-the-Contras dealings themselves, and then later in the course of the investigations. The very complexity of the arguments used to second-guess Walsh draws a compelling picture of how difficult a job he was assigned and how unlikely he was ever to achieve something that consensus could call success.

Some of this difficulty grew out of the obstacles that came with the territory of Walsh's investigation—particularly the inconstancy of a Congress that couldn't make up its mind about how far it dared go in punishing a popular president. The joint congressional committees that investigated Iran-Contra set themselves a deadline that precluded a very thorough job. In return for striking deals with its witnesses that undermined Walsh's later prosecutions, Congress got very little. North was allowed to testify without prior questioning by the committees' investigators and to edit his diaries heavily before they were presented as evidence. And when faced with the antic patriotism North displayed in his testimony, most committee members lost their nerve. The chief fear of the congressional hunters was that they would actually catch their quarry. "They were very much afraid of Reagan's reputation, and that there would be a backlash if they got too close to him," says Georgetown law professor Sam Dash, who served as chief counsel to the Senate Watergate Committee. "The manner of their presentation, how they called their witnesses, and how they failed to thoroughly investigate, confused the public rather than cleared things up, so that at the end the public wasn't sure who the black hats were and who the white hats were. . . . At the end, the public was terribly confused as to what the Iran-Contra affair was all about."

Walsh was left with the heavy expectation that he would be able to get at the truth that the senators and representatives had not pressed for. One former staffer for the committees said, "A lot of [the committee members], I think, just threw up their hands and said, 'Walsh will have to get this; we'll never get it.'" The unspoken corollary was that it would also now be up to Walsh's investigation to achieve the moral conclusiveness the congressional hearings had not, to establish not just who had broken the law in Iran-Contra, but *why* it was wrong. But of course Walsh's assignment under the law was not to lay out a broad concept of Iran-Contra's importance; it was to prosecute specific crimes by specific individuals. And over time, it became clear that he could not prosecute the underlying events of Iran-Contra, only the efforts of administration officials to cover it up by destroying, altering, or withholding evidence, or by lying to various investigators, both before and after the arms sales became known. A significant obstacle was the amount of classified material involved in prosecuting officials from the nation's top national security circles. Walsh was forced to drop the most sweeping count of his indictment of North and Poindexter—a broad conspiracy charge attempting to establish that the Iran-Contra operation itself had been illegal—when North argued that he couldn't defend himself without the use of documents that the Reagan administration was unwilling to declassify. Many of the "secrets" the administration withheld were absurdly public facts, widely reprinted in newspapers around the world. But the Classified Information Procedures Act allowed White House and Justice Department intransigence to rule the day. Walsh's indictments and convictions over the years have shown that the crimes that can be proved here tend to be particular, date-specific, narrow offenses. Important crimes, in the scheme of constitutional law, that add up to genuine violations of congressional prerogatives, but not crimes that give an opportunity to present, in any coherent narrative, the kind of concerted lawlessness that lay at the heart of Iran-Contra.

The great irony in the way Congress abandoned its role to Walsh was that Congress itself was—or should have been—the complaining party in Iran-Contra. At issue were the Reagan administration's systematic efforts to circumvent the role in foreign relations that Congress derives from its power of the purse. "Iran-Contra was first and foremost a constitutional crisis," says Reid Weingarten, who was drafted by Walsh to handle the prosecution of middleman Richard Secord.* "Congress was the victim, and Congress dropped the ball."

---

*A retired air force major general and business partner of Albert Hakim, Secord pled guilty to lying to Congress in November 1989.

Or rather, passed it off to Walsh. But this was a setup: as much as it wanted to be relieved of its responsibility, it didn't especially want Walsh to succeed where it had failed. Some members have continued to support him and share his views of Iran-Contra's seriousness. But since 1987, many prominent members have edged further and further away from reckoning with Iran-Contra. In 1989 the Senate confirmed president George H. W. Bush's former vice presidential national security advisor Donald P. Gregg as ambassador to Korea, despite unresolved questions about whether he had known of North's secret operations to support the Contras. Then in 1991, former CIA deputy director Robert M. Gates was confirmed as director of central intelligence, despite conflicting testimony at his confirmation hearings over whether he had told the full truth about when and how he learned of North's activities. In each case, the confirmation was an admission that senators didn't really want to pursue Iran-Contra into the Bush White House—and a signal that association with the scandal no longer carried any taint.*

Clearly, a good part of the country shared this disinclination to know too much. On the one hand, national polls have shown overall support for Walsh's efforts. But on the other hand, voters in the presidential election of 1988 ignored considerable evidence that as vice president Bush had known of and supported the arms-for-hostages trade. A vast, silent political referendum had been held and had

---

*Covering Gates's confirmation hearing for the *Washington Post*, Marjorie took note of a "fortyish couple in matching yellow shirts" who wandered in to watch while Gates answered a question about Iran-Contra:

> On Gates talked, in tones as level as the land he came from. *Yes, sir. No, sir. I should have done more, sir.* After about ten minutes the couple was eyeing the clock; after fifteen, they were scuffling toward the door in the bent-over posture of children, gleeful but embarrassed, sneaking away from their chores. Off to the linear narratives of the Mall, the history people come to Washington to see: in which Lincoln follows Washington and dinosaurs live and then perish, where Apollo follows Mercury until man reaches the moon.

Two presidential administrations later, Gates sailed through Senate confirmation to replace Donald Rumsfeld as defense secretary.

concluded that, well, yes, Iran-Contra was bad. But not perhaps as bad as some other things. In the end there would be no serious political sanctions at all against an administration that presumed to hijack the prerogatives of Congress, if the executive was popular enough. It was over; it could be allowed to slip back into our wake, if only we didn't have to acknowledge too directly what we were winking at. Walsh alone ignored this consensus, because Walsh was not about politics. Only Walsh, with his anachronistic sense of duty, slogged on, insisting that it was a serious matter—a serious *crime*—for members of the executive branch to lie to Congress and other investigators. He had an assignment, which charged him to keep investigating for as long as he kept turning up possible crimes.

In the utilitarian political universe of Washington, consistency like Walsh's is distinctly suspect. It began to seem rigid of him to care so much. Hence the gathering critique of his efforts as vindictive, extreme. *Ideological.* Thus by June of last year, when he indicted Weinberger for lying about the existence of his extensive contemporaneous notes about the affair, Walsh's critics were able to depict him as a scalp hunter, determined to bag someone of Weinberger's lofty title. Hadn't Weinberger, after all, opposed the arms sales in the first place? Not only Sen. Warren Rudman, who had been the Republican co-chairman of the congressional joint investigating committees, but also Sen. Daniel Inouye, his Democratic counterpart, publicly questioned Walsh's wisdom in bringing the indictment. For them to give Walsh the benefit of the doubt, men like these would have had to sustain a sense of outrage that simply isn't thought productive in Washington; it has no functional benefit to them. And the rest of the country, in order to care, would have had to be able to pierce the curtain of complexity that surrounds the whole affair.

Except for the all-out partisans, most of the critics acknowledge the difficulties that have beset Walsh's investigation. They also grant the strange, self-perpetuating quality of an investigation that prosecutes a cover-up. The more Walsh investigated, the more people lied to him; the more people lied to him, the more he was duty bound to prosecute their obstructions. Yet even many Walsh sympathizers tend to feel that the length of his investigation has

undermined the credibility of his work. The most devastating comments to this effect come from former associates in the independent
counsel's office, half a dozen of whom spoke about their misgivings
for this story, on the condition that they be allowed to do so anony-
mously. Most decline to say precisely when he should have been
able to wrap it up, but they have watched Walsh make decisions
from up close, they say, and don't entirely trust him to move as
quickly or as fairly as he might. "I admire him because he is tough as
nails," says one former associate counsel. "On the other side, I . . .
was concerned about toughness being substituted for wisdom." "Especially since there are so few limitations on an independent counsel," says another, "it is important for an independent counsel to
show his own sense of limitations. And that's one area where Judge
Walsh could have shown a greater sense of constraint."

Some former associates hint, uncomfortably, that they believe
Walsh may have been unconsciously motivated to continue because
his own alternative—returning to Oklahoma City, a place where he
has few roots, and picking up a greatly truncated law practice—was
bleak. "Has he consciously extended his duties as independent
counsel because of that?" wonders one former colleague. "No, absolutely not. Would he be appalled if it were suggested to him? Absolutely. . . . Has it possibly been a factor? I can't say no." In fact,
Walsh resisted retiring in 1981, when he reached the age of seventy.
His firm's retirement policy was absolute. Not only did he have to
quit practice at Davis Polk, but he was not allowed to continue
practicing anywhere the firm could define as a competitive arena.
(Actually, he could have accepted a senior sinecure, becoming "of
counsel," to the firm; "which is a very nice arrangement," he sniffs,
"but you don't practice.") So he moved to Oklahoma City—which
was his wife's native city, but far from the Atlantic seaboard he
loved—in order to retain what he could of his professional life, joining the big firm of Crowe & Dunlevy there.

If fear of semiretirement may have been an unconscious contributor to the investigation's slowness, a more obvious one was Walsh's
civil litigation background. In addition to pondering his decisions for
a long time, "he would have people write a lot of memos about

things, and do work that seemed kind of busywork, and peripheral to what we should be doing," says one former Iran-Contra lawyer. "They were the dot-every-i, cross-every-t school of litigation, where you have to protect against every possible eventuality and know every possible argument that could be made. But as a practical matter, a lot of it was a waste of time." Critics of the independent counsel law have long complained that it is inherently unfair for the government to pursue a prosecution with the single-minded standards of a private litigator. A normal prosecutor, who operates in a universe where he must address a range of crimes, has built-in limitations on how far he can press a case. Practical decisions about relative costs and benefits—X more dollars spent on punishing white-collar crime mean X fewer dollars to spend on pursuing rapists, for example—are the essence of prosecutorial discretion. But Walsh, with an unlimited budget to pursue only one set of crimes, without making any judgments about the relative benefits, can go after his targets with the luxuriant thoroughness of a blue-chip hired gun. This is one of the points that Walsh's political enemies stress. And it must be said that he has given them ample rope with which to hang him, showing a certainty—especially where his budget is concerned—that borders on arrogance. If Washington has been too political in sweeping Iran-Contra under the rug, the opposite can be said of Walsh. In some of his actions, he has not been political enough.

In a recent General Accounting Office report, Walsh was cited for receiving overgenerous reimbursements from the government for enjoying such private-sector frills as his room at the Watergate—including reimbursements for days he kept the room for his law books and belongings but was not staying in Washington—and a routine use of first-class travel for his trips to Oklahoma City. Altogether, the report said, he had been compensated by at least $44,000 more than the reimbursement rate he was entitled to. The report did not challenge Walsh's claim that he had acted in good faith in these violations; in most cases, it said, he had relied on rulings by the Administrative Office of the U.S. Courts, which nominally supervises the finances of independent counsels. And today the government pays for neither extra nights at the Watergate nor for the difference between coach and first-class travel. (Walsh still flies first class, but says his frequent-flier mileage covers the difference.) He shrugs off criticism that his business expenses seem more in keeping with the regal standards of private lawyers than with what taxpayers can fairly expect to pay public servants. "The problem is that the Independent Counsel Act doesn't have any restrictions," says Walsh. "And the legislative history seemed to leave it to the judgment of the independent counsel." In his case, his manner suggests, that judgment is unassailably trustworthy.

More troubling still was the revelation that Walsh's office had spent $52,600 last December—before Bush's pardon of Weinberger—to perform a mock trial of the former defense secretary. Used to assess such things as the attitudes of the likely jury pool in a given trial setting and what lines of argument that population is likely to find appealing, mock trials are common tools among private lawyers, but almost unknown among government prosecutors. Given that Walsh was already under fire for his indictments of Weinberger *and* for the amount of money his investigation had cost, the expenditure played into the hands of the critics who argued that he would do anything to nail his defendant. When he is questioned about this, just a flash of the combative, thin-skinned Walsh is revealed. He says his critics made him do it. "From the time of the indictment, back in June, it seemed to me there's been a series of attacks on the office, on me, on [deputy independent counsel] Craig Gillen; and favorable statements about ex-secretary Weinberger. . . . All of these are factors and present problems in selecting juries and in developing an effective case. . . . The added problems caused by Senator Dole and those who've been criticizing us made it necessary," he concludes.

It was the Weinberger case, of course, that provided the most fateful example of Walsh's allergy to pragmatism. From the beginning, Walsh's adversaries had seized on the Weinberger case as a weapon. Given Weinberger's age (then seventy-four), his long government service, and his original opposition to the Iran-Contra dealings, it was easy for anyone not steeped in the facts of Walsh's investigation to see Weinberger as a sympathetic figure. When Walsh brought a revised indictment that included a reference to President Bush's presence at a crucial meeting and his support for the arms-for-hostages policy, and filed it only four days before the November election, he made it equally easy for others to question his motives. While there was a detailed legal rationale for bringing the indictment, its timing revealed a political obliviousness that went beyond principle and into the realm of deafness. It wasn't just that Walsh had failed to anticipate the furious publicity that would attend this indictment in the midst of a campaign. (Though according to associates, he was astonished by the controversy.) It was also a stark illustration that Walsh, sequestered inside his guarded office, had failed to understand the denial that permeates America's understanding of Iran-Contra. As Walsh was well aware, the Weinberger notes contained in the indictment didn't actually reveal anything new: earlier evidence— from contemporaneous records by the then secretary of state George Shultz, Poindexter, Bush aide Craig Fuller, and others—had also undermined Bush's claims to have been "out of the loop" concerning the trading of arms for hostages. But Walsh didn't seem to know that his fellow Americans had never chosen to accept this fact—not until he presented it to them at a moment when George Bush was deeply unpopular for other reasons.

Walsh insists that even if he had understood that he was dropping a bombshell into that pool of willful ignorance, he would have indicted Weinberger that day anyway. (Other prosecutors, but not Walsh, might debate whether holding up the indictment until after the election would have been a greater or a lesser sin than indicting in the midst of a campaign.) But as it was, the timing of the indictment, and the legalistic explanations of it that emanated from the counsel's office, gave Bush his most crucial piece of political cover for the pardons of Christmas Eve. By then the abandonment of Walsh was complete. House Speaker Tom Foley and future secretary of defense Les Aspin, both members of the original joint committees, were sounded out in advance about whether they would raise a fuss if Weinberger were pardoned. Both reportedly indicated that they would not object. Walsh was left to argue, to a world uninterested in listening, that he had had a strong case against Weinberger, that he hadn't *wanted* to indict the man, but had no choice when faced with the evidence and Weinberger's adamant refusal to admit any wrongdoing.

It was finally obvious what a great gulf divided the legal narrative of Iran-Contra, as it had built up over these years of investigation, and the fractured folk narrative that Washington had chosen to pretend was a thing of the past. Mary Belcher, Walsh's spokeswoman, describes the day of the pardons with a curious choice of words. "It was sort of like a death in the family," she says. "There's so much to do, and the emotions follow later."

There is little, now, to keep Iran-Contra from sliding entirely into the grave. George H. W. Bush has joined Ronald Reagan in retirement. None of the contenders to lead the Republican Party in the future has any connections at all to the case. And now that the White House has changed parties, none of the bit players is up for a job that is likely to revive the ghosts. Walsh will write his final report—presumably, a report of Walshian care and comprehensiveness. It seems likely to be the taxpayers' best value for their money, for Walsh did develop a far more detailed and complete understanding of Iran-Contra than posterity would receive without his efforts. But the truth is that when Walsh finally goes home, he will leave a perceived loser. What was the final fruit of all that effort? "The most important [result] is the message to senior national security officials that they can't take policy making off the books, that they have to obey the Constitution and the laws, that they have to answer to Congress," says Tom Blanton, executive director of the National Security Archive, a nonpartisan research institute in Washington. "That message, I think, hasn't been so successfully sent by the Walsh process. Because it's taken so long; because so many people have gotten away with slaps on the wrist; and because of Bush's pardons, which send a larger message: take care of the president, and we'll take care of you. . . . Walsh can write as hard-hitting a final report as he wants, but the cover-up worked. The people who lied have gone free." And even if he won some of his battles, Walsh might inadvertently have lost the war. For the law that created the independent counsel has expired, pending another congressional effort at renewal this spring; and Walsh has become a poster child for those who would like to see it buried permanently.* Like so many facts about his six-year ordeal, this, too, is not precisely Walsh's fault. Like everything else, it is a by-product of the fateful marriage between the world's most political case and the world's most methodical lawyer.

If Walsh has been bruised by the experience, he bears it in his customary solitude. "I think he's been brutalized publicly, and I don't think he deserves it," says Reid Weingarten. "My sense was he's a stoic, but that it hurt him." Stoically, Walsh insists that his investigation has been a success. "A personal success, I'm not so sure," he admits, with his apologetic laugh. "But a success in the interest of the government, yes, because it has shown that deterrence by criminal prosecution can be made effective in the national security area."

If this stiff, gray man could ever speak in the voice of the poet, the rime of this ancient mariner might sound more like that of Coleridge:

> Since then, at an uncertain hour,
> That agony returns:
> And till my ghastly tale is told,
> This heart within me burns.

—*April 1993*

---

*It was renewed, but later allowed to expire in 1999 amid even greater public weariness over a series of interminable Clinton-era investigations that culminated in Kenneth Starr's investigation of the Lewinsky affair.

THE STORY OF A BAD BOY

(LEE ATWATER)

A political campaign, he instructs, is "not unlike Ulysses. I mean there's thousands of sirens"—sah-*reens,* he styles them, in his rasping drawl—"on thousands of rocks, diverting you. And that's why a campaign plan, and a strategy, is so critical." Before setting sail, he continues, you have to ask the people around you to do as Ulysses's crew did to protect their captain. "You have got to sit down and make assessments and in effect get the people running the campaign saying, all right, here we are, *tah me to the mast.*" His face, with its great big eyes and tiny little mouth, has a strange, quivering fragility, like that of a child with a fever. He talks with the whole face—eyebrows up, then down, eyes popping, then limpid, with sincerity. His voice would be pleasantly smoky but for the hectic pace of his talk, and for the rapid-fire, guttural laughter that follows any point he is especially tickled by.

He talks about electing the governor of South Carolina and playing guitar with B. B. King, and about his passion for Machiavelli and Plato. About the years in his twenties when he sat at the knee of Strom Thurmond soaking up knowledge, driving the senator to events all over the state for the chance to spend those learning hours in the car; about what it was like—although he does not put it this way—to have had the privilege, last year, of tying the vice president of the United States* to the mast against the sirens of censure. The

---

*George H. W. Bush.

seat of his chair is on fire as he talks. He squirms, bounces, shifts from hip to hip, sinks down and props his feet on the edge of the table, then sits bolt upright to punctuate a point. When he gets to the good parts, his hands flash out, fingers splayed, palms facing toward him, to punctuate each phrase with an outward jerk of the wrist.

But enough about him. What do *you* think of him? "So," he asks suddenly, casual as a singing telegram, "have you found any unique dark past of mine?" He sits much stiller when he listens, his brow puckered into a pit that could grip a small marble. He seems to listen not so much for the words as for that dog whistle of danger, pitched in a key only his ears are exquisite enough to hear. This is Harvey LeRoy Atwater in his element, armed and ready for a fight he conducts every hour of every day, whether or not he has an adversary.

He sees all around him a world of Lee Atwaters, not to be trusted.

I.

All of a sudden he's out in the public, where he's being shot at just the way the candidate's always getting shot at.
　　　　　　　—SOUTH CAROLINA GOV. CARROLL A. CAMPBELL JR.

Atwater is especially watchful now, after ten months on the job as chairman of the Republican National Committee. For he has spent much of that time trying to manage his way out of a box. He made this box himself, of course. It was Atwater who fashioned its planks from the knotted pine of southern politics, who hammered in the barbed nails of a relentless political technique. It was Atwater, working obsessively, who planed and sanded it, who polished the wood with his assiduous self-promotion. And it was Atwater who finished off the lid with the cheap lumber of the 1988 presidential campaign and the convict labor of Massachusetts prisoner Willie Horton. For a few months after former Bush campaign manager Lee Atwater was anointed party chairman by a grateful president-elect, it seemed he had built a pedestal, lifting himself, at thirty-eight, to a kind of national ubiquity. Within the tiny political community he thinks of as his peer group, his new post was a long-sought affirmation of his skills as a strategist, a grown-up promotion from his old persona as Peck's Bad Boy of the tactical realm. And outside the Beltway, he had taken to a new level the strange evolution of his species, becoming one of the few American politicians to be widely famous, in the television-celebrity, name-recognition sense of fame, without ever having to run for or govern anything. Suddenly people stopped him on the street to ask him for his autograph. His name was a question on *Jeopardy!* With his much-hyped blues guitar and public passion for horror movies, he was the first baby boom politician who was really *of* the baby boom. To GOP activists—especially young ones—he had become a hero, the man who made it cool to be a Republican.

But he had aroused too much bad feeling along the way. In March, students at predominantly black Howard University occupied the administration building to protest Atwater's election to the board of trustees, holding him accountable, as manager of Bush's 1988 campaign, for what the student newspaper called "the most racist strategy in a national presidential campaign in the 20th century." Mainstream Republicans began to grumble over Atwater's avidity for the limelight, and grumbled louder when he posed for an antic photo in *Esquire* with his sweatpants pooled around his ankles. And then in June, Atwater aide Mark Goodin resigned after the RNC issued a mailing insinuating that Tom Foley, the new Democratic Speaker of the House, was gay. Although Atwater denied participation, he was widely held responsible—and widely denounced. "Thanks to the Lee Atwaters of the world, national politics is looking more and more like the coastline of Valdez, Alaska," said his Democratic National Committee counterpart, Chairman Ron Brown, at the time.* "He certainly became a lightning rod," says Frank Fahrenkopf Jr., Atwater's predecessor as RNC chairman. "And he probably contributed to the opportunities to make those criticisms."

---

*In March 1989 the *Exxon Valdez* spilled more than ten million gallons of crude oil in Prince William Sound, Alaska.

If he built his box himself, however, he is surely kept in it by the passions of others. Atwater, the master of making elections turn on potent symbols, has himself become a symbol. To his enemies, he represents the ascendancy of cynicism and sewer politics, the triumph of image over not only substance but reality. They say, in the boyish vernacular of the trade, that he is chronically "over the line." Atwater's friends concede that he will do *almost* anything to win. But most think he is feared simply for his talent. To his GOP allies, he symbolizes a voyage out of the thirty-five-year wilderness of minority status in the House of Representatives and a permanent extension, to the state level, of the party's presidential winning streak. They argue, in George Bush's immortal words, that Democrats hate Atwater because "he's getting in their knickers." As a skilled, nervy, and intensely focused warrior with a priceless understanding of traditionally Democratic voters, he is necessarily a threat to the opposition. In neither version is Lee Atwater the only example of the phenomenon he symbolizes. But he is certainly the most vivid and most visible. And either way, whether he is seen as a guerrilla testing the limits of acceptable political warfare or a renegade who has trampled the boundaries, his career has come to define where those boundaries lie. This is why he is watched so closely. And this is why it is worth examining the forces of character and history that have conspired to box him in.

II.

A prince, therefore, must have no other object or thought, nor acquire skill in anything, except war, its organization, and its discipline. The art of war is all that is expected of a ruler; and it is so useful that besides enabling hereditary princes to maintain their rule it frequently enables ordinary citizens to become rulers.

—Niccolo Machiavelli, The Prince

When Lee Atwater married Sally Dunbar in 1978, after a five-year courtship, they had a one-night honeymoon in a Charleston motel. He had to be back at work the next day on Thurmond's reelection campaign. Two years later, when he was working on Ronald Reagan's crucial primary campaign in South Carolina, Sally sometimes took their infant daughter, Sara Lee, to see her father at campaign headquarters—because he slept there. Sally Atwater smiles as she relates these stories. She smiles as she confirms the tale that she does almost all the driving in the family, because learning his way around would cost her husband too much concentration that he could better spend on politics. She smiles as she tells of moving into a new house. "I gave him instructions that day," she says, and holds up her hands to shape a small slip of paper. "'This is where you will live this afternoon. Please show up.'"

The concept of workaholism does not begin to describe Atwater's single-minded pursuit of his calling. It would be more accurate to see him as a kind of idiot savant of American politics, with a hyper-developed acuteness in this one realm. "What I try to do," he says, echoing Machiavelli's instruction, "is not ever learn anything I can't put to use. You got to be conscious about that in life. . . . That's why I'm very introspective after a campaign. You look back on what you did, and then analyze, 'Okay, what did I do there that I can systematize and use in the next campaign?' . . . People that are good in anything either consciously or subconsciously do that. I think it's better to be conscious about it."

Atwater came to politics through a summer internship in Strom Thurmond's Senate office, but his discipline predated his passion for politics by a year or so. He was a dismal student in high school, but as a freshman at Newberry College, a small Methodist school thirty-seven miles from his hometown of Columbia, South Carolina, he underwent a dramatic conversion from pudgy, beer-guzzling fraternity guy to driven, straight-A student with grand ambitions. "It was a very distinct change, almost like throwing a switch," says Carlos Evans, an Alpha Tau Omega fraternity brother. "At a very distinct point in time, he made up his mind that he was going to be somebody someday. And everything he did from that point on was directed to that end." He decided to run fifty miles a week—ten each Saturday and Sunday, and six miles a day for the rest of the week—and to read two books every week. He stopped drinking on all but special occasions, lost weight, and began the self-teasing discipline of smoking cigarettes only on Fridays. He has cut down the mileage, in deference to his aging knees, but in all other respects has pursued the whole regimen for nineteen years. Today, "he's God's most perfect political machine," says Mark Goodin, the longtime Atwater protégé who resigned in the wake of the Foley memo. "It's like a machine that begins to function from the minute it turns on, and runs until the moment some little timing mechanism turns it off." Atwater is fond of saying that "everything's a microcosm of everything else." By which he means: everything is like a campaign. Even retroactively, he compares or relates almost everything to this central activity of his life.

Was it hard on him to move around, he is asked, when his father's job as an insurance adjuster involved frequent transfers before the family settled in Columbia? No, he says, because "it was very good for me politically. . . . We moved to the key, critical political points of the state: Charleston, Aiken, Columbia, and Spartanburg. So I had a good understanding of the state because of the places I'd lived." He is talking about events that took place before he was ten years old. Minutes later, he is asked about the household accident that killed his three-year-old brother, Joe, when Lee was five. Lee was in the next room playing with his toy soldiers one afternoon as Joe was watching their mother deep-fry doughnuts. Stepping down from the wastebasket he was standing on to watch the cooking, the little boy pulled the pot of bubbling fat down on top of himself and was fatally burned. Lee witnessed his brother's suffering. "It had a big impact on me, there's no question about it," he says. "I can close my eyes and see it." But he declines to answer questions about what that impact was, contenting himself with this observation: "Well, to the extent you go into anybody's life, there are a few defining events, just as there are in campaigns. You can go back and analyze."

Seeing the world through this lens, he must necessarily greet people as potential constituents, susceptible to a variety of appeals. "I don't know how many layers you have to peel back to get to the real Lee Atwater, or whether the layers *are* the real Lee Atwater," says one former colleague from the Bush campaign. It makes Atwater a strangely isolated extrovert. He has always been socially popular, a lover of crowds. "The worst thing that could ever happen to Lee," says Jim McCabe, one of his oldest friends, "is to be totally off by himself, isolated somewhere." He keeps up with many friends from boyhood and college, ranging from bankers to bar owners, inviting them by threes and fours to family weekends at the Atwaters' cabin in Virginia's Shenandoah Valley. These old friends—the only ones with whom he drinks alcohol—are the friends who can help him relax. "Because there's no angle," he says. "There's no angle." But according to Sally Atwater, even these weekends have political meaning for her husband. "He talks to 'em, he'll talk about their daily life, that kind of thing—where their goals are. So he's always doing the politics." "He's surrounded by lots of people," says National Republican Congressional Committee co-chairman Ed Rollins, "and lots of people you certainly would think are his friends. But when you're so possessed that you work as much as he does, you pretty much are a loner. I've been his friend. But you know, friendship takes time."

III.

Once you saw him do it a few times, all those games, you thought, "I wonder which one I'm part of?"

—A FORMER OFFICIAL OF THE 1988 BUSH CAMPAIGN

The year after Atwater found politics, he became a record-setting recruiter for the South Carolina College Republicans. First he persuaded his best-looking fraternity brothers to drive to the local women's colleges to recruit new members, who would be enlisted, in turn, to recruit at all-male schools. When the guys set out for Winthrop College, an hour and a half away, Atwater would equip them with three pens—one red, one blue, and one black—and instructions to rate the girls as date material while they were at it, for the benefit of the whole fraternity. "The red were the best-looking girls, the blue were the mediocre, and the black were 'Don't call'," remembers fraternity brother Evans. "That was 90 percent of the incentive. Why else would a group of guys take time to drive to Winthrop College?" Motivation and reward: Atwater has always been fascinated by the leverage inherent in knowing what people need and want—or can be induced to want. High school classmate Joe Sligh recalls thinking that Atwater, then most notable for his interest in the worlds of rock music and professional wrestling, would one day make his living as a promoter. "He is a promoter," says Sligh. "And whether he'd be promoting George Bush or Andre the Giant or the Allman Brothers, he would have done it well." As a junior at A. C. Flora High School, Atwater invented a sort of alternative newspaper—really a single-page, mimeographed bulletin that was his own running challenge to the rules of high school social structure—called *Big At's Comedy Ratings*. It offered a changing list of the funniest students in the school. Because Atwater was a popular student, admired for his wit, the "ratings" evolved into a certification of popularity. The fun of it, Atwater's friends remember, was that he often anointed the unlikeliest people he could think of, simply to sit back and enjoy the social anxiety that would result. "After a couple of issues, people would do stupid things just to get on this rating," says a classmate, Warren Tompkins. "He told me later that that's when he first learned the power of the press—that you could manipulate people's thought processes by something you printed."

"I think Lee was always a studier of people," says his former campaign deputy, Ed Rogers. "He was always more of an outsider, looking at people's behavior, and stimulating behavior, than he was part of the group." As early as junior high school, he was fascinated by all-star wrestling, with its bellowed insults and theatrical aggression. He calls it "the only honest game in town" and has often spoken of its application to politics, telling *Dossier* magazine that he sometimes advises candidates to tune in to one of the choreographed festivals of mutual abuse that constitute prefight interviews: "It's a caricature of a politician's press conference," he says. Which makes the audience a parody of the citizenry. And Atwater's interest in the audience is what college fraternity brother Eddie Gunn remembers best. "We enjoyed watching the matches," he says, "but we especially enjoyed watching the fans. They took it so seriously, like they thought it was real." Over the years, Atwater would learn to codify such knowledge as this. He earned a master's degree in mass communications, then did years of field training in the whole apparatus of modern opinion molding—the polling and the focus groups, and how you mix paid media (which is advertising) with "earned" media (which is surrounding your candidate with one hundred members of the Boston police department for a shot that will make network news). But none of this formal training has ever been more valuable than what he had already taught himself about the people who believe all-star wrestling is real and buy fat remedies from the back pages of the *National Enquirer*. "He's a very acute observer of human behavior," says a former senior official of the Bush campaign, who confesses to having studied him in meetings. "You could tell the difference between the meetings where he came in not especially knowing what he wanted out of it, and the meetings where he *knew*. And in those I'd just sit and watch him work it around, work it around, to where he wanted it. Manipulating it."

Atwater's one apparent blind spot, in the matters of human nature, is that he believes everyone else works the same way. Eric Alterman, a journalist who last spring profiled Atwater for the *New York Times Magazine*, tells of accompanying him back to Columbia, South Carolina, for a St. Patrick's Day parade. In advance of the event, where he was to be parade marshal, Atwater became suspicious that the reporter was plotting with old South Carolina adversaries to arrange a demonstration against him in order to make the scene, and therefore the article, more colorful. Never mind that such a tactic could destroy a journalist's career. "It's not easy to convince a guy who's sure you're just as Machiavellian as he is," says Alterman.

IV.

I think he *needed* the reputation. Otherwise he would have been just like every other mojo.

—SALLY ATWATER

Atwater's reputation as a bare-knuckle tactician has tended to obscure how much he contributes to the campaigns he works for. Beneath all the smoke is a very intelligent man, with a political mind of great dexterity. It's commonly said that Atwater can see around corners. South Carolina governor Carroll Campbell, perhaps Atwater's closest political ally, says, "He's got a sixth sense about what's around that corner that you'd better be ready for." "When you cut away all the theater and all the drama and all the mystique," says Janet Mullins, media director for the 1988 campaign, "you've got someone who really is that good at getting someone elected. . . . He's far and away much smarter than most other people in this business." Atwater is more committed to his business than most, for one thing. He cut his teeth as a Columbia political consultant in a decade of managing local races, down to the mayoral and county council level, in South Carolina and neighboring states. He has never missed an election cycle. Even in 1982, as a White House operative, he was careful to stay closely involved in a handful of House races. He has been intermittently active in a political consulting firm since 1985, but a former colleague from Atwater's years in the White House political office says he is fundamentally different from such people as his former partners at Campaign Consultants, Inc. "Charlie Black wants to be rich. Roger Stone wants to be rich. Lee Atwater doesn't want to be rich. He wants to be master of the game." The Atwaters live in an unpretentious brick house near Foxhall Road, and their two daughters, Sara Lee and Ashley Page, attend public schools. Atwater is generously paid, of course; he makes $125,300 at the RNC and gives occasional paid speeches for as much as $15,000 a throw. But the finances of this game have been so distended that in Republican political circles in Washington, in 1989, these numbers lend some credence to his claim that he is not motivated by money. Furthermore, some Republicans say that Atwater's reputation as a sharp operator has obscured his talents as a strategist. In the Bush campaign, for example, it was Atwater who insisted—over the objections of several other senior advisors—on the "firewall" strategy of pouring major resources into the South early on, which paid off in Bush's sweep of the Super Tuesday primaries.

Friends say Atwater is anxious for recognition as a big-picture man, and piqued when his trickster reputation gets in the way. "The one uncompleted mission of his, in terms of his communicating to the world who he is, is the sense that he's a larger political thinker than just someone who can figure out how to spook an opponent before he goes into a debate," says John Buckley, spokesman for the National Republican Congressional Committee. And yet Atwater is best known for that whiff of brimstone that follows him from one campaign to another.

To understand both his talents and the controversy that has followed him, you need to understand two things about southern politics. The first is that, as recently as twenty-five years ago, the Republican Party scarcely existed in the South. "Republicans in the South could not win elections simply by showing various issues and talking about various issues," Atwater has said. "You had to make the case that the other guy, the other candidate, is a bad guy." In other words, you had to go negative. So Atwater mastered the art of making the voter pull the lever *against* the other guy. Bush's campaign against Massachusetts governor Mike Dukakis—hitting hard on such issues as gun control, the Pledge of Allegiance, and the Massachusetts furlough program that turned lifer Willie Horton loose—was, of course, a textbook example of driving up the opponent's negatives.

The furlough issue also drew on the second major theme of southern GOP politics in the past twenty-five years: race. The rise of the party in that time has been largely among southern whites alienated by the Democrats' embrace of civil rights—especially in such heavily black states as South Carolina, which today has some of the most racially polarized election returns in the country. Race and negativism meet at the "wedge" issue, the kind of emotionally laden topic that splits off elements of the traditional Democratic coalition. Wedge issues might include such things as school prayer, the death penalty, and laws governing pornography. Atwater is the master of this art. A negative campaign, of course, is not the same thing as a dirty campaign. But often, when it is not to a candidate's advantage to be seen going negative, the inflammatory issues are raised covertly. This is the essence of the worst of the stories that follow Atwater.

The demonology always includes the 1980 South Carolina congressional race in which he did some polling for Rep. Floyd Spence. Spence's opponent, Tom Turnipseed, alleges that selected white voters received calls from telephone pollsters pointedly informing them, in the course of one question, that Turnipseed belonged to the NAACP. In the course of campaign spatting over this and other contentious issues, Atwater revived the issue of Turnipseed's treatment, as a teenager, with electroshock therapy. "I'm not going to respond to that guy," he said. "In college, I understand they hooked him up to jumper cables." Atwater denies raising the question of Turnipseed's NAACP membership and has repented of the ugly remark. He "feels terrible" about it, he told the *New York Times*. Which is pretty much the same thing he said six years later in apologizing to a Jewish businessman in Columbia, Samuel Tenenbaum, for referring to him as "a Gestapo-type politician." Tenenbaum, a Democratic fund-raiser, had been trying for years to tag Atwater with a story from 1978, when Carroll Campbell, then a state senator and a longtime Atwater client, was running for the U.S. House of Representatives against Max Heller, the popular Jewish mayor of Greenville. It is one of the most serious counts raised against Atwater, surrounded by some of the most tantalizing evidence; it is also a tale no one has ever shown to be true. In brief, it is alleged that the Campbell campaign enlisted a third-party candidate to inject anti-Semitism into the race, passing to him a poll showing that Heller could be defeated if voters were told that he did not believe in Jesus Christ. The third candidate hammered this point home, Heller's support fell, and Campbell won the election. Both Campbell and Atwater vehemently deny the story—indeed, Atwater denies all involvement in the campaign; reporters have picked over and over the incident without proving it.

Atwater expresses anger that these and other incidents are hashed over in every history of his career. But according to friends and colleagues, the man most responsible for promoting the down-and-dirty Atwater persona has long been Lee Atwater. Many people tell of Atwater's boasting to them of campaign exploits. "Some of this is Lee's own fault, to the extent that he enjoys the myth of the sharp operator," says the NRCC's John Buckley. William Carrick, a Democratic consultant who shares roots in South Carolina, adds that it was also part of Atwater's service to his clients to project himself as "the bad guy, the Machiavellian, backroom, behind-the-scenes operative who does things that are sort of somehow independent of the candidate's oversight." It boosted his gunslinger's reputation, and for years no one cared enough who Lee Atwater was to make his tactics an issue in subsequent campaigns.

V.

If I can make Willie Horton a household name, we'll win the election.

— LEE ATWATER

Atwater's biggest problem is that he and Willie Horton became household names together. The Horton case was the perfect weapon in the Bush campaign's effort to paint Michael Dukakis as a pointy-headed Massachusetts liberal out of touch with plain common sense. Horton, under life sentence for murder, had been allowed out of prison for weekends under a state furlough program and had terrorized a Maryland couple, torturing and stabbing the man and raping the woman. Horton is black, the couple is white, and the campaign was accused of using the issue as an unsubtle pitch to America's worst racial fears and prejudices. Atwater and others have protested that Horton's race was incidental to the furlough issue, and that the campaign itself never used Horton's photograph—and promptly denounced any state parties or independent groups that did. But at a party meeting in July 1988, Atwater delivered a damning monologue that marked the Horton issue as a classic instance of southern-style racial politics. "There is a story about a fellow named Willie Horton, who, for all I know, may end up being Dukakis's running mate. . . . The guy [Dukakis] was on TV about a month ago, and he said, 'You'll never see me standing in the driveway of my house talking to these [vice presidential] candidates.' And guess what? Monday, I saw in his driveway of his home Jesse Jackson. So anyway, maybe he [Dukakis] will put this Willie Horton on the ticket after all is said and done."

After the election, Bush's campaign managers were quick to distance themselves from Willie Horton—or from "the furlough issue," as they are careful always to call it. Some have succeeded better than others: rarely, for example, does Bush himself or secretary of state James A. Baker III, who was the campaign's chairman, come in for a full share of the discredit.* That Atwater is most frequently blamed is due in part to his eagerness to take credit for the campaign. But it is also because Atwater is a product of the southern GOP. "This crowd which produced Lee Atwater did so at a time when race-baiting was the embryonic fluid of the Republican Party in South Carolina," says Charles T. Ferillo, a Democratic consultant in Columbia. "He plays a very subtle game in the politics of race," says Earl Black, a former graduate school professor of Atwater's at the University of South Carolina and an expert on southern politics. With blacks voting solidly for Democrats, the challenge to Republicans has been to scoop up disaffected, traditionally Democratic white voters who are revolting against the pace of change in the South—without appearing to appeal to bigotry. "You have to avoid overt appeals to race," continues Black, a Democrat. "But that doesn't rule out other means of achieving the desired result."

Atwater's three major allies in South Carolina politics all have charged histories in the area of race; two were pioneers in building the southern GOP through racial politics. The first, Harry Dent, was the sharp Dixie pol largely responsible for crafting Richard Nixon's so-called Southern Strategy in 1968. That year Nixon, with crucial support from Thurmond, managed to win enough white Democratic votes in the peripheral South to neutralize both George Wallace and Hubert Humphrey—largely through such means as publicizing Nixon's opposition to busing schoolchildren and his support for

---

*See "The Game," p. 55.

"freedom of choice" plans, which were often a subterfuge to evade desegregation orders. Atwater has called that "a model campaign," saying, "I've used that as a blueprint for everything I've done in the South since then." The second mentor was Thurmond himself, the Dixiecrat who led a third-party presidential campaign in 1948 on a states' rights platform, saying, "There's not enough troops in the Army to break down segregation and admit the Negro into our homes, our eating places, our swimming pools and our theaters." He called the 1964 Civil Rights Act "extreme to the point of being revolutionary," and in that year switched from the Democratic to the Republican Party to support Barry Goldwater. Atwater's third major influence, as much ally as mentor, is South Carolina Governor Campbell. At forty-nine, Campbell is widely cited as an exemplar of New South Republicanism. Atwater has supported his career since 1974, when he ran unsuccessfully for lieutenant governor, and most recently helped him win a narrow victory for the governorship in 1986. Campbell's roots in racial politics have a more modern look than Thurmond's, but they date back to 1970, when he led a group called the Citizens Committee to Prevent Busing. After many years of stalling by state and local authorities, a federal court had ordered immediate desegregation of schools in two South Carolina counties, and Gov. Robert E. McNair had responded with a courageous televised speech telling his state, "We've run out of courts, and we've run out of time, and we must adjust to new circumstances." Campbell led a petition drive urging that McNair join with other southern governors in refusing to comply, and organized a march from his native Greenville to the capitol in Columbia. Campbell's foes charge that he exacerbated a dangerously inflamed situation for political advantage; he had lost a race for the state House of Representatives the year before, they point out, and won a seat in 1970.

Southern politics has changed radically in the last twenty years, and all three of these mentors have taken more moderate public stances since that time, enabling Atwater to argue that they represent the progressive strain of the southern GOP. Atwater further argues that when he is charged with racial politics, he is simply the victim of a general belief that all white southern men are racists.

"It's just an absolute fact," he argues. "We're sitting ducks, and anybody can take a shot at us about anything." Since he became party chairman, he has made minority outreach his most visible priority. But skeptics abound. "Atwater's interest in being on the board of Howard and appearing around the country talking about the black vote is a cover," charges longtime adversary Ferillo. "He is attempting to sanitize his past and present political instincts."

Democrats have argued that Atwater hopes to kill at least four birds with the one stone of minority outreach:

1. It will make Democrats spend time and effort defending their most faithful base—the more visibly they can be made to do this, identifying themselves more and more with blacks in the eyes of conservative whites, the better;

2. It will assuage the misgivings of moderate-to-liberal Republicans, especially in the North and Midwest, who are alarmed by the racial polarization of the two parties;

3. It may at least lower black animus against the GOP, so that it is more difficult to mobilize minorities *against* Republican candidates—an especially important goal in southern state and local races, where black turnout has been a major Democratic advantage in recent years; and

4. If the GOP should actually happen to pick up some votes, so much the better.

That the program simultaneously addresses the party chairman's major public relations problem only adds to its charm, in this analysis. It is a cynical construction of Atwater's aims, to be sure, but adversaries point out that he has pursued a similar strategy in the past. In 1978, Strom Thurmond faced the most serious challenge he had seen in years, from a popular young Democrat named Charles "Pug" Ravenel. Already, for some years, Thurmond had soft-pedaled his segregationism. Now, with Atwater as his field director, he launched an all-out campaign for the black vote—sending his six-year-old daughter to public school, announcing federal grants in the black community, and more. He didn't gain many black votes, but suddenly Ravenel's panicked campaign was flying in Martin Luther King Sr., Andrew Young, and other prominent blacks to protect its flank. "The Ravenel campaign looked like it spent all its time going after black voters," recalls William Carrick. Carrick, who has known Atwater for years, says, "I don't think Atwater's racist himself. He's not personally a bigot. . . . I read Willie Horton in the light of, these guys had their backs up against the wall and they were looking for wedge issues, and the ultimate wedge issue for the 1980s and 1990s is race, and they used it."

Atwater seems genuinely startled to find himself, at this late date, handcuffed to Willie Horton. He is working at minority outreach the way he works at everything he undertakes: hard and systematically. And very publicly. Speaking on Martin Luther King Jr.'s sixtieth birthday last January at King's Ebenezer Baptist Church in Atlanta, he said, "I was too young to appreciate the significance of his life, the bravery of his work, or the tragedy of his death. . . . But I know now. I know *now* that Martin Luther King Jr. is a towering giant in our history. . . . I share his dream of a united America and a brotherhood of man. And in the days ahead, as I shoulder my new responsibilities, the memory of Dr. King's life will prod me on." Atwater has devoted so much energy to conciliation that it comes as something of a shock to visit his office. In a place of honor on the wall, along with many other uncomplimentary editorial cartoons, is one that shows a smarmily beaming Atwater under a "diploma" from "Willie Horton University."

VI.

I'm a classical liberal thinker, and I think power is evil.

—LEE ATWATER

Lee Atwater has ideological beliefs of a kind. Conservative. Somewhat libertarian, though he isn't at pains to spell out where this puts him on various social issues dear to the far-right wing of the GOP. "I've had two criteria" in selecting candidates, he says. "They've got to be a good person . . . and they've got to be conservative." But government interests him only as the end that enables the means. A passion for waging politics over making policy hardly makes Atwater unique among campaign technicians, but he is remarkable for his disdain of the kingdom to which he holds the keys. "He has a large measure of distrust—even a contempt—for large institutions," says a onetime Atwater associate. And he sees most of what goes on in Washington as a circus of self-interest. "Bull permeates everything," he is fond of saying, and he has an infallible meter for the kind of hypocrisy and self-delusion that abound in politics and government. This is the core skepticism that makes him love the resentful anarchy of *The Three Stooges*, and it is part of what makes him a brilliant populist politician. But it is also his great limitation. He is like one of those new airport security machines that, in order to detect the presence of small plastic explosives, must be calibrated so broadly that it can also be set off by a Shetland sweater. Thus everyone with wool in his suitcase becomes a terrorist; and for Lee Atwater, an official culture that thrives on *some* self-delusion is through and through a lie. Politics alone is pure. Like professional wrestling, it is unabashed manipulation—the only honest game in town. "The big tragedy with Lee is that if he applied all the energy he applies to the gamesmanship of politics to making the government work, both he and the government would be better off," says Carrick. "He doesn't really care what happens after election day. It's a permanent campaign mentality."

Atwater decided a year or so out of college that he would never be a candidate for office. "I made a conscious decision not to try to acquire [power] for myself," he says. When it is suggested that he now holds considerable power, he answers, "But not power in the sense that I'm not governing. . . . The ultimate power in this country resides in the hands of those who are elected, and who are governing. And I'm very conscious about that, and that's one of the reasons I don't lobby. I would be getting out of the role I've established for

myself. Because then I would be, in effect, participating in the process of governing." It is, of course, preposterous to suppose that this
chief political advisor to the president is not "participating in the
process of governing." Atwater talks to the president at least twice a
week and to White House chief of staff John H. Sununu "every day,
for one reason or another," according to Sununu's executive assistant, former Atwater aide Ed Rogers. Atwater's advice is informally
solicited by many people on the White House staff and in the cabinet. When he became RNC chairman, the White House political
operation's center of gravity essentially moved to RNC headquarters
on Capitol Hill, and Atwater maintains a network of protégés
throughout the White House staff, including Rogers; Jim Wray, who
runs the Office of Political Affairs; and Jim Pinkerton, deputy assistant to the president for policy planning. But he is, he insists, simply
a political operative. And whatever advice he offers—on personnel,
or managing the press, or the politics of the capital gains tax—seems
to have no reality to him beyond the political.

This fixation makes his close relationship with Bush in some ways
puzzling: a Greenwich Yalie whose attitude toward politics has always reeked of noblesse oblige might seem the last person to identify
himself with a middle-class gut-fighter who has no use at all for public service. Mutual self-interest is obviously the genesis of their
bond, and many political observers have pointed out that Atwater
has been a useful foil for a candidate and a president who wishes to
have the benefits of hardball politics while remaining a gentleman.
But neither of those things explains how Atwater has somewhat
transcended the powerful barrier that exists, in George Bush's mind,
between people like George Bush and people like Lee Atwater. Bush
is renowned (though hardly alone) in political circles as a man who
sees political operatives as hired help. "There is a sense of compart-
mentalization and categorization that goes on . . . in the mind of a
man like Bush," says David Keene, who worked on Bush's presidential effort in 1980. Before Bush lost the nomination to Reagan, he
told Keene, "I do want you to understand that, if I win, we don't
want any people like you in the government." This is often cited as

a reason why Bush had to overcome a powerful internal block to appoint a Lee Atwater to the RNC chairmanship—a job once held by none other than George Herbert Walker Bush. Generally overlooked, though, is that this is also a major reason *for* the comfortable bond between the two men. Lee Atwater knows his place and wouldn't have it any other way.

The job of chairman was to be the job in which he could have it all: affirmation as an important player. Power and publicity, without the responsibilities of office. The enticement of new political games to be learned with the big new toy that is the national party. And the chance to marry more closely than ever a united party and a White House political operation. "Lee has had a plan to get to where he is today for about ten years," says Ed Rollins. "And this is a town where long-range planning is lunch." But somewhere he miscalculated, and today he finds himself, instead, in his box.

VII.

Every time he tries to break out of the box that he's constructed for himself, he tends to get hurt.

—GOP POLITICAL CONSULTANT DAVID KEENE

It is one of those soupy July evenings in Washington, above 100 degrees—the kind when nothing but passion or duty could compel souls out of doors. Accordingly, only a few dozen people have come to the Ellipse to sit in the bleachers of the Democratic Party, while a beautiful young throng fills the Republican side. They're here to cheer on the RNC softball team, coached by Atwater, against the Democratic National Committee team coached by Ron Brown. The scene is like some civic sacrament in a banana republic. GOP team members sport newly minted, numbered T-shirts on which the Republican elephant, wearing sunglasses, plays guitar. Many fans wear T-shirts with the legend, "Lee Atwater's Red, Hot and Blue Revue, 1989 World Tour," which refers both to the Arlington rib joint of which he owns a small part and a series of concerts listed on the

T-shirt's back. A select few people, at the top of the status hierarchy, stalk the sidelines with shirts saying "Atwater's Cast Party, Presidential Inaugural," which dates back to the rhythm and blues concert he arranged last January. The man himself takes the field wearing jeans, a loud shirt of vaguely Hawaiian extraction, and the emblem of his rule—a cap reading "Late Night with David Letterman."

"It's a cult," sums up his old friend Jim McCabe. "Lee has literally developed a cult following."

It is all part and parcel of his efforts to peddle the other, more palatable side of the Atwater myth: the blues-pickin,' bad old good old boy, the southern lad who made it in the big city by saluting the flag, speaking his mind, and never letting the bastards get him down. This is Atwater the performer, about whom old friends reminisce with astonishing unanimity, describing an exhibitionism that was held in relative check for the fifteen years of Atwater's career as a behind-the-scenes operative—and that in January burst back into full flower. "If he goes for a few days without getting his name in the newspaper, he's like a heroin addict who hasn't had his methadone," says one person who knows Atwater well. "Right after he became chairman he was amazed by his own fame. . . . He was mesmerized by it." "Nothing's really changed," says high school friend Joe Sligh. "He's always promoted other people. Now, I guess, he's promoting himself."

Even before the Foley incident, several close political advisors had told Atwater that he should lower his profile. After that controversy, with his fame clearly shading into notoriety, he began turning down interviews about anything more personal or flamboyant than the RNC's candidate recruitment program. Aides have started emphasizing his work with Champ Cookies, a program to give inner-city kids the chance to work for "dough money, not dope money." More recently, he has thrown the RNC into collecting donations for the babies of women addicted to crack cocaine. But even now, after months of good behavior—of being tied to the mast, when necessary, by aides at the RNC—Atwater remains a prisoner of his past success. Having advertised himself for years as the baddest political operative in America, he must now persuade the world that he doesn't deserve the ruthless reputation he cultivated so tirelessly. Having achieved the position from which he can be involved in any and every level of American politics—even, if he wishes, in any race—he is now at risk of becoming the focus of any campaign he is visibly involved in. Somehow he has to deliver for the throng of Republican activists who greeted his appointment with excitement—but without recourse to many of the tactics that earned him his winner's reputation.

His most immediate problem, the one that follows him to work every day, is his potential to *be* a problem. Bush has been careful to demonstrate his confidence in Atwater, but in the wake of so much controversy, the chairman is inescapably a potential liability to the White House. No advisor is brilliant or useful enough to justify a president's having to answer for him more than once at a nationally televised press conference, as Bush was forced to do in the wake of the RNC attack on Tom Foley. The Foley episode, notes the NRCC's John Buckley, "made clear that anything was going to provoke a response among Democrats, and the less aggressive members of the Republican community, to go after him. And having withstood that fire, I think he understands exactly where he stands right now." As he approaches his second year on the job, Atwater continues to keep his head down, working hard at the necessary nuts and bolts of party building in advance of the crucial redistricting election of 1990. After an Atwater remark became an issue in a Florida special election in August, he was careful to avoid public entanglement in any of the high-profile campaigns decided November 7. Down to his Hermès tie and tassel loafers, he is doing a creditable imitation of the buttoned-down lawyers and legislators he followed into the job.

After these months of good behavior, many of Atwater's allies are baffled that he continues to be demonized. In the words of one friend, "Lee Atwater didn't create negative campaigning; he's just someone who has been real good at it. That environment has been the ambient noise of every campaign for the last twelve years." Atwater may not have invented the science, his enemies reply, but he is unique in the ruthlessness he has brought to politics on the national level.

Both sides are partly correct: he is singular, and he is one of many. He is a freak of political nature, but one who could never have flowered so well as in this place and time. Yet both sides also miss a larger point. American politics has changed so fast, and the ambient noise has grown so loud, that in a sense Lee Atwater has become the indispensable man. As the designated villain of American politics, he has quieted fears that his brand of cynicism may be the universal currency of elections today.

Never mind that the empty, read-my-lips politics of flag preservation and no-tax pledges has already crept from elections into governance. Never mind that races earlier this month in Virginia, New Jersey, and New York City degenerated into charges of lying and pandering, tax dodging and rapist coddling without any visible leadership from the chairman of the RNC. As long as one man can be said to embody all the problems of American politics, they will seem limited problems. As long as Lee Atwater is locked in his box, we may cherish an illusion that the line marking the outer frontier of acceptable politics is, at least for now, standing still.

—November 1989

POSTSCRIPT (SIXTEEN MONTHS LATER): IN MEMORIAM*

His ambition was a teenage boy's restless daydream, dreamt in the sweat of a late Saturday morning playing air guitar on his back while his parents bugged him to get up, and the path to stardom meant somehow getting past bagging groceries at the Winn Dixie out on the highway. For Lee Atwater, becoming chairman of the Republican

---

*Four months after Marjorie described the "box" that Atwater's success put him inside, that dilemma became, abruptly, the least of his problems. While delivering remarks to a breakfast fund-raiser for Sen. Phil Gramm, Atwater collapsed; rushed to the hospital, he was diagnosed with an advanced-stage brain tumor. Atwater died a year later at forty, prompting Marjorie to write this appreciation.

National Committee after running George Bush's presidential campaign was like being one of the Beatles, only in a necktie and loafers. You could tell by looking at him both the size of that old, adolescent hunger and his pleasure in its fulfillment, and this was surely the scent that drew to his side, any time he went out, flocks of earnestly sweating young men in yellow neckties who stammered, "Mr. Chairman, Chairman Lee, I just wanted to shake your hand."

Harvey Leroy Atwater was a man who could have invented himself—have invented, indeed, a whole new form of fame—only in America. He was a scoundrel, one of the darkest figures to dominate our recent politics, a man with a comprehensively cynical view of his fellow creatures. But he was an original, as fully alive a person as I have ever met. In 1989 I spent two months researching and writing a long profile of Atwater, and this was the paradox I never resolved.

Nothing could prepare you for the sheer oddness of Lee Atwater's vitality: the nervous electricity of gesture, the protuberant blue-green eyes, the tiny, madly mobile mouth. He projected such intensity as to seem drugged, or a little unbalanced, until you realized that in a certain limited sense he *was* unbalanced. He tended to shine his focus so exclusively onto the political business at hand as to surrender the ballast by which most of us live, shelling out attention or effort here and there but always reserving the great mass of ourselves.

He made it in the most improbable way, learning to dress at Brooks Brothers and keep his funky white-trash wickedness, too; he won the gloss of being an important Republican, an essential helper to the preppiest president since Franklin D. Roosevelt—and played gigs with Percy Sledge and B. B. King on the side. In describing him, friends trotted out the same shopworn adjectives applied to almost all public figures by their friends. He was disciplined, he was focused, he was driven. But ultimately he didn't want the same things most people want from politics. He wanted power, and he wanted fame, and he didn't mind money, and by the time he ran George Bush's campaign in 1988 he came to see that gaining some respectability would be a good career move. But he didn't crave the oblivion so many people seem to seek from power and politics—the assurance, by "arriving" here, that his was a good and gainful life. In Washington people tend to become institutions, and too often this relieves them of any responsibility to remain people. But Atwater never seemed to believe the cant he talked, the cant everyone talks in politics.

He was a dissembler and a trickster, but he was not a self-deluder. "I've figured out, in my own way, and in my own life, in my own values, how the system's [expletive]," he told me. But "always, no matter what I'm saying and doing, I know what my values are and what I believe and what I'm doing and what life means to me, and why I'm doing what I'm doing." That far, I believed him. This is admittedly a limited piece of praise. For if it made him less synthetic, his lack of illusion also certified him as a more purely cynical politician than most. He had a fundamentally bleak vision, favoring politics over government because he thought that at least politics was honest in being about manipulation, about illusion, about winning and losing.

His willingness to take credit for the seamiest ways his candidates won power—the negative campaigns, the racial insinuations, the tricky tactics—were both a part of his utility and the engine of his fame. He did it for George Bush; he had done it for earlier sponsors, including Sen. Strom Thurmond and South Carolina Gov. Carroll Campbell. In running campaigns that played on racial divisions, he was something worse than a bigot; he was a man who pretended to be a bigot in hope that it would sell. But Atwater was also a convenient fiction. He drew so much fire that everyone else—including many political consultants who used similar tactics and the candidates who should have borne ultimate responsibility for the campaigns Atwater ran—managed to seem fairly pure by comparison. If we look back on his career with any depression, it should not be at the thought that he embodied the ugliness of our recent politics. There are men and women enough, living and working, to remind us of the dreary facts of our lives. It should be over how rarely we can say of our politicians, as we can of him, that he knew who he was.

—*March 1991*

THE INGENUE

(LAURA INGRAHAM)

On this, her friends and her enemies agree: it all began with the leopard-print skirt. The *New York Times Magazine* of February 12, 1995, featured, on its cover, an article about what it called a new "opinion elite," a group of young, self-consciously hip conservatives versed in the postmodern arts of irony and image and bent on challenging their eternal stereotype as maladjusted guys with bad haircuts. The cover photograph showed five of the men and women discussed in the article, but the eye was ineluctably drawn to the one who had been given pride of place in the foreground—a dishy blonde wearing a figure-hugging black velour shirt, a very tight, very short leopard-print skirt, and a facial expression that dared you to give her any lip about it.

Laura Ingraham was at that time only in her second year at the Washington office of Skadden, Arps, Slate, Meagher & Flom, a former law clerk to Supreme Court justice Clarence Thomas who had spent her early twenties as one of the hundreds of true believers staffing the middle levels of the Reagan administration. Her greatest claim to a leadership role in forming conservative opinion was the occasional op-ed piece she turned out in between her briefs and motions. But the *Times Magazine* cover gave her an instant cachet, a platform from which to launch a new career as the conservative "It" girl. Not only did it bring her to the attention of a press corps suddenly hungry for a way to explain the conservative tide that had

231

swept into Congress three months earlier; it also made her understand, for the first time, just how far she could go on her high-concept package of looks, brains, and right-wing politics.

By spring of the following year she had left the law firm for the full-time pursuit of life as a media phenom. And by the end of last summer she had snared some of the most highly sought commentary berths in broadcasting: the political-analyst slot on the *CBS Weekend News* from which Joe Klein had been ejected after he was unmasked as the author of *Primary Colors*;* a regular gig as "contributor" to MSNBC, the collaborative cable–Internet venture between NBC and Microsoft; recurring appearances as a guest on the *Charlie Rose* show and Don Imus's morning radio program; and a role as substitute for the regulars on *The McLaughlin Group*. Not least, she had created the kind of buzz in the executive suites of two networks that veteran broadcasters would kill for. "We love Laura Ingraham," says Jonathan Klein, executive vice president of CBS News, who calls her potential "limitless." At NBC, anchor Tom Brokaw and news chief Andrew Lack have both taken an unusual interest in the career of a woman who is only a bit player at the network's fledgling cable outlet. Brokaw told me that he and Lack were chagrined, when CBS signed Ingraham in early August, that they hadn't thought in time of carving out a role for her at NBC itself. It is an oversight they hope one day to remedy, Brokaw says: "We would like very much for her to be part of the NBC News family. There's no secret about that."

How did a thirty-three-year-old of limited experience become, overnight, such a valued source of wisdom? In the annals of single-minded self-invention, Ingraham's ascent rivals that of her pal Arianna Huffington. Even a good friend of hers comments, "It is amazing how she has managed to propel herself into the spotlight, by force of will, so quickly." The conservative writer David Brock, a close friend of Ingraham's who also appeared on the *Times* cover,

---

*Klein had publicly denied writing this roman à clef about Bill Clinton.

and who first brought her to the attention of the *Times* reporter, salutes her rise in simpler terms. "I should have worn the skirt," he says with a laugh.*

Phil Griffin, executive producer of MSNBC's evening talk show *InterNight,* describes Ingraham's appeal this way: "The main thing is, she cuts against the cliché. She's young, smart, hip, and conservative. . . . She's sort of the perfect image of somebody different." Ingraham's fellow conservative Lisa Schiffren summarizes this syndrome, from personal experience, as "the Talking Dog thing—it's really hard to get articulate, Ivy League–educated, smart women who are really conservative."

And Ingraham is really conservative—anti–affirmative action, anti–abortion rights, anti–gun control, anti–big government. Her signature is a kind of muscular antifeminism, which grants (and profits from) the many achievements of the women's movement but blasts today's feminists as weaklings whining for special favors. "More and more women look upon feminism," she wrote in 1995, "as a fad of yesteryear—something to be left behind, like the mood ring and Flower Power stickers." Above all, Ingraham has shown a genius for politics as performance art. For years, she drove a light-blue Porsche whose vanity plate read FAR RITE. At the end of 1995, to counter the Renaissance Weekend popularized by Clinton and his circle, Ingraham and another conservative attorney organized the first annual Dark Ages Weekend in Miami, drawing luminaries such as Robert Bork, Ralph Reed, and Gordon Liddy with promises of hard liquor, cigars, and, Ingraham told a reporter, "wenches running around with sides of beef." And when David Shribman of the *Boston Globe* interviewed her for yet another article about influential young conservatives, Ingraham came to lunch in a full-length fur—made, she assured him, from "baby squealing foxes." (Ingraham's outspokenness did not extend to granting *Vanity*

---

*At the time this profile was written, Huffington and Brock were, like Ingraham, conservative Republicans. Today they are liberal Democrats.

Fair an interview for this article. She declined immediately and asked her friends to do the same.*)

Like all really good images, Ingraham's is one she has been polishing for a long time. The fourth child and only daughter of very conservative parents, Ingraham grew up middle class in Glastonbury, Connecticut, a small city in the orbit of Hartford. As a freshman at Dartmouth in the early 1980s she found soul mates at the *Dartmouth Review,* whose staff later gained national notoriety for such antics as tearing down shanties that had been built on the college green to protest apartheid. As the paper's first female editor, Ingraham sent a reporter with a concealed tape recorder into a support group meeting of the Gay Students' Association; she published the transcript with an editor's letter calling the GSA "cheerleaders for latent campus sodomites." At Dartmouth she dated Dinesh D'Souza, who later came to fame as the author of *Illiberal Education,* the first big book about political correctness on campus. (Dedicated to Ingraham in its 1991 hardcover edition, it was later undedicated, if there is such a thing, in its paperback form, after the couple had broken up.) After college, Ingraham got a job working for Undersecretary of Education Gary Bauer, whom she later followed to his job as White House policy advisor. Bauer, who was one of the most far-right planets in the Reagan policy universe, is now president of the Family Research Council, a leading voice of the Christian right.**

---

*Ingraham failed to mention this refusal when she described being approached by Marjorie in her book *The Hillary Trap: Looking for Power in All the Wrong Places* (Hyperion, 2000):

> It all started with a voice sweet as congealed syrup, on my answering machine. It was *Vanity Fair's* Marjorie Williams . . . a fortysomething feminist with a tousled sandy crop and deceptively kind eyes. Guess what, she crooned: She'd been assigned to do my profile. She was so looking forward to meeting me. She just knew we'd have *soooo* much to talk about.

**Bauer later quit this position to seek, unsuccessfully, the Republican presidential nomination in 2000. Subsequently he became president of American Values, another Christian right group.

When the Reagan era ended, Ingraham went to the University of Virginia law school, making law review, and in 1992 and 1993 she clerked in Thomas's chambers—where, according to someone who knew her, she often boasted that she was the most conservative of the thirty-six law clerks at the court. Even in her twenties, says a right-wing journalist, Ingraham "had a very highly developed sense of her own place in the Washington food chain." And her clerkship enabled her to meet almost anyone she wanted. "You're talking about somebody who is the world-champion networker," says a noted conservative. She is also, apparently, an accomplished name-dropper. In law school she was apt to tell people that she was a good friend of William Bennett, who had been secretary of education when she worked at the department, and that she played racquetball with justice Antonin Scalia, whose son she knew socially. "She does drop names, there's no question about that," says one friend. "It's kind of cute, actually."

After she joined Skadden, Arps, Ingraham became a member of the Independent Women's Forum, a group that advertises itself as "taking on the old establishment of feminist organizations." She was eagerly adopted as a winning spokesperson, tapped, for example, when the Forum was invited to testify before Congress against affirmative action. Led by successful careerists like herself—many of them the wives of prominent male conservatives—the IWF has been described tartly by the social critic Wendy Kaminer as "the women's auxiliary to the conservative elite." It seems to embrace all the most advantageous gains of the women's movement and then anathematize the more controversial or inconvenient bits, exuding an I-got-mine contempt for anyone still mired in problems old-fashioned enough to call for some form of social redress.

If liberated antifeminism seems an inherently self-canceling state, that is only one of the broad contradictions posed by Ingraham's stance as the Happening Conservative. It is hard, for example, to conceive of any meaningful construction of the term "culture war"—a phrase Ingraham has been known to bandy—that could place a conservative on the same side of the battle line as Don Imus, with his sodomy jokes and leering comparisons of Ingraham to Sharon Stone.

Another puzzle is Ingraham's apparent history of antigay rhetoric, going beyond even the overtly homophobic attitudes she promoted at the *Dartmouth Review*. *New York Times* reporter Michael Specter, for example, recalls meeting Ingraham about seven years ago, when he was covering the AIDS crisis for the *Washington Post*. "Oh, yeah," he recalls her saying, "you're the guy who defends homosexuals for a living in the *Washington Post*." Yet the brother to whom Ingraham is closest is gay, as is David Brock, one of her best friends, who dismisses any notion that she is intolerant. "This is somebody," he says, "who can go to a gay bar with me and have a completely good time." One way of resolving these contradictions is to assume that Ingraham's conservatism contains a large element of theater. She has often bragged to liberals about owning a handgun and keeping it (depending on whom she was talking to) in her purse, beneath her bed, or under her pillow. It is striking that her conservative friends tend not to remember hearing about her gun. "I'm a lifetime member of the NRA, and she never told me," says entrepreneur Michael Crane. "There probably is no gun, and she does it to annoy liberals." (Indeed, Brock says she has not owned a handgun since she began living in the District of Columbia, where it is illegal.) The gun—whether or not it ever existed—has clearly been most useful as a way of drawing attention. A man who met Ingraham in law school remembers her mentioning her gun in one of their first encounters, which took place near a window. Outside, groundhogs could be seen on one of the University of Virginia lawns. "She said she wished she had her handgun handy so she could 'take one of them out,'" says this classmate. "I always thought she was a poser."

But there is nothing posed about Ingraham's emotional intensity: the word "intense," or one of its variations, comes up almost as frequently in interviews about her as the leopard-print skirt. She has, says one acquaintance, "an intensity that is frightening." A colleague from the Reagan era recalls that even in a Department of Education softball game she projected "this kind of manic, 'I'm going to rip your face off' attitude." Another woman who knows her from conservative circles notes that "the [TV] producers like her because of the fact that she's very aggressive and doesn't back off. But she translates that also into personal relationships."

A case in point, widely whispered about in Washington, was her breakup with Richard Sauber, a lawyer with whom she had a relationship in the early 1990s. The two met when she worked as a summer associate at his firm during law school, and they ultimately began living together. When, after a few years, Sauber decided to end the relationship, Ingraham apparently wouldn't take no for an answer. "I don't want to be interviewed," Sauber said when I asked him to discuss the story. But he has told it in the past to friends, who describe Ingraham as having reacted with something like the outrage of an angry, thwarted child. For five or six weeks, according to these sources, she would appear unannounced at Sauber's door and would call him constantly, insisting that they talk things over again. She telephoned his friends, asking them to intercede with him. Two or three times she let herself into his house, at one point restoring some framed pictures of herself to the spots from which he had removed them. One day he came home to discover that the floor of his foyer was wet, the garden hose nearby; he assumed, he told friends, that Ingraham had aimed the hose through the mail slot to spite him. Finally, he told her that he would call the police if she entered the house again. "A lot of people were concerned about her," says one of her friends.

The Sauber episode echoes the bursts of intense anger that have punctuated her political life. While she was an assistant in the Education Department, for example, Ingraham and other conservative Dartmouth alumni tried to elect a slate of their own candidates to the college's board of trustees. When she learned that a Washington attorney had formed a group to oppose the conservative candidates, she fired off a letter to the managing partners of the lawyer's firm threatening an investigation of his activities and signed it with her official title and address. Her boss made a formal apology to the lawyer. Her career, too, rings with violent rhetoric, as when she told a gathering at the right-wing Heritage Foundation that "conservatism errs in failing to go in for the kill." Even today, her copy tends to strike a bloodthirsty note. The Republican Party, she wrote a few weeks before the November election, must banish those who ran the Dole campaign: "Odds are that in two years they'll be back knocking at the door of the next front-runner, offering advice. But that door should be slammed, nailed, bolted, even welded shut."

It is this note of attack, this quality of raising her voice just one or two decibels higher than necessary, that makes her an interesting high-wire act on TV. During the GOP convention, when Ingraham appeared on Comedy Central's free-for-all *Politically Incorrect with Bill Maher,* ragging on attorney general Janet Reno, the comedian Chris Rock remarked on the air that, "with all due respect, ma'am, you are the meanest bitch I've ever seen." On Imus's show the week before the election, Ingraham launched into an extended riff about how foolish it was of Dole to pander to the so-called soccer mom, a phenomenon she depicted as the invention, like all other bad things, of mewling feminists. So what if mothers feel stressed out and over-worked, she asked—who doesn't? In the old days, Ingraham opined, women had to worry about their children going off to war or suc-cumbing to typhoid. Now, she continued, their big worry is "whether to take the Lexus or the Range Rover to pick up the kids." With problems like those, she concluded, "*I* want to be a soccer mom."

"You will never be a soccer mom," deadpanned Imus, "because you scare men."

All through 1995, while turning out opinion pieces for the *Wall Street Journal,* the *Washington Post,* the *New York Times,* and others, Ingraham pondered how she could follow up the coup of the leopard-print skirt. Finally, in early 1996, she decided simply to quit the law and become a full-time media personality. Senior partner Robert Ben-nett praises her work on white-collar crime cases at Skadden, Arps, but makes it clear he did not beg her to stay. "I never viewed her as somebody who really I could see spending the rest of their life practic-ing law, and I told her that," he recalls. "She has the talents that could make her a first-rate trial lawyer, if she got the experience and put the time in. But I remember saying, 'I don't know, can you wait that long?'" At the very least, her departure is a testament to her nerve. As of last June, she had nailed down only her MSNBC job, which report-edly pays less than $50,000 a year. She had just bought a town house worth almost $400,000 in northwest D.C., financed with a 90 percent mortgage. But she set about building her new life with characteristic intensity. One TV executive marvels, "She just has a way of putting on her radar screen who's important, who can help her, and going for it." Her big break came when an acquaintance at CBS—Washington-based producer Bill Owens, who had once interviewed her for a story—invited her as his guest to the Radio and TV Correspondents' Association Dinner, a major annual social event that lures network brass down to Washington. CBS executives, who had watched Ingraham on a recent 60 *Minutes* segment about the Independent Women's Forum (and who, of course, had seen the *Times Magazine* cover), lined up to meet her. According to someone with whom she has discussed her career, Ingraham greeted executive vice president Klein and news-division president Andrew Heyward with her signature provocation. "She told them, in no uncertain terms, what she thought of the network and how they needed to do better and what they could do to get there"—letting them know "that they could do better with a fresh face." In no time, she was being called up to New York and introduced to various producers. Ultimately she was hired as an analyst, at a salary that a CBS source pegs at "a little past the six-figure mark." Aware of all the networks' reputations for hiring new talent and then ignoring it, Ingraham held out, according to a CBS source, for a contractual guarantee that she would be assigned a high-level mentor. "It suddenly dawned on me," says the source, "that this was a person who knew her way around." Ingraham is now officially under the wing of Lane Venardos, vice president for hard news. A similar boldness snagged her an occasional seat on the *McLaughlin Group*. Ingraham was introduced to John McLaughlin at a party held by *George* magazine in San Diego during the Republican convention and told him that he needed to get some younger people on the show. He, too, was charmed by this approach. "What I admired about her is she's absolutely fearless," he says. "She doesn't trim at all."

Talk to enough people about Ingraham and a theme announces itself: the chance meeting at a party, the challenging attitude, the new conquest. It points up an intriguing part of Ingraham's appeal, which is her ability, even as she ingratiates herself in traditionally female ways, to be one of the boys. Intensely athletic—she recently ran in the New York City Marathon—she has been known to hail an important executive at a party with a playful cuff to the solar plexus. Ingraham's berth at MSNBC, in the meantime, has been worth more than money. It is the appetite of new outlets such as this one that has made opinion mongering a full-time job. MSNBC actually schedules its contributors to stand by in the studio in three-hour shifts throughout the day, like doctors, to perform emergency punditry on whatever news events might roll in. Though the new network has, at this point, a tiny audience, it has given Ingraham exposure in all the right places. Because it has a camera in Imus's Queens studio to broadcast him on cable, she gained entrée to his radio show, which is widely listened to in media circles. More important, MSNBC gave Ingraham contact with powerful new patrons at the parent network.

I called Tom Brokaw after hearing that he'd been seen having a late-night drink with Ingraham in the bar of the Royalton Hotel, following one of the presidential debates. He said he met Ingraham at— yes—a party, thrown by NBC on the last night of the Democratic convention in Chicago. She was there with rising NBC star Brian Williams, who doubles as MSNBC's anchor.* Brokaw was making his last "fast lap around the room," he recalled, when "she just walked over and introduced herself," then offered "a couple of snappy one-liners" about the president's acceptance speech. "I had seen her on MSNBC, and she really stood out," Brokaw said. "I was amused by her, and I thought she kind of held her own and was quite fearless."

Needless to say, Ingraham's quick conquest of television has created plenty of grumbling inside the walls she has breached. "If Laura Ingraham were a guy with glasses, would we have hired him? I don't think so," complains one broadcast veteran. Such sniping contains a good deal of professional jealousy and outrage that she has skipped the meat and spinach of apprenticeship in either journalism or political campaigning and gone straight to the dessert course of highly paid punditry. In some, she inspires an annoyed sense that journalism is becoming nothing more than a catchall form of celebrity, a

---

*Williams later replaced the retiring Brokaw as anchor of NBC *Nightly News*.

way of staying perpetually in the public eye. But Laura Ingraham's critics might comfort themselves that her rise thus far offers two delicious ironies. The first is that her success is, in the final analysis, a simple case of affirmative action at work. She is the Conservative Woman. The vogue word in TV news these days is "voice," as in "Laura Ingraham is a fresh voice." But this is only the latest euphemism for the quota system that has crept into all mainstream journalism. Ingraham, says CBS's Klein, is part of a "campaign to add distinctive voices. . . . We're talking to a black conservative writer. And we're talking to a black liberal writer. And we're talking to a variety of others." Whether this self-conscious balancing act is a good thing or a bad thing is hotly debated in newsrooms and studios across the country; what it definitely is not is the ideal that Ingraham and her fellow conservatives purport to believe in—a hierarchy of merit and experience alone. In taking her well-burnished persona to the heights of broadcast journalism, Ingraham is, above all, proving herself adept at the diversity politics she claims to loathe.

And the final irony is still revealing itself every time Ingraham appears on CBS above a caption that says, simply, "Analyst." If Ingraham continues to rise, television—which has already softened her hair, her clothes, and her makeup—will sand away ever more of the sharp edge for which it sought her out in the first place. It is bound to be fun to watch. "Who knows where she's going to go after the election? Because there's not going to be quite the same interest in that kind of voice," said MSNBC producer Phil Griffin a week or so before election day. "But we'll see.

"Listen," he concludes, "the world of the pundit is forever, you know."*

—January 1997

---

*Ingraham didn't last at CBS and MSNBC, but she went on to host a nationally syndicated talk radio program. In *Power to the People* (Regnery, 2007), Ingraham wrote, "I was a fish out of water in the television news business. I didn't come from their world and I didn't buy into their worldview. They knew it and I knew it." Ingraham later returned to TV with a show of her own, *Just In*, on Fox News.

BEFORE THE FALL

(COLIN POWELL)

It's been a long, hard day of inspiration in the Palace of Auburn Hills, the neo-Aztec sports arena where the Detroit Pistons play their home games. Some thirteen thousand people slump in the seats they've paid an average of $80 apiece to occupy as participants in "Success 1995," an all-day motivational seminar. By five o'clock, the audience has heard from Olympic skater Bonnie Blair, chat-*meister* Larry King, sports broadcaster Ernie Harwell, and motivation coach Zig Ziglar. Sales guru Tom Hopkins has walked them through the seven Cs of customer service, and conference organizer Peter Lowe, a peppy young redhead with an Eddie Haskell manner, has offered them some bibilical affirmations that helped him to enlist Jesus in his own success (and invited them to "pre-invest, for 11 months, for $99.95 plus shipping and handling," in the "Success-Talk" tapes his firm also markets). The very air of the arena feels spent when finally Lowe introduces the day's top draw: Colin Luther Powell, poster child for the brand of wishful thinking that has brought this crowd to this place.

A zaftig blonde singer belts out Lee Greenwood's Reagan-era anthem of national pride, "God Bless the U.S.A." Red, white, and blue spotlights play over the crowd, and fireworks suddenly erupt on the arena's stage. At last Powell—a natty figure in a good blue suit— bounds lightly up to the podium, a happy accomplice in this carnival patriotism. "I tell you," he begins, "if that doesn't make your heart go pitty-pat, you ought to lie down and get someone to throw some dirt on you, 'cause you're *dead*." From that moment, the crowd is reawakened, happy, and eating from Powell's hand. Listening, one understands why the general finds himself discussed, promoted, even venerated as the next Eisenhower, a wild-card candidate for the presidency. At fifty-eight he is a remarkably personable man—gracious and funny, self-possessed in a way that is rare in any business. Unlike almost anyone else in the dense establishment, a somber breeding ground for self-importance, he is unafraid to reach for notes of feeling and compassion; unlike almost anyone practicing politics today, he can speak of the spirit and the family without seeming to recite cynical boilerplate. "One of the reasons people talk about him," says GOP political consultant David Keene, "is that they can look at him and see him as president. That's a very important quality, and he's got it, no question about it. It's one of those necessary-but-not-sufficient things that go into the mix." For about forty-five minutes, Powell speaks in soaring terms of communism's death, of his pride in the young men and women who fought in the Persian Gulf War, and of the urgent need to turn to the mending of America's social fabric. Implicitly, he appeals for racial healing, and issues a call to conscience. "We cannot enjoy what we have if others do not share in our good fortune," he says, sounding as if he means it. It is only when he has finished speaking that you find yourself groping to think of anything remotely memorable in his remarks.

At this point, Powell's "candidacy" is mostly the fevered creation of a political press corps starved, a full year in advance of the 1996 election, for something to call news. Yet polls show him beating Clinton in a head-to-head race in which Powell is the Republican nominee and running strongly against Clinton and Republican Bob Dole were he to campaign as an independent. Other polls, designed to measure more generally Powell's level of appeal, conclude that he is the most widely admired political figure in America, whether the respondents are liberal, conservative, or in between. "At a time when distrust of politicians is at a record high, he is an example of personal integrity and trust," says Andrew Kohut, director of the

Times Mirror Center for the People & the Press, which has polled extensively about Powell. "The downside is that people don't know a damned thing about what he stands for."

It is almost a truism, by now, that Powell represents a sort of pleasant fantasy—a blank page onto which, lacking information about his opinions on the knotty issues of the day, we can all cast our fondest hopes. Powell himself may have said it best: "Some people," he said jokingly last fall, "refer to me now as the political Forrest Gump." But there is much to learn from asking just what itch it is that Colin Powell scratches. The enthusiasm for Powell goes beyond a perception that he's a war hero and symbol of a military that has rebuilt itself in the wake of Vietnam to become one of the most esteemed institutions in America. Powell's history as the first black chairman of the Joint Chiefs of Staff makes him a politically ideal construct: the conservatism suggested by his army career balances out any liberalism hinted at by his skin color—and vice versa. His long service at the top levels of the defense bureaucracy makes him seem reliable enough for the presidency, while his complete innocence of political office lends him the "outsider" quality that tops all other virtues in voters' minds today.

Nowhere is Powell's anodyne excellence more attractive than in the area of race, where he carries an especially powerful—and mixed—message. In a year when the Supreme Court has made historic rulings against race-based remedies for discrimination, and affirmative action is the hottest of political hot buttons, his life proves anything you want it to. Powell is cited by some as proof that affirmative action isn't needed—and by others as evidence of how well it works. His potential as racial healer is hailed, in both good and bad faith; it is also exaggerated, as suggested by the existence of two Republican draft-Powell movements in Washington, one of them led by blacks, one of them by whites, each group certain it holds the key to the true Colin Powell.

In fact, there is very little reason to think that Powell will run for president next year. "I would give you a hundred-to-one shot that he's not going to run," says a good friend. "It's a huge risk. And it's a risk he doesn't need to take." Yet Powell, with a reported $6 million book advance to earn out, has seen an advantage in passively encouraging the various activists who are talking him up. These dreamers feel that his five-week, twenty-two-city book tour will be the perfect launch for a presidential campaign, but it can't have escaped the cagey general that the reverse is also true. All this presidential talk is sure to sell some books. A master synergist, Powell is already using his speeches (for which he gets paid up to $60,000) to plug *My American Journey*. "I've spent the last year and a half working on my memoirs," Powell tells his Detroit audience at the end of his talk. "It'll tell the story of a young kid, a young black kid, born in Harlem, raised in the South Bronx, who in this great country was able to rise—even in an age of segregation, of Jim Crow—to a very high position in the armed forces of the United States. And I hope it will be read as a story of what you can do in this great country."* But in order to regard Colin Powell as a racial Everyman, up from destitution with a vision that might transform this race-riven land, you have to seriously misrepresent his background, his career, and perhaps his very nature. In fact, it's less illuminating to scrutinize what Colin Powell has made of his life than to examine what all the rest of us have made of Colin Powell.

On November 5, 1987, the select congressional committees wrapping up their joint investigation of the Iran-Contra scandal voted out twenty-seven recommendations. One of those recommendations was that the president never again appoint an active-duty military officer as national security advisor. Also on November 5, Ronald Reagan picked Colin Luther Powell, a three-star army general—and one with substantial early involvement in the mechanics of shipping arms to

---

*Powell's *My American Journey* (Random House, 1995) spent twenty weeks on the *New York Times* best-seller list and sold 1.4 million copies.

the mullahs—for the job. Already the committees had stepped carefully around Powell, finding reasons not to make him testify in public, on national television, along with his sweating civilian counterparts from the Defense Department. Now that the whole principle of civilian control of the National Security Council was up for grabs again, did any senator or representative throw a fit? Warn the White House off the appointment? Even grumble to a newspaper reporter? No member of either committee raised an objection. As a Senate source told the *Washington Post*'s Walter Pincus at the time, "There was united agreement he was a superb officer." "There is just no taste for going after this man," sighs a Reagan administration official who got no similar breaks. "I don't really hardly know anyone who dislikes Colin Powell."

For the public at large, it was Powell's stewardship of the Pentagon during the Gulf War that marked what a former colleague calls "the emergence from 'Colin Powell, extremely talented guy' to 'Colin Powell, political rock star.'" In interviews for this story, several of his friends and former colleagues referred, almost unconsciously, to a time "before he was Colin Powell." But Powell had already been, through most of the 1980s, a virtually untouchable figure within Washington—the closest thing the capital has recently known to a true sacred cow. "He's got this great outside reputation, but he's also the consummate insider," notes Richard Haass, who was senior advisor on the Middle East to George Bush's National Security Council. The Colin Powell of popular legend is a meat-and-potatoes man, a down-to-earth army guy who repairs Volvos for a hobby and whose favorite foods are said to be ground beef and peanut butter and jelly. This man entered the army through the ROTC—the first chairman of the Joint Chiefs ever to do so—and worked his way up the traditional ladder of infantry command. He served two tours in Vietnam, earning a soldier's medal for rescuing his commanding officer and three others after a helicopter crash despite a broken ankle, and landed some of the most prestigious grooming assignments in the army—a stint at the National War College, for example. It was this Colin Powell, a plainspoken soldier, who memorably informed the nation of his plans for Saddam Hussein's army: "Our strategy to go after this army is very, very simple. First we're going to cut it off, and then we're going to kill it."

While the bare facts of that legend are true—especially its emphasis on Powell's abiding passion for the military—it obscures the real man, who pursued a career path that took him away from field command and into the meetings and dining rooms of official Washington. This Powell went through business school during his army career and gained his first real exposure to the inner workings of power as a lieutenant colonel, when he was picked as a White House fellow in the Nixon administration. He held bureaucratic assignments in the Carter administration, at the Pentagon and the Energy Department, and then, in the Reagan administration, as the top military aide to secretary of defense Caspar Weinberger (whose eye he had caught as a White House Fellow), and later as the deputy national security advisor and the national security advisor. While Powell returned to the field from time to time for the short command assignments he needed in order to earn his general's stars, it was his Washington career that led to his promotion, over the heads of fourteen more senior generals, to serve as George Bush's chairman of the Joint Chiefs of Staff.

Powell has cut a sophisticated, somewhat elegant figure on the capital's social A-list through three administrations. Guests at Ben Bradlee and Sally Quinn's annual New Year's Eve party last winter were startled to look up at midnight, as the band launched into "Auld Lang Syne," and find Powell in smooth, cheek-to-cheek partnership with Lauren Bacall. Powell's wife, Alma—attractive, well dressed, with the iron poise of a senior military wife—is herself firmly ensconced among the city's socially powerful, serving, for example, on the board of trustees of the Kennedy Center for the Performing Arts. Upon Powell's retirement in 1993, the couple settled into a $1.3 million house in the elite, predominantly white suburb of McLean, Virginia.

The hallmarks of Powell's career have been great political finesse and a very conscious caution. Powell is not one of the defense intellectuals who rose to power under Reagan and Weinberger, seeing in their unprecedented military buildup a chance to advance some personal conviction about arms control or force structure. "I don't think he ever came into a job and said, 'These are the three things I want to do,'" says a friend. His instincts, says a Bush administration official, are to "lie low and do what you can." With one exception—husbanding the reputation of the army he loves and protecting the lives of its fighting men and women—Powell has never seemed a man with a burning agenda of any kind. For most of his Washington career he was simply one of the city's premier process jockeys, who ride the best horse they can find and ride it to win. As part of this art, Powell has deftly generated the most consistently glowing press in recent memory. ("Powell has become a folk hero," wrote the *Los Angeles Times* after the Gulf War, "a living, breathing recruiting poster with a beerbarrel chest, a blacksmith's arms and the bearing of a centurion.") Normally a subtle creature who works behind the scenes, the mediaconscious Powell briefly broke cover in Bob Woodward's 1991 book, *The Commanders*, which made it clear that Powell had been carefully spooning out his own, self-protective version of events leading up to the conflict with Iraq even as Bush's inner circle was meeting in its early councils of war. Soon after he became chief, Woodward noted, Powell made a point of installing a direct phone line from his desk to the desk of Pete Williams, the Pentagon spokesman.

People who try to describe what made Colin Powell so good as an insider cite the classic attributes of workaholism, clubbability, and guile. The one rarer quality they grope to define is Powell's great and natural smoothness. "My sense of Colin Powell," says Frank Gaffney, assistant secretary of defense in the Reagan administration, "is that if Colin Powell were angling for something, you'd never know it." "Colin is forceful," notes Haass, "yet he doesn't have *edges*." Conversations with Powell's friends and former colleagues all point to the conclusion that Powell has a shrewd understanding of his own appeal—down to the usefulness of his chameleon quality. "He is an elastic figure in people's minds. But I don't perceive him as an elastic person in his beliefs or behavior," says Richard H. Kohn, former chief of air force history and now a professor of history at the

University of North Carolina at Chapel Hill. "He simply has the charm and ability and intellect to avoid being pinned down."

The curious thing about Powell is that this chameleon quality seems to extend even to the impressions of people who know him very well. "We've talked about how the army is not an affirmative-action organization," says Kenneth Adelman, a good friend of Powell's who ran the Arms Control and Disarmament Agency during the Reagan administration. "You can't argue that you need affirmative action to do well. Because the army proves you don't." Yet Powell's cousin J. Bruce Llewellyn argues precisely the opposite—also on the basis of conversations with Powell. "He's for affirmative action," Llewellyn says with certainty. "He wouldn't have gotten where he is in the army if it hadn't been for affirmative action. . . . He's said that a lot."*

One set of Powell supporters titles itself the Exploratory Draft Colin Powell for President Committee. With its offices in Prince George's County, Maryland, the most heavily black of the suburban counties surrounding Washington, the group grew out of a black Republican scholarship organization. Its honorary chairman is Lionel Hampton, and its most visible spokesman is W. Ronald Evans, a fifty-eight-year-old entrepreneur who has interest in real estate and

---

*In My American Journey, Powell's discussion of affirmative action is, in fact, somewhat self-contradictory:

> If affirmative action means programs that provide equal opportunity, I am for it. If it leads to preferential treatment or helps those who no longer need help, I am opposed. I benefited from equal opportunity and affirmative action in the Army, but I was not shown preference. The Army, as a matter of fairness, made sure that performance would be the only measure of advancement. When equal performance does not result in equal advancement, then something is wrong with the system, and our leaders have an obligation to fix it. If a history of discrimination has made it difficult for certain Americans to meet standards, it is only fair to provide temporary means to help them catch up and compete on equal terms. Affirmative action in the best sense promotes equal consideration, not reverse discrimination. Discrimination "for" one group means, inevitably, discrimination "against" another; and all discrimination is offensive.

the auction business. Evans worked for Nixon at the Small Business Administration and for Reagan at the Department of Energy's Office of Minority Economic Impact. Evans resists the description of the draft group as a predominantly black effort, noting that "we have Hispanics, Asian Americans, Native Americans working with us. . . . We have tried to take the color off it." Yet Evans also declares of Powell, "Certainly, he's going to be very, very positive in the civil rights area because of whence he came." Evans believes that "it puts us a hundred years behind if affirmative action is abolished." For all the efforts of the group Evans represents, African Americans have complicated reactions to Powell, who would by no means be assured of a large black vote.* Powell's real strength—his plausibility as a candidate—has far more to do with his appeal to America's white majority.

Some see in him a chance to cast a vote for racial comity. "Without minimizing the number of people who are racially intolerant, there are actually a sizable number of Americans who really would like to see things go better in the area of race," says Paul Sniderman, a professor of political science at Stanford University who has done extensive research on racial attitudes. "A lot of people would really see this as their chance to support a historic accomplishment." Yet there's also reason to believe that white admiration for Powell does more to deny and paper over the existence of racism than it does to ameliorate it. Juan Williams, a black journalist who has written often about politics and civil rights, says, "A lot of his attraction to whites is that it allows them to say, 'I'm not a racist; I like Colin Powell. I don't have a problem with blacks; I have a problem with blacks who don't share my *values*.'" In this view, Powell's chief symbolic importance is to send the falsely reassuring message that if *he* made it big, then so can anyone else. "There is a very mistaken

---

*Neither, at first, was Barack Obama, whose 2008 presidential candidacy revealed similarly divergent aspirations for racial progress among black and white supporters.

notion that if you see one black man who has succeeded, then society is open for all black people," says Clifford Alexander, a black attorney and businessman who served as secretary of the army during the Carter administration.

Accounts of Powell's career tend to exaggerate the humbleness of his roots as "a ghetto child," born in Harlem and "raised in the poverty-ridden South Bronx." ("We get poorer and poorer," Powell's sister has wryly noted, as media interest in Powell grows.) The more disadvantages he can be seen to have started with, the more his great success validates the American Dream. It is clear in the comments of some of Powell's close friends and supporters that they believe their admiration for Powell absolves them of the harsher racial judgments they may harbor of blacks in the aggregate. "I think he could be a fabulous president," says one of his closest friends. "Yes, partly because he's black, and having a competent black president would be wonderful." There is, in the remark, that unconscious condescension—the weary suggestion that fair-minded whites are so tired of giving opportunities to blacks who waste them. No one embraces this attitude more openly than Powell's number-one white booster, Charles J. Kelly Jr., who is the self-appointed force behind what he calls Citizens for Powell. Kelly is sixty-six, a retired financier who as a young law student was involved in Citizens for Eisenhower. His confederates in the Powell effort include Eisenhower biographer Stephen Ambrose and Tex McCrary, the eccentric public-relations maestro who also boosted Ike's 1952 campaign. Kelly exudes both an indelibly Midwestern civic-mindedness—"sort of Babbitt on the Potomac," in the words of an acquaintance—and nostalgia for a simpler era. He works almost full-time on his efforts to line up supporters for Powell, traveling around the country to meet with CEOs and chambers of commerce, drafting cogent memorandums to persuade reporters and potential backers that Powell can win the Republican nomination. He belongs to Washington's most establishmentarian group, the Metropolitan Club, and he and his wife rent a wing of Ben Bradlee and Sally Quinn's enormous house in Georgetown.

Sitting on Bradlee's spacious grounds on a warm July morning, Kelly explains that America is more than ready to elect its first black president. "If I talk to rednecks, and cabdrivers, and so on, they don't see him as the black problem, which is associated with irresponsible behavior." Kelly and I have stumbled almost accidentally onto this line of conversation, but he is suddenly deeply engaged. "Powell represents a litmus test in America," he says. "What is the meaning of racism in America? Is racism skin-color prejudice? Does a car full of teenagers dressed in urban-guerrilla costumes with a loudspeaker blaring offensive lyrics in traffic—is revulsion at that racist revulsion? Or is it revulsion at the offensive incivility of the process, at the arrogance of these youths? Which no one will speak to, for fear of being called racist—or for fear of their lives. . . . From everything I've been able to determine, the prejudice is behavior-related." Powell himself has admonished audiences of minorities that racial progress demands a greater assumption of personal responsibility. But he always stresses, too, that racism remains a crushing fact of life in America, embracing the reality that prejudice, behavior, and perception act on one another in boundlessly complex ways.

Some white Powell enthusiasts, however, are peddling the comforting belief that racism is a thing of the past. If black men with bachelor's degrees now earn seventy-six cents for every dollar earned by their white counterparts, they're just not trying hard enough. Powell helps the problem, Kelly says, "just by standing there. His presence says, 'Kwitcherbitchin. If I can do it, you can do it. Don't run around talking about how the world owes you a living. Just don't whine about it. Get on with your lives.'"

Even beyond the dubious value of promoting any one person as symbolic of tens of millions of others, there are particular problems with seizing on Colin Powell for this role. For Powell has an exceptional background in two very important dimensions. While it is true that Powell was born in Harlem and grew up in the Hunts Point section of the South Bronx, blocks from the Fort Apache police station, which would one day come to represent the worst of urban blight, this was the geography of another era. And as the son of Jamaican immigrants, he had an upbringing closer to the experiences of other up-and-coming immigrants—notably the Jewish families that surrounded his in Hunts Point—than to the experience of most American blacks. Blacks of West Indian heritage, in general, have had a distinctive profile in black American life, producing—especially in the early days of civil rights—a number of the nation's black leaders and stars: Harry Belafonte, Sidney Poitier, Kenneth B. Clark, Shirley Chisholm, Malcolm X. They have been, on the whole, more financially successful than other African Americans—though why and to what extent are matters of great controversy. One study found that in 1980 the male U.S.-born children of West Indian immigrants were almost twice as likely as other African Americans to be professionals. As early as the 1930s, some American blacks referred to West Indians as "black Jews." Powell has numbered among his cousins in his extended family a federal judge, a New York State judge, an aerospace engineer, a biochemist at the National Institutes of Health, and two former U.S. ambassadors. His cousin J. Bruce Llewellyn sits on the board of Chemical Bank and co-owns Philadelphia's Coca-Cola bottling plant with former NBA star Julius Erving. (Llewellyn scoffs at the idea that Powell would put himself through the hell of presidential campaigning "for a job that pays $200,000 a year.")

Powell's parents moved from Harlem to Hunts Point three years after his birth in 1937. They rented a big four-bedroom apartment, and both worked in the garment industry—his mother as a seamstress, his father as a shipping clerk who eventually rose into lower management. His was, then, closer to a middle-class childhood than the "ghetto" upbringing some associate with him. His parents, who had emigrated separately in the 1920s, during the first great wave of West Indian immigration to the United States, both thought of themselves originally as British subjects. They attended an Episcopal church (as Powell still does) and had been raised in a culture that—although it, too, bore a harsh legacy of colonial slavery—had freed its slaves a generation before America did and had then placed great emphasis on educating them. "His Jamaican background is the strongest factor in his personality," Powell's sister, Marilyn Berns, has said. And his family's identification with that heritage was so powerful that they were somewhat shocked, Powell told one reporter, when he married Alma, whose roots are in Birmingham, Alabama.

Though the early 1940s marked the start of a black movement into the South Bronx, the young Powell was also surrounded by Jews and other immigrants. He worked for Jews all through high school, in a children's furniture store, and picked up so much Yiddish that he still sprinkles his conversation with it. Ultimately, his parents also tracked the Jewish exodus from Hunts Point, leaving to buy a house in Queens. But for a very brief time, as Powell biographer Howard Means documents, Hunts Point was something like the melting-pot ideal that has so often been touted, and so rarely been achieved, in America.

The other way in which Powell must be discounted as a racial Everyman is that he accomplished his stunning rise in the army, an organization that has no parallel outside the military. Paradoxically, the army has both a terrible record on race relations and—in just the two decades since Vietnam—a very positive one. With the elimination of the draft in 1973, the military began confronting what was clearly a festering problem in its ranks, and, by most accounts, did quite a good job. "After the 1970s, the military addressed its three biggest problems: Vietnam, drug use, and racial tensions," says Tom Ricks, who covers defense for the *Wall Street Journal.** "Society as a whole never grappled successfully with those three things. And while the military still has some problems with drugs and racism, it has addressed those as well as they're going to be addressed in the American context." The army, it is widely agreed, did the best job of all the services. And Powell came up through the ranks just as the army was beginning to understand it needed talented blacks in positions of authority. Undoubtedly he benefited from the informal affirmative action that was promoted as official service policy—a conscious effort, short of numerical quotas, to correct its biases in promotion. When Clifford Alexander became the

---

*He later moved over to the *Washington Post.*

first black secretary of the army in 1977, he recalls, there were only ten black generals. By the time he left, there were thirty—one of whom was Colin Powell. Not even Powell's detractors believe he was *unfairly* promoted up the ladder, but even some of his warmest supporters point out that he probably got an edge of four or five years. Certainly his race muted the criticism that might otherwise have greeted his promotion to Joint Chiefs chairman over the heads of fourteen more experienced four-stars.

Powell himself said, in 1990, that his race has "probably helped me more than it's hurt me." He has also touted the army's great success in proving the possibility of racial integration. Where others see the half-empty glass of a military disproportionately filled with minorities who can find few other jobs, Powell sees the half-full glass of an organization that extends opportunities—as well as discipline—to many of his race. A staple of his speeches, for years, has been a highly romanticized account of a TV interview that Sam Donaldson conducted in the desert, on the eve of the Gulf War battle, with a young black man who spoke of his multiracial unit as "my family." "That is the essence of what it is to be an American," Powell told his recent listeners outside Detroit. "We have to restore, in every school and every workplace, every office and every factory . . . that sense of family." The subtext underlying Powell's appeal—the message that listeners read into his airy speeches—is that he would be able, because of his career history and his skin color, somehow to accomplish this. The problem with this hope is that many of the army's methods are of limited use in civilian life. Once it decided that reducing racial tension was a priority, the army had an impressive arsenal of coercive tools it could bring to bear, and a rigid hierarchy that could simply will away the "glass ceiling" that is still the rule in the private sector. When all else fails, racial cooperation can be (and sometimes has been) ordered down the throats of reluctant recruits.

If Powell should run for president, discussions of his record as a senior steward of military policy are likely to focus on three areas.

The first is his conservatism in the use of force, bred from his army's harrowing lessons in Vietnam. Powell's caution is probably anything but a political liability. Most Americans undoubtedly would prefer an army of Colin Powells to an army of Curtis LeMays,* and he may have an ironic appeal to the pacifists who were his army's critics twenty-five years ago. But there remains a question about whether his vision of arms would limit U.S. leadership in the world.

The second, related question about Powell's tenure as chairman is whether he arrogated too much power to himself, tilting the balance against civilian rule of the military. An influential line of criticism to this effect has blossomed recently, arguing that during the first year of the Clinton administration, while Powell was serving out his last eight months before retirement, he dramatically defied and manipulated the president over several issues—especially gays in the military. And whether or not Powell was right in urging Clinton to stay out of Bosnia, many observers were uncomfortable with how openly Powell stated his opinions on this in public forums, effectively tying Clinton's hands.

Finally, a presidential campaign would likely bring new scrutiny to the subject of Powell's involvement in Iran-Contra. As Defense Secretary Weinberger's top military aide, he carried out orders to transfer missiles from the Defense Department to the Central Intelligence Agency, knowing their eventual destination was Iran. While the record suggests that he and Weinberger had a shared disdain for the plan, investigations depict Powell as helping to implement a policy he knew was illegal, with his foremost priority being to make sure that the Defense Department left as few fingerprints on it as possible. In his final report, independent counsel Lawrence Walsh also criticized Powell for helping to conceal from early investigators the existence of Weinberger's diary, which eventually cast serious doubt on Weinberger's version of events.**

---

*Gen. Curtis LeMay, a hard-line Cold Warrior who rose to air force chief of staff, is credited with coining the phrase, "bomb them into the Stone Age."
**See "The End of the Affair," p. 179.

But even the most controversial moments of Powell's military career tell us little about how he would respond to the larger world of domestic politics. Powell, who has long been a registered independent, said in a May speech, "I don't find yet that I fit neatly into either party. I have very strong Republican leanings on economic matters and international-affairs matters, but I'm still a New Deal kid from Harlem and the South Bronx. Franklin Roosevelt's picture was in my home." It's not only that Powell has declined partisan identification. He's indicated that he has few political convictions of any kind. "Now that I am retired and traveling around the country," he said as recently as January, "I expect I will develop a political philosophy." Such is Powell's aura that statements like that are often greeted as if they contained a mystery, cloaking some coherent worldview that he will reveal in his own good time. Only a few people have criticized them as the confessions of political immaturity that they are, coming from a man who has observed three presidents at close range. "I don't think, at fifty-eight, you ought to be saying things like that," says Clifford Alexander. "I would hope he's been enough of an observer of the American scene to have opinions. It's a little like Clarence Thomas having no opinion of *Roe v. Wade*, when he was in law school when it was handed down."* However, Powell should probably be taken at face value. He really *doesn't* have a political philosophy, because he has never been engaged by issues that aren't compassed by his beloved army. And this is just the first of the major obstacles that stand between Powell and the presidency.

The conventional wisdom in Washington holds that Powell—proud, reputedly thin-skinned, accustomed to command—may not be prepared for the rigors and indignities of a national campaign. But if one thinks it through carefully, that's the least of his problems. Given everything we know of Powell's nature and strengths, it's

---

*That's what Thomas told the Senate Judiciary Committee at his Supreme Court confirmation hearings in 1991.

hard to see how a Powell run in 1996 adds up. Many Powell believers would like to see him run as an independent, but his friends are the first to rule this out. "I don't see any possibility he'll head some kind of third-party effort," says Ken Adelman. "He's just more of an institutional guy." Not only is it the hardest way to run for president, without benefit of party help in fund-raising and organization, but Powell doesn't seem an angry enough character for a campaign that, by definition, would have to appeal to those voters most furiously alienated by the system. Running for the Democratic nomination is out of the question, with an incumbent president in the race. It's difficult to imagine Powell doing so, in any case. His professional patrons have all been Republicans, and conservative Republicans at that. Most of his political friends are Republicans, and most of the money he could easily attract is Republican.

That leaves the Republican nomination as Powell's best route to the White House. But while polls show that he could beat Clinton, gaining the nomination would be nearly impossible. One problem is Bob Dole's formidable lead. The GOP rarely upsets the campaign of a strong front-runner, and though Dole's support isn't deep, it is at this point very broad. Moreover, Powell is positioned all wrong to be the alternative for Republicans who can't stomach Dole. "Unfortunately for Powell, those people aren't going to go to him," says political consultant David Keene. "They're the Buchanan types. They're much more conservative than he is." Certainly Powell is out of step with the antitax, small-government energy that is the unquestioned engine of the current Republican ascendancy. "You have to understand: the typical American army general believes in the U.S. government, which has been very good to him," says Tom Ricks. Professional soldiers are sheltered from some of the most abrasive elements of American life; they live most of the time in small utopias that tend to their medical care, discount their groceries at the PX, and sometimes even educate their children. It would be amazing if Powell did have Newt Gingrich's or Pat Buchanan's visceral sense of the fears that plague the American middle class.

Finally, the Republican Party is deeply invested in some of the few themes that even a man as flexible as Powell probably can't swallow. Friends believe that he is pro-choice and that he is put off by the religious right; more than that, Republican attitudes on racial policy, especially some candidates' increasingly vocal attacks on affirmative action, would only place Powell in conflict with the great majority of the nation's black voters—including much of his extended family. J. Bruce Llewellyn says, "I personally don't think he'd want to be the nominee of a party that's trying to dismantle everything we've gained in the last thirty years." Powell has never tried to evade or soften his racial identity, and his past behavior suggests that retaining the goodwill of the black community is important to him. As chairman, he was always careful to give interviews to magazines such as *Ebony* and *Jet*. More recently, he made a point of attending festivities celebrating Myrtle Evers-Williams's swearing-in as head of the National Association for the Advancement of Colored People. In all the years he was sheltered by his uniform, he was able to contain or ignore the conflicts among his loyalties. Even if Powell was uncomfortable with the 1988 Bush campaign's notorious symbolic use of Willie Horton,* it was—literally—his duty not to express opinions on President Bush's handling of civil rights matters. But in the realm of politics, such conflict would be flushed to the surface. To run for the White House, Powell would effectively have to renounce some key piece of his past life.

There is one more alternative—the only way, barring a major upheaval in American politics, that Colin Powell is at all likely to ascend to the presidency. He could win the Republican vice presidential nomination in 1996: a perfectly Powellian solution. The vice presidency itself is a largely symbolic job, in which the chosen candidate is expected to be visible but not too visible, distinctive enough to be an asset but never so controversial as to be a liability. It would allow him to continue down the path to the presidency

---

*See "The Story of a Bad Boy," p. 205.

while withholding his ultimate commitments. And if Powell has any lust for the White House, history tells him that the vice presidency remains the best way to get there—especially on a ticket with Dole, whose age might well limit him to one term. But the vice presidency, of course, is a matter of chance, hinging on who wins the presidential nomination, and by how much, and what sort of regional and ideological strengths a running mate may need to bring to the ticket. Friends also believe Powell covets an appointment as secretary of state. The true model for Powell, some say, is not Eisenhower but the apolitical George C. Marshall, the army-bred author of the Marshall Plan, perhaps the most revered secretary of state in the twentieth century. For now, Powell has bided his time, keeping all of his options wide open. He has maintained his mystery by forbidding video and audio coverage of most of his profitable speeches. His book tour—kicked off by an interview with Barbara Walters, for which the two journeyed to Jamaica—will bring his maximum hour of attention and opportunity.

Whatever Colin Powell means to you, it's not hard to see him as someone with extraordinary potential to do good: a man in his prime, a man of enormous presence and great skill and some apparent understanding of the ills of others. Friends spin endless scenarios of the fine efforts to which Powell may bend all these assets—invariably including, in their accounts, some effort to better the lot of the minority poor. Yet some of the same friends express an uneasy feeling that Powell, master of caution, may hoard all that potential too carefully. "I don't know why he's busting his butt on money now," says one. "I told him, 'It seems like a stupid way to organize your time.' Once he got the book money, I always thought it was peculiar he did so many speeches. . . . It's not *building* anything." Put another way: it's hard to picture George Catlett Marshall heading the bill at a Peter Lowe seminar, let alone at the seven that Powell has done in the past two years. Great expectations surround Powell, and it will be fascinating to see how long he will be content to package faith and optimism as weightlessly as Zig Ziglar and Larry King do, waiting for the highest use of his talents to be revealed to him. Pure potential, unspent, is finally an empty thing. "He stands for togetherness and tolerance, and America as a place of opportunity," says J. Bruce Llewellyn. "But then again, everybody stands for those things."*

---

*Powell did not run for president or vice president in 1996, but during president George W. Bush's first term he realized his ambition to become secretary of state. In that capacity, he gave a speech prior to the 2003 Iraq invasion laying out evidence that Saddam Hussein harbored chemical and biological weapons. After the invasion, however, no such weapons were found.

Since stepping down as secretary of state, Powell has resumed participation in Zig Ziglar's motivational seminars.

ACKNOWLEDGMENTS

Reputation, like *The Woman at the Washington Zoo*, was a labor of love. I remain grateful to Peter Osnos, founder and editor-at-large at PublicAffairs, for initiating those labors and imposing discipline on them; to Susan Weinberg (who succeeded Peter as publisher) for coaxing *Zoo* onto the best-seller list and for lavishing generous attention on its sequel; and to Lindsay Jones for editing both books with deftness and care. Thanks also to Sharon DeJohn, Pete Garceau, Lindsay Goodman, Lisa Kaufman, Melissa Raymond, Laura Stine, Trish Wilkinson, and Lindsay Goodman. Marjorie's agent, Andrew Wylie, again provided helpful guidance on editorial matters in addition to managing the business end, assisted ably by Jeffrey Posternak.

Veronika Jiranova typed into a computer several pieces that weren't available electronically, and *Vanity Fair's* Bruce Handy and John Ortved hunted down a few more that still lingered in *Conde Nast's* computer system. Mark Feeney, Ann Hulbert, Patsy Noah, Dana Stevens, and Bob Thompson reviewed the manuscript in its entirety. Others who helped in various ways include Leah Allen, David Atkins, Bill Barol, Philip Bartolf, Matt Cooper, Marcelle DuPraw, Antonio Elmaleh, Abby Frankson, Beth Frerking, Peter Ginna, Paul Glastris, Bonnie Goldstein, James Grady, Donald Graham, Jerome Groopman, Rachel Halterman, Jennifer Haverkamp, Susan Hewitt, Michael Hopkins, Paul Jackson, Mickey Kaus, Jeff Kehne, Charles Lane, Jon Leibowitz, Paul Leonard, Ruth Marcus, John Mintz, Sara Mosle, Ruth Marcus, Jim Naughton, Robert and Marian Noah, Peter and Paula Noah, Charles and Beth Peters, David Plotz, Thorne

Rankin, Wistar and Tom Rawls, Thomas E. and Mary Kay Ricks, Robin Rue, Jack Shafer, Alan Shearer, Steve Shere, Laura Stone, Jill Timmons, Jacob Weisberg, Anne Williams, Rosina Williams, Sally Williams, Susan Williams, Diane Willkens, Dave Wood, and Emily Yoffe. Rosa Brooks, whose relationship to this project isn't simple, offered tactful sympathy, loving support, and reason to be happy.

Publishing *Reputation* would be impossible were it not for the success of *Zoo*. I therefore thank those who participated in and/or arranged book-related events on the last go-round: Jill Abramson, Monica Adler, Ann Louise Bardach, Barb Barnhart, Nick Burd, Susan and Robert Burch, Constance Casey, Carla Cohen, Cleve Corner, Meghan Daum, Anne Davenport, Chris Desser, Jennifer Egan, Beth Frerking, J. Elise Gaul, Mary Lou Hartman, Nancy Jacobson, Elizabeth Kastor, Michael Kinsley, Jaime Leifer, Paul Leonard, Ruth Marcus, Kirk Marckwald, Marie Monrad, Maureen Orth, Katha Pollitt, Dale Russakoff, Cliff Sloan, Helen Schulman, Sally Bedell Smith (who also dedicated her joint biography of Bill and Hillary Clinton, *For Love of Politics*, to Marjorie), Patty Stonesifer, Kara Swisher, Kathleen Townsend, Anne Williams, Jacob Weisberg, and Pam Wiley. I don't intend to publish any further collections of Marjorie's work, so thanks in advance to those who perform similar favors for *Reputation*.

If Marjorie were here, she would thank those who granted her interviews on and off the record, starting with the profile subjects themselves. She would also thank the people who edited and helped conceptualize her stories. My knowledge of the latter group is incomplete, and in some instances I had to guess the identities of the relevant editors, so thanks and apologies to anyone I've left off the honor roll that follows.

At the *Washington Post*: Bob Thompson edited three of the profiles included in this book, and his continuing dedication to Marjorie's legacy moves me beyond words. Others who guided Marjorie's work at the *Post* in various ways include Henry Allen, Rick Atkinson, Dan Balz, Benjamin C. Bradlee, the late Ann Devroy, Leonard Downie, Sandy Flickner, Donald Graham, Mary Hadar, Fred Hiatt, Robert

Kaiser, Ken Ikenberry, the late Mary McGrory, Sally Quinn, Gene Weingarten, Linton Weeks, and Tom Wilkinson.

At *Vanity Fair*: Graydon Carter oversaw the reporting and writing of eight profiles included in this book, qualifying him, perhaps, as its true editor. Certainly the playful tone and shrewd selection of profile subjects echo Carter's sensibility. Others who illuminated and/or cheered Marjorie's path include Judy Bachrach, Tina Brown, Bryan Burrough, Klara Glowczewska, Bruce Handy, Wayne Lawson, Dee Dee Myers, Maureen Orth, Elise O'Shaughnessy, Sally Bedell Smith, and the magazine's great fact-checking staff.

At American Express and *Departures* magazine: Laurel Kamen recommended Marjorie when *Departures* needed someone to freelance a travel piece about Washington. The assignment helped fund a six-month journalism hiatus while Marjorie nursed and bonded with our firstborn child. Gary Walther and Kathleen Fitzpatrick, then the two top editors at *Departures*, presumably deserve some credit for the delightful way this Washington primer, circa 1993, turned out.

For miscellaneous friendship and services rendered, Marjorie would thank Robert Barnett, Juliana Capois, Monique DuPree, Joni Evans, Stephen "Felix" Mantell, Alice Mayhew, the late Debbie Moses, Daniel Okrent, Sheila and the late Corlies Smith, Willa and the late William Stackpole, Mary Sulerud, and Abigail Wiebenson. Marjorie would also thank the people with whom she participated for two decades in group psychotherapy.

Alan and Beverly Williams, now deceased, would dispute some of their daughter's harsher judgments in *Zoo*, but Marjorie's love for them ran bone-deep, as did her love for her sisters, Wistar, Anne, and Rosina, and for her stepmother, Robin Rue. Marjorie's friendship with Beth Frerking, and, at earlier stages of her life, her friendships with the late Julie Browder (her childhood neighbor in Princeton) and Vicky Stein (with whom she negotiated the treacherous shoals of Manhattan publishing) were enormously vital and sustaining. She would thank all three.

Finally, Marjorie would thank the kids and me. My reply, once again, is to thank you for spending your life with me. Will and Alice are now both teenagers. Like you, they are smart and warm and beautiful and funny, and in a thousand ways they would delight and fascinate you and make you proud. We miss you—*I* miss you—some days more sharply than others. But I'm moving on, as you'd want me to, and learning to savor the gift of being alive.

RIGHTS AND PERMISSIONS

INDEX

Marjorie Williams was born in Princeton, New Jersey, in 1958 and died in Washington, D.C., in 2005. She was a contributing editor to *Vanity Fair*, a feature writer and columnist for the *Washington Post*, and a frequent contributor to *Slate* and the *Washington Monthly*. Williams is the author of *The Woman at the Washington Zoo: Writings on Politics, Family, and Fate*, a *New York Times* best seller  and winner of the PEN/Martha Albrand Nonfiction Award. She is survived by her husband, Timothy Noah, a senior writer at *Slate*, and her children, Alice and Will.

CREDIT: MARY CROSS

PublicAffairs is a publishing house founded in 1997. It is a tribute to the standards, values, and flair of three persons who have served as mentors to countless reporters, writers, editors, and book people of all kinds, including me.

I. F. STONE, proprietor of *I. F. Stone's Weekly*, combined a commitment to the First Amendment with entrepreneurial zeal and reporting skill and became one of the great independent journalists in American history. At the age of eighty, Izzy published *The Trial of Socrates*, which was a national bestseller. He wrote the book after he taught himself ancient Greek.

BENJAMIN C. BRADLEE was for nearly thirty years the charismatic editorial leader of *The Washington Post*. It was Ben who gave the *Post* the range and courage to pursue such historic issues as Watergate. He supported his reporters with a tenacity that made them fearless and it is no accident that so many became authors of influential, best-selling books.

ROBERT L. BERNSTEIN, the chief executive of Random House for more than a quarter century, guided one of the nation's premier publishing houses. Bob was personally responsible for many books of political dissent and argument that challenged tyranny around the globe. He is also the founder and longtime chair of Human Rights Watch, one of the most respected human rights organizations in the world.

· · ·

For fifty years, the banner of Public Affairs Press was carried by its owner Morris B. Schnapper, who published Gandhi, Nasser, Toynbee, Truman, and about 1,500 other authors. In 1983, Schnapper was described by *The Washington Post* as "a redoubtable gadfly." His legacy will endure in the books to come.

Peter Osnos, Founder and Editor-at-Large